BILLIARDS: THE OFFICIAL RULES & RECORDS BOOK
2005 Edition

Published by Billiard Congress of America (BCA)

Our Vision:
*To make billiards the number one
participation sport in the world.*

Our Mission:
*To provide exceptional value to our members by
promoting and growing cue sports worldwide.*

BILLIARD CONGRESS
OF AMERICA

D0029641

Billiard Congress of America
4345 Beverly Street, Suite D, Colorado Springs, Colorado 80918 USA
Phone: 719.264.8300 • Fax: 719.264.0900 • Web: www.bca-pool.com

Editor: Amy Long - BCA • Design and Production: Ginni Francis - BCA
Photography: Tom Keller and David Kelly - Medium Pool
Brad Armstrong Photography • Billiard Creative Agency • BCA Archives
Printing: Kendall Printing Company - Greeley, Colorado

The BCA thanks the following individuals and
organizations for their invaluable contributions to this book:
Allison Fisher, Tom Rossman, Mike Shamos, Nick Varner,
C.J. Wiley and Medium Pool

TABLE OF CONTENTS

BCA BOARD OF DIRECTORS

VOTING

Mike Baggett
Cue & Case Sales
BCA Treasurer

Roger Blank
Connelly Billiards
BCA Secretary

Pat Conners
AMF Billiards

Dan Dishaw
American Cuemakers
Association

Clay Etheridge
Showcase Billiards

Barry Hart
Viking Cue Mfg., Inc.

Gregg Hovey
Olhausen Billiard Mfg., Inc.
BCA 2nd Vice President

John Nusser
J-S Sales Co., Inc.

Reneé Poehlman
American Poolplayers
Association, Inc.

Bob Radford
Antique Billiard Supply

John Stransky
Brunswick Billiards
BCA President

ROOM OPERATOR

Mark Griffin
Gaslamp Billiard Palace

Greg Hunt
Amsterdam Billiard Club

RETAIL

Michael Brownstein
Recreation World, Inc.
BCA 1st Vice President

BCA NATIONAL OFFICE STAFF

Stephen D. Ducoff ......Executive Director..Ext. 106

Ginni Francis ....Graphic Designer/Production Manager............................Ext. 103

Tracy Hart....................Associate Director of Trade Services & Development ....Ext. 110

Eileen Johnston ....Director of Finance ....Ext. 122

Carolyn Lewis..............Director of Trade Services & Development ....Ext. 128

Amy Long ....Director of Marketing..Ext. 104

Linda Mojer ....Communications Director ....Ext. 120

Kathy Simmons ....Member Services Administrator ....Ext. 116

Gabriele Stephenson....Director of Executive & Member Services.........................Ext. 102

Staff members may be reached at **719.264.8300**
or through our website: **www.bca-pool.com**

BILLIARD EDUCATION FOUNDATION

MISSION STATEMENT

The purpose of the Billiard Education Foundation is to further a standard of excellence and leadership within the billiard community by engaging in activities related to the educational and cultural advancement of tomorrow's leaders.

BILLIARD EDUCATION FOUNDATION

The Billiard Education Foundation (BEF) is a 501(c)(3) non-profit charity organization administered by the BCA. The BEF raises money through various fundraisers such as the BEF Challenge the Stars benefit, in which billiard fans can challenge their favorite pro to a game of 9-Ball. BEF funds are used for developing programs consistent with the BEF's mission.

The BEF Academic Scholarship Program is an annual program administered by the BEF Scholarship Committee. Applications are made available in the fall on the BCA website (www.bca-pool.com), with a postmark deadline of the following March 15.

The program is divided into three categories: Excellence in Education scholarship ($5,000 awarded over a two-year term), BCA scholarships (7 x $1,000 awarded annually) and Dr. Cue "Artistic Pool" scholarship ($2,500 awarded annually).

The objective of the BEF Academic Scholarship Program is to grant scholarships to high school seniors who have benefited from the sport of billiards and are pursuing a college education.

BCA OFFICERS AND COMMITTEES 2004-2005

John Stransky - **President** • Michael Brownstein - **First Vice President**
Gregg Hovey - **Second Vice President** • Mike Baggett - **Treasurer**
Roger Blank - **Secretary**

Executive
John Stransky*
Michael Brownstein
Gregg Hovey
Mike Baggett
Roger Blank
Stephen Ducoff**

Finance/Grants
Mike Baggett *
Michael Brownstein
Pat Conners
Greg Hunt
John Nusser
Bob Radford
Eileen Johnston**

Long Range Planning
Gregg Hovey*
Roger Blank
Pat Conners
Dan Dishaw
Barry Hart
John Hoffman
Greg Hunt
Doug Kelly
Reneé Poehlman
Amy Long**

Promotions
Reneé Poehlman*
Mark Griffin
Gregg Hovey
Greg Hunt
Mike Panozzo
Amy Long**

Trade Show/Services
Roger Blank*
Mike Baggett
Michael Brownstein
Pat Conners
Dan Dishaw
Clay Etheridge
W.T. Glasgow, Inc.
Barry Hart
Greg Hunt
Doug Kelly
Monty Kuntz
Aaron Lundeen
Carolyn Lewis**

Membership/Nominating
Mike Brownstein*
Clay Etheridge
Mark Griffin
Barry Hart
Henry Hayes, Jr.
John Nusser
Gabriele Stephenson**

Hall of Fame
Mike Panozzo*
Conrad Burkman
J.R. Calvert
Dan Dishaw
John Nusser
Mike Shamos
Tom Shaw
Stephen Ducoff**

Instructor
Bob Radford*
Fran Crimi
Randy Goettlicher
Rick Poyser
Kathy Simmons**

Bylaws (ad hoc)
Reneé Poehlman*
Gregg Hovey
Ivan Lee
Bob Radford
Shari Stauch
Stephen Ducoff **

Certification/Specificatic (ad hoc)
Mike Baggett*
Roger Blank
Erik Brownstein
Pat Conners
Marvin Eisenhauer
Clay Etheridge
Mark Griffin
John Hoffman
Gregg Hovey
Bob Radford
Stephen Ducoff **

*Committee Chair
**Staff Liaison

BCA VOTING MEMBERS 2004-2005

ABC Billiards & Accessories
AMF Billiards & Games
Ace Product Management Group
American Cuemakers Assn.
American Heritage Billiards
American Poolplayers Assn.
Amisco Industries
Anheuser-Busch
Antique Billiard Supply
Ardesia Biggio S.R.L.
Art Gallery
Atlas Billiard Supplies
BCA Pool League
Barney's Billiards
Bassford
Beach Mfg.
Beasley Creations - Tee & Cue
Billiard Lighting Warehouse
Blatt Billiards
Bottelsen Dart Co.
Brunswick Billiards
C.L. Bailey Co.
California House
Canada Billiard & Bowling
Cannon USA
Carrom Co.
Celebrity Pool Tables and Accessories
Champion Shuffleboard
Classic Sport Co.
Clicks Billiards
Connelly Billiards
Container Marketing
Craftmaster Pool Tables
Creative Inventions
Cribbs dba Bonzini USA
Crystal Leisure
Cue & Case Sales
Cue Tech Pool Schools
CueStix International
D & R Industries
DFS International
DLT International
DMI Sports
Dart World
Diamond Billiard Products

Dimplex North America
Domus Slate
Douglas Furniture of California
Drawknife Billiards
Dufferin Billiards
Eagles Industries Corp.
Elephant Balls
Escalade Sports
Falcon Cues
Frank's Center
Gamenamics
Gameroom Concepts Unlimited
GLD Products
Goodtime Novelty
Gorina Cloth USA
Great American Recreation
Greenfields Pool & Sports Bar
Groovystuff
Hampton Ridge Billiards
Happ Controls
Hi-Lite Mfg.
Hillsdale House
Hood Leather Goods
Imperial International
Impresa
Italian Trade Commission
Iwan Simonis
J. Pechauer Custom Cues
J & J America
J-S Sales Co.
JSA Corp. - Hippopotamus
Joss Cues
KASSON
Landmark Lighting
Legacy Billiards
Leisure Bay Industries
Lion Sports
Lou Sardo Products - Tight Rack
Luby Publishing
Mali & Co.
Mazzco Billiard Supply
McDermott Hand Crafted Cues
Midnight Flame Lighting
Mueller Recreational Products
Neonetics

Northstar Products Co.
Olhausen Billiard Mfg.
Palason Billiard
Playcraft Industries
Predator Products
Presidential Billiards LP
Primo Craft Billiards
ProLine Billiards, Etc.
Quasimoto
R. A. M. Lighting
RC Designs International
Regent Sports Corp.
Saluc S.A.
Shanghai Longsbeng Billiards
Shelti
Showcase Billiards
Showood
Sims Vibration Laboratory
Stealth Cues
Sterling Gaming
Stylite Lighting
TBS Group Corp.
Tempo Industries
The Level Best Co.
Tiger Products
Toltec Co.
Tree Products by Cranford
Trica
Tweeten Fibre Co.
Valley-Dynamo LP
Venture Entertainment Prod.
Victoria Billiards
Northwoods Billiards
Viking Cue Mfg.
Vitalie Mfg.
Willard's Cue Products
World of Leisure Mfg. Co.
Z-Lite Jenamees

For more information about
BCA Business Membership
please visit www.bca-pool.com.

MESSAGE FROM THE PRESIDENT

Dear Billiard Enthusiast,

Great news - billiards continues to attract new players. The Sporting Goods Manufacturer's Association (SGMA) reports that over 40 million Americans played billiards last year and that sales of billiard equipment was up 4%.

The Billiard Congress of America (BCA) is dedicated to making cue sports the number-one participation sport in the world. It's a lofty goal, to be sure, but one worth pursuing. Each year, the BCA offers a variety of programs to encourage more people to play - either in their home or at one of the more than 3,000 billiard rooms throughout the U.S.

Our main event is the International Billiard & Home Recreation Expo, the world's largest business-to-business trade show for the industry. We also host the BCA Open 9-Ball Championships. This prestigious event invites the top-64 men and top-64 women professional players from around the world competing for $164,000. The finals and semi-finals of both divisions are shown each year on ESPN and ESPN2. A current television schedule can be found at www.bca-pool.com. Tune in!

As a pool player, we invite you to visit our website (www.bca-pool.com) to see what the BCA has to offer. In addition to tournament and Hall of Fame information, we have a great shopping cart with apparel, posters and other billiard-related items. You'll also find direct links to our business members who represent the top names in tables, cues and accessories. If you're in the market for billiard items, make the BCA website your first stop.

Here's to playing by the rules!

John E Stl

John Stransky, President
Billiard Congress of America

A BRIEF HISTORY OF THE NOBLE GAME OF BILLIARDS
by Mike Shamos

The history of billiards is long and very rich. The game has been played by kings and commoners, presidents, mental patients, ladies, gentlemen, and hustlers alike. It evolved from a lawn game similar to the croquet played sometime during the 15th century in Northern Europe and probably in France. Play was moved indoors to a wooden table with green cloth to simulate grass, and a simple border was placed around the edges. The balls were shoved, rather than struck, with wooden sticks called "maces". The term "billiard" is derived from French, either from the word "billart", one of the wooden sticks, or "bille", a ball.

The game was originally played with two balls on a six-pocket table with a hoop similar to a croquet wicket and an upright stick used as a target. During the 18th century, the hoop and target gradually disappeared, leaving only the balls and pockets. Most of our information about early billiards comes from accounts of playing by royalty and other nobles. It has been known as the "Noble Game of Billiards" since the early 1800's, but there is evidence that people from all walks of life have played the game since its inception. In 1600, the game was familiar enough to the public that Shakespeare mentioned it in Antony and Cleopatra. Seventy-five years later, the first book of billiard rules remarked of England that there were "few Towns of note therein which hath not a publick Billiard-Table".

The cue stick was developed in the late 1600's. When the ball lay near a rail, the mace was very inconvenient to use because of its large head. In such a case, the players would turn the mace around and use its handle to strike the ball. The handle was called a "queue"- meaning "tail"- from which we get the word "cue". For a long time, only men were allowed to use the cue; women were forced to use the mace because it was felt they were more likely to rip the cloth with the sharper cue.

Tables originally had flat vertical walls for rails and their only function was to keep the balls from falling off. They resembled riverbanks and even used to be called "banks". Players discovered that balls could bounce off the rails and began deliberately aiming at them. Thus a "bank shot" is one in which a ball is made to rebound from a cushion as part of the shot.

Billiard equipment improved rapidly in England after 1800, largely because of the Industrial Revolution. Chalk was used to increase friction between the ball and the cue stick even before cues had tips. The leather cue tip, with which a player can apply side-spin to the ball, was perfected by 1823. Visitors from England showed Americans how to use spin, which explains why it is called "English" in the United States but nowhere else. (The British themselves refer to it as "side"). The two-piece cue arrived in 1829. Slate became popular as a material for table beds around 1835. Goodyear discovered vulcanization of rubber in 1839 and by 1845 it was used to make billiard cushions. By 1850, the billiard table had essentially evolved into its current form.

The dominant billiard game in Britain from about 1770 until the 1920's was English Billiards, played with three balls and six pockets on a large rectangular table. A two-to-one ratio of length to width became standard in the 18th century. Before then, there were no fixed table dimensions. The British billiard tradition is carried on today primarily through the game of Snooker, a complex and colorful game combining offensive and defensive aspects and played on the same equipment as English Billiards but with 22 balls instead of three. The British appetite for Snooker is approached only by the American passion for baseball; it is possible to see a Snooker competition every day in Britain.

Billiards In The United States
How billiards came to America has not been positively established. There are tales that it was brought to St. Augustine by the Spaniards in the 1580's but research has failed to reveal any trace of the game there. More likely it was brought over by Dutch and English settlers. A number of American cabinetmakers in the 1700's turned out exquisite billiard tables, although in small quantities. Nevertheless, the game did spread throughout the Colonies. Even George Washington was reported to have won a match in 1748.

By 1830, despite primitive equipment, public rooms devoted entirely to billiards appeared. The most famous of them was Bassford's, a New York room that catered to stockbrokers. Here a number of American versions of billiards were developed, including Pin Pool, played with small wooden targets like miniature bowling pins, and Fifteen-Ball Pool, described later.

The American billiard industry and the incredible rise in popularity of the game are due to Michael Phelan, the father of American billiards. Phelan emigrated from Ireland and in 1850 wrote the first American book on the game. He was influential in devising rules and setting standards of behavior. An inventor, he added diamonds to the table to assist in aiming, and developed new table and cushion designs. He was also the first American billiard columnist. On January 1, 1859, the first of his weekly articles appeared in Leslie's Illustrated Weekly. A few months later, Phelan won $15,000 in Detroit at the first important stake match held in the United States. He was a tireless promoter of the game and created the manufacturing company of Phelan and Collender. In 1884 the company merged with its chief competitor, J.M. Brunswick & Balke, to form the Brunswick-Balke-Collender Company, which tightly controlled all aspects of the game until the 1950's.

The dominant American billiard game until the 1870's was American Four-Ball Billiards, usually played on a large (11 or 12-foot), four-pocket table with four balls - two white and two red. It was a direct extension of English Billiards. Points were scored by pocketing balls, scratching the cue ball, or by making caroms on two or three balls. A "carom" is the act of hitting two object balls with the cue ball in one stroke. With so many balls, there were many different ways of scoring and it was possible to make up to 13 points on a single shot. American Four-Ball produced two offspring, both of which surpassed it in popularity by the late 1870's. One, simple caroms played with three balls on a pocketless table, is sometimes known as "Straight Rail", the forerunner of all carom games. The other popular game was American Fifteen-Ball Pool, the predecessor of modern pocket billiards.

The word "pool" means a collective bet, or ante. Many non-billiard games, such as poker, involve a pool but it was to pocket billiards that the name became attached. The term "poolroom" now means a place where pool is played, but in the 19th century a poolroom was a betting parlor for horse racing. Pool tables were installed so patrons could pass the time between races. The two became connected in the public mind, but the unsavory connotation of "poolroom" came from the betting that took place there, not from billiards.

Fifteen-Ball Pool was played with 15 object balls, numbered 1 through 15. For sinking a ball, the player received a number of points equal to the value of the ball. The sum of the ball values in a rack is 120, so the first player who received more than half the total, or 61, was the winner. This game, also called "61-Pool", was used in the first American championship pool tournament held in 1878 and won by Cyrille Dion, a Canadian. In 1888, it was thought more fair to count the number of balls pocketed by a player and not their numerical value. Thus, 14.1 Continuous Pool replaced Fifteen-Ball Pool as the championship game. The player who sank the last ball of a rack would break the next rack and his point total would be kept "continuously" from one rack to the next.

Eight-Ball was invented shortly after 1900; Straight Pool followed in 1910. Nine-Ball seems to have developed around 1920. One-Pocket has ancestors that are older than any of these; the idea of the game was described in 1775 and complete rules for a British form appeared in 1869.

From 1878 until 1956, pool and billiard championship tournaments were held almost annually, with one-on-one challenge matches filling the remaining months. At times, including during the Civil War, billiard results received wider coverage than war news. Players were so renowned that cigarette cards were issued featuring them. The BCA Hall of Fame honors many players from this era, including Jacob Schaefer, Sr. and his son, Jake Jr., Frank Taberski, Alfredo DeOro, and Johnny Layton. The first half of this century was the era of the billiard personality. In 1906, Willie Hoppe, at the age of 18, established the supremacy of American players by beating Maurice Vignaux of France at balkline. Balkline is a version of carom billiards with lines drawn on the table to form rectangles. When both object balls lie in the same rectangle, the number of shots that can be made is restricted. This makes the game much harder because the player must cause one of the balls to leave the rectangle, and hopefully return. When balk-line lost its popularity during the 1930's, Hoppe began a new career in three-cushion billiards which he dominated until he retired in 1952. Hoppe was a true American legend - a boy of humble roots whose talent was discovered early, a world champion as a teenager, and a gentleman who held professional titles for almost 50 years. One newspaper reported that under his manipulation, the balls moved "as if under a magic spell", to many fans, billiards meant Hoppe.

While the term "billiards" refers to all the games played on a billiard table, with or without pockets, some people take billiards to mean carom games only and use pool for pocket games. Carom games, particu-larly balkline, dominated public attention until 1919, when Ralph Greenleaf's pool playing captured the nation's attention. For the next 20 years he gave up the title on only a few occasions. Through the 1930's, both pool and billiards, particularly three-cushion billiards, shared the spotlight. In 1941 the Mosconi era began and carom games declined in importance. Pool went to war several times as a popular recre-ation for the troops. Professional players toured military posts giving exhibitions; some even worked in the defense industry. But the game had more trouble emerging from World War II than it had getting into it. Returning soldiers were in a mood to buy houses and build careers, and the charm of an after-noon spent at the pool table was a thing of the past. Room after room closed quietly and by the end of the 1950's it looked as though the game might pass into oblivion. Willie Mosconi, who won or success-fully defended the pocket billiard title 19 times, retired as champion in 1956.

Billiards was revived by two events, one in 1961, the other in 1986. The first was the release of the movie, "The Hustler", based on the novel by Walter Tevis. The film depicted the dark life of a pool hustler with Paul Newman in the title role. New rooms opened all over the country and for the remainder of the 60's pool flourished, until social concerns, the Vietnam War, and an increase in outdoor activities led to a decline in the game. In 1986, "The Color of Money", the sequel to "The Hustler" with Paul Newman in the same role and Tom Cruise as an up-and-coming professional, brought the excitement of pool to a new generation. The opening of upscale rooms catered to a new type of player, whose senses may have been offended by the old cliché of poolrooms.

While the game has had its heroes since the early 1800's, it has waged a constant battle for respectability. In the 1920's, the poolroom was an environment in which men gathered to loiter, fight, bet and play, so they were often the target of politicians eager to show their ability to purge immorality from the communities. Most rooms now bear no resemblance to those of earlier times. The atmosphere of many new rooms approaches that of chic restaurants and night clubs. They offer quality equipment, expert instruction, and the chance for people to meet socially for a friendly evening. These rooms have helped contribute to the greatest interest in billiards in over a century.

Women have played billiards since its beginning in the 15th century. Since the late 1800s, there have been women who took the game and their talents to new levels. May Kaarlus turned heads with her trick shot artistry at the turn of the century. Ruth McGinnis could give most men a run for their money and toured with the legendary Willie Mosconi in the 30s. And in the early 70s, it was grandmother Dorothy Wise, winning five U.S. Open tournaments, who kept the women's dream of professional pool alive and well. It wasn't until 1976 and the formation of the Women's Professional Billiard Association (WPBA) that women players officially organized. The WPBA works with the BCA to further the careers of great players from Jean Balukas, winner of seven U.S. Opens, to Allison Fisher, winner of over 50 major titles since 1995. Today, women's billiards boasts unprecedented television coverage and sponsor support in major events, including the ESPN-televised BCA Open 9-Ball Championships. In a sport once considered the last bastion of male dominance, women are now at the forefront of exposing pool to a wider audience.

Mike Shamos is the Curator of The Billiard Archive, a nonprofit organization set up to preserve the game's history.

BCA EQUIPMENT SPECIFICATIONS

TABLE SIZES:

3 1/2' x 7', 4' x 8', and 4 1/2' x 9' with the play area measuring twice as long as it is wide (± 1/8") from the cloth covered nose of the cushion rubber to the opposite cushion rubber. 4 1/2' x 9' tables with a Play Area of 50" x 100" is the recognized size for professional tournament play.

TABLE BED HEIGHT:

The table bed playing surface, when measured from the bottom of the table leg, will be 29 1/4" minimum to 31" maximum.

POCKET OPENINGS & MEASUREMENTS (Cloth covered rails):

Pocket openings are measured from tip to tip of the opposing cushion noses where direction changes into the pocket. This is called the mouth.

Corner Pocket: Mouth ....4 7/8" minimum to 5 1/8" maximum
Side Pocket:Mouth ....5 3/8" minimum to 5 5/8" maximum

The angle at the corner pocket entrance on each side of the pocket is 142° (±1°). The angle at the side pocket entrance on each side of the pocket is 103° (± 2°).

Vertical Pocket Angle:.................12° minimum to 15° maximum

Shelf: The shelf is measured from the center of the imaginary line that goes from one side of the mouth to the other where the nose of the cushion changes direction to the center of the vertical cut of the slate pocket radius.

Corner Pocket: ....1 5/8" minimum to 1 7/8" maximum
Side Pocket: ....0" minimum to 3/8" maximum

Drop Point Slate Radius: The pocket radius measured from the vertical cut of the slate to the playing surface.

Drop Point Slate Radius ....1/8" radius minimum to 1/4" radius maximum

PLAYING BED:

The playing surface must be capable, either by its own strength or a combination of its strength and that of the table base frame, of maintaining an overall flatness within ± .020" lengthwise and ± .010" across the width. Further, this surface should have an additional deflection not to exceed .030" when loaded with a concentrated static force of 200 pounds at its center. All slate joints must be in the same plane within .005" after leveling and shimming. The bed must be covered with a billiard fabric, the major portion of which is made of wool, with proper tension to avoid unwanted ball roll-off. It is recommended that professional tournament size tables have a three-piece set of slate with a minimum thickness of 1" and a wooden frame of at least 3/4" attached to slate. BCA will sanction tournament play on home and coin-operated tables with one-piece slate providing the Play Area requirements are met. All playing surfaces must be solidly secured to base frame with screws or bolts.

CUSHION:

Cushions should react so that they conform under controlled conditions to the three cushion angles prescribed in the "diamond" (or site) system shown in the diagrams on page 139 to ± 1 ball width. The speed of the table cushions should be such that placement of a ball on the head spot, shooting through the foot spot, using center ball english, with a level cue and firm stroke, the ball must travel a minimum of 4 to 4 1/2 lengths of the table without jumping.

POOL BALL SPECIFICATIONS:

Molded and finished in a perfect sphere in the following weight and diameter:
Pocket Billiard Balls
Weight: 5 1/2 to 6 oz. ....*Diameter: 2 1/4"
*Diameter tolerance: ± .005"

POOL CUE SPECIFICATIONS:

Player may bring a maximum of 3 cue sticks to a match
Width of tip: ....No minimum/14 mm maximum
Weight:......................................No minimum/25 oz. maximum
Length: ....40 inches minimum/no maximum
The cue tip may not be of a material that can scratch or damage the addressed ball. The cue tip on any stick must be composed of a piece of specially processed leather or other fibrous or pliable material that extends the natural line of the shaft end of the cue and contacts the cue ball when the shot is executed.

The ferrule, if of a metal material, may not be more than 1 inch in length.

INSTRUCTIONAL PLAYING TIPS

By Jerry Briesath and Richard Rhorer*

There are many variations of the game of billiards, but the fundamentals of good billiard playing are inherent in every format of the sport. This section deals with these fundamentals. The following instructions and illustrations are for right-handed players.

Cue Selection: Try several cues and start with the one that feels most comfortable to you. It is difficult for a beginning pool player to know which weight cue to get. Keep in mind that most professional pool players use a cue that weighs between 18 and 20 ounces. The shaft size of a cue mainly has to do with personal

preference and the size of your fingers. Shaft sizes for pool cues basically run between 12 to 14 millimeters. Most professional pool players play with a shaft size of 12 1/2 to 13 1/2 mm.

Figure 1

Proper Grip Of a Cue: Hold cue lightly with thumb and first three fingers (Fig. 1). When the cue is gripped properly, it should not touch the palm of your hand (Fig. 2). It is very important to maintain a light grip on the cue at all times. Gripping the cue too tightly while stroking through the cue ball is a common mistake that must be corrected.

Figure 2

Where To Grip The Cue: When you are bent over in your shooting position and the cue tip is almost touching the cue ball, the shooting hand should be directly under the elbow. It is okay to have the shooting hand an

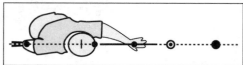

inch or two ahead of the elbow at impact. It is never recommended to have the shooting hand behind the elbow at impact (Fig. 3).

Figure 3

Mr. Briesath and Mr. Rhorer are both BCA Master Instructors with dozens of years of experience coaching students and managing tournaments. The BCA is also grateful to professional players Allison Fisher, Nick Varner and CJ Wiley for their assistance.

CUE STANCE: Face the shot. Before you even bend over to shoot, there is a lineup of three points - the chin, the cue ball and the exact place you want the cue ball to go. Turn your body slightly to the right without your chin leaving the point of lineup. Bend over at the waist, put your bridge hand down 7 to 10 inches from the cue ball so that your chin is 2 to 8 inches directly above the cue stick. Adjust your feet to distribute your body weight approximately 50/50 (as shown in Fig. 4). A generally accepted stance when you are in your shooting position is to have the tip of the right toe directly under the line of the cue and the

Figure 4

left toe slightly to the left side of the line of the cue. This should allow a 4 to 6 inch gap between the hip and the cue for freedom of movement. A common mistake made by beginners in their shooting position is to have the shoulders and chest facing the cue ball. A preferred technique is to turn the left shoulder out in front and the right shoulder back, thus turning the chest more to the right. This makes a better body alignment (Fig. 5).

Figure 5

BRIDGES: One of the most overlooked fundamentals of the game is a solid bridge. The difference between a good player and a mediocre player can often be

Figure 6

traced to the bridge or their bridges. Nothing is of greater importance in billiard play. If the shot you are executing is to be accurate, your bridge must be natural, yet give firm guidance to the cue. Adapt the following formulas for your correct bridges. There are two basic bridges - an open bridge and a closed bridge.

Figure 7

Open Bridge: An open bridge is one formed by placing the hand firmly on the table, cupping the hand, pressing the thumb against the forefinger forming a "V" (Fig. 6). The cue is now placed on the "V" (Fig. 7). To adjust the height of the bridge, simply pull the fingers toward you to raise the bridge (Fig. 8), or pushing the fingers away to lower the bridge (Fig. 9). This allows you to strike the cue ball high, medium or low while maintaining a solid bridge. This bridge is recommended for beginners. Professionals use this bridge on many shots that don't require a lot of power or cue ball spin.

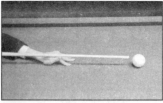

Figure 8

Stretch Shots: When stretching out for a shot where a long bridge is required (12 inches or more), it is important to use an open bridge. Keep the backswing and follow-through very short and use minimum speed (Fig. 10).

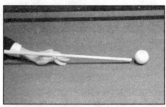

Figure 9

Closed Bridge: Place your entire bridge hand flat on the table. The heel of your hand should be down firmly (Fig. 11). Bend your forefinger so that its tip touches your thumb, thus forming a loop (Fig. 12). Place the cue tip in the loop formed by forefinger and thumb, resting the cue against the inner groove of these two fingers. Extend the cue through the loop formed by the above. Now pull your forefinger firmly against the cue, but with the loop just loose enough so that you can stroke the cue back and forth easily. As you do the above, keep your middle, ring and small fingers spread out and firmly pressed against the table. They form the

Figure 10

bridge tripod which must be firm yet natural. You have the correct bridge when the cue passes through easily, accurately and with firm guidance and support.

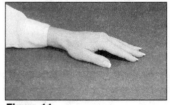

Figure 11

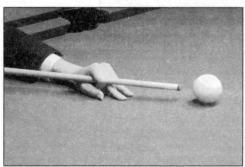

Figure 13

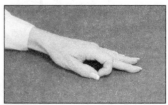

Figure 12

The bridge length is the distance between the loop of the forefinger and the cue ball on a closed bridge or the thumb and the cue ball on an open bridge. Most professional pool players use a bridge length of 7 to 10 inches. Whether you use an open or closed bridge, the heel of your hand should be firmly on the table at all times. The bridge hand must not move while you are striking the ball.

Figure 14

Bridge for Follow Shot: Using a Standard Bridge, elevate the tripod fingers slightly. Keep cue level (Fig. 13).

Bridge for Draw Shot: Using a Standard Bridge, lower the tripod fingers until your thumb rests on the bed of the table. Keep the cue level (Fig. 14).

Figure 15   **Figure 16**

Figure 17

Figure 18

Figure 19

Rail Bridges: If the cue ball is four inches or more away from the rail, set your bridge hand on the rail. Place your thumb under the index finger (Fig. 15). Put the cue on the rail against the thumb, and bring your forefinger over the shaft (Fig. 16). Keep your cue as level as possible when stroking your shot. If the cue ball is closer than 4 inches to the rail, place the cue between the thumb and forefinger. Place the other three fingers on the rail (Fig. 17).

Bridge for Over Ball Shot: When it is necessary to shoot over an object ball in order to stroke the cue ball, the following bridge should be used. Bracing all four of your fingers on the bed of the table behind the obstructing object ball(s), raise the hand as high as necessary and place the cue on the support made by your index finger joint and the thumb (Fig. 18 and 19). This is an uncomfortable bridge, but a necessary one and should be practiced.

Figure 20

Mechanical Bridges: If a shot is beyond reach with any of the aforementioned bridges, a mechanical bridge should be employed. Don't sacrifice a shot because you cannot use the mechanical bridge; it is very easy. Set the bridge on the table 6 to 8 inches from the cue ball. Place your hand on the bridge. Place the shaft of your cue in the notch at the front part of the bridge. (Use higher notch for "follow", lower notch for "draw" or "stop"). Place your thumb under the base of the cue and your four fingers over the top of the cue. Your elbow will be sticking out to the side as you stroke; the bridge will be to the left if you are right-handed. Be sure to lay the bridge flat on the table if possible (Fig. 20) and secure it with your left hand. Now use the same system as for any other shot.

Learning A Stroke: Remember, "Practice doesn't make Perfect; Perfect Practice makes Perfect". A stroke is a throwing motion. A good throwing motion starts with a slow backswing with a smooth acceleration through the cue ball. A common mistake by amateur and beginning players is to drop the elbow while stroking through the cue ball. It's important to note that the throwing motion must take place only in that part of the arm below the elbow. The less the elbow moves up and down, the more precise the stroke. It should be a pendulum swing from the elbow down.

Cueing The Ball: For the beginning player, it is important to adjust the bridge so that the cue tip strikes the cue ball a little above center, never to the left or right, while learning accuracy and speed control. As skill level progresses, it will be necessary to learn to strike the cue ball at other places - higher, lower, left, right, etc.

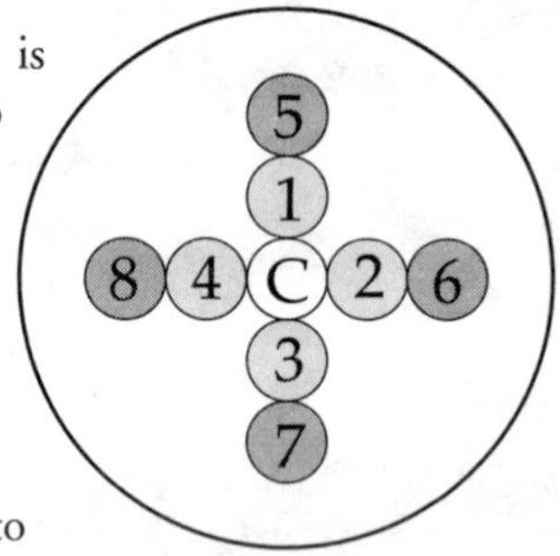

The most important things to learn after a player has progressed past the beginner stage are (1) how to make the cue ball follow, (2) how to stop the cue ball on a straight-in shot and (3) how to make the cue ball draw or reverse direction off the object ball. (See Diag. 2 for further details) The smoother the stroke, the lower or higher the cue ball may be struck without miscuing. Most good players can strike the cue ball almost two full tips off center without miscuing.

Diagram 2

Keep in mind that extreme spin requires a very good stroke and smooth delivery. When following the cue ball, the higher the tip strikes the cue ball, the more over-spin imparted to the cue ball; likewise for backspin. In pool there is one stroke.

10

Figure 21

You use the same stroke to follow the ball as you do to stop or draw the cue ball.

A common mistake people make when they want to stop or draw the cue ball, is they think they have to jab or hit the cue ball and stop the cue tip immediately on impact with the cue ball or even hit the cue ball and pull the stick back. That is not the way to stop or draw the cue ball. To make the cue ball stop, you must put enough backspin on it by shooting below center to cause it to arrive at the object ball with no spin. The cloth is always trying to rub the backspin off the cue ball. The farther the cue ball is from the object ball, the lower or harder you must shoot to cause the cue ball to stop or come back. (Diag. 2 shows positions 1-4 and also 5-8, extreme spin.) When using backspin on the cue ball, it is important to understand the concept that the backspin you put on the cue ball is caused by the tremendous friction the chalk creates between the tip and the cue ball. You must understand that the cue stick imparts backspin to the cue ball as you throw it 4 to 6 inches through the lower part of the cue ball. (Fig. 21 shows how the cue stick follows through 4 to 6 inches after contact with the object ball.)

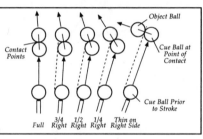

Diagram 3

HITTING THE OBJECT BALL: The first thing the pocket billiard player must learn is that his eyes should be on the object ball as he executes the shot. During the aiming process his eyes go back and forth between the cue ball and the object ball. When you are ready to pocket the object ball, your eyes are on the object ball. To shoot a ball into a pocket, the simplest way to determine your point of impact on the object ball is to draw an imaginary line from the center of the pocket that bisects the object ball. Where this line extends through the object ball is your contact point. It is the point at which the edge of the cue ball must contact the edge of the object ball. You must aim so that these two contact points will meet (Diag. 3).

Figure 22

POINT OF AIM, POINT OF IMPACT: In Figure 22 and 23, you can see there is a white dot on the object ball.

Figure 23

This mark is where the cue ball must contact the object ball in order to pocket the ball. The white dot is called the Point of Impact. The white dot on the table is the Point of Aim. No matter where the cue ball is, the cue stick and the center of the cue ball are aimed at the Point of Aim in order to contact the Point of Impact on the object ball.

A keen eye and judgement are important here. Your skill in hitting the Point of Aim will determine your status in pocket billiard circles. Once again, there is no better experience than practice. Accomplish this phase by placing your cue ball close to the object ball, then gradually increase the distance between the two balls. Time and practice will increase your accuracy in striking the cue ball correctly and hitting the object ball where you aim, thus driving it to the exact target area desired.

LEARNING A GOOD SHOOTING SYSTEM: The first thing you have to remember when you play pool is that you don't control the balls. All you control is your body and your cue. What the balls do is only a result of how well your body moves the cue. There are two things you have to get out of the way before you can shoot any shot. You have to make sure the cue is aiming straight and you have to make sure your arm can move the cue straight back and forth the full length of your bridge (7 to 10 inches).

A good practice technique for this is to place the cue ball on the spot and shoot it down the table into a corner pocket. Be sure to get your stance and aim correct. Then take a couple of smooth, slow warm-up swings the full length of the bridge. Stop at the cue ball and check your aim by letting your eyes go down the line of the cue to the target and back a couple of times. If the aim looks perfect, lock your eyes on the target, then after a slow backswing, "throw" the cue smoothly 4 to 6 inches through the cue ball directly over the dot. If after executing the shot, the cue is to the left or right of the dot, repeat this system until you can shoot the ball into the pocket and the cue finishes its motion 4 to 6 inches straight ahead and directly over the dot. It is imperative that your head remain perfectly still during the shot. This is an important practice to help develop your accuracy and stroke. The warm-up swings should be slow and smooth in both directions, training the arm to make the cue go straight. After every two or three warm-up strokes, be sure to stop at the cue ball and check your aim. If it looks perfect, take a smooth backswing, and then accelerate 4 to 6 inches through the cue ball at any speed you want to shoot. It's very important that you always maintain the same slow backswing no matter how hard you accelerate through the ball. Never go back faster just because you want to shoot harder. It's just like throwing a ball; to be accurate, you go back slowly, then you throw hard.

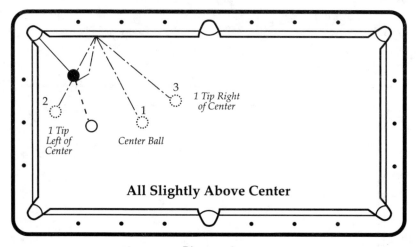

Diagram 4

It is important to learn to stroke through the ball at all speeds. Although you have more control at slower speeds, sometimes position play will require you to shoot a ball harder. Keep in mind-slow backswing, accelerate forward.

ENGLISH (Left or Right). When we talk about english, we are generally referring to left or right spin on the cue ball. By putting left or right spin on the cue ball, you immediately do three things that can cause you to miss a shot. Beginning with right hand english, when you strike the cue ball on the right hand side, the cue ball (1) immediately deflects off the tip to the left of the line of the cue stick. As the cue ball proceeds down the table, it may (2) curve back to the right just a little bit. It will never curve back as much as it deflects unless you elevate the cue, which we're not going to talk about here. With a level cue and right hand english on the ball, it will first deflect to the left. It might curve back a little to the right depending on the distance. The third thing is that the english might throw the object ball. Right hand english can throw the object ball a little to the left of the contact line. The curve back is dependent on the speed and the distance that the cue ball is traveling.

We've mentioned three things that happen when you use right hand english: the deflection immediately off the tip, the curve back to the right and throwing the object ball to the left. Of these three, the curve is usually very slight. The throwing of the object ball is very slight. The biggest factor in causing people to miss with english is the deflection off the cue tip. It is important to remember that when using right hand english, aim slightly to the right of where you would normally aim on the object ball. When using left hand english, you must aim slightly to the left of where you would normally aim on the object ball left or right hand english is almost never used to pocket an object ball, but rather for playing posi-

13

tion on another object ball. The purpose of applying sidespin to the cue ball is to change the angle at which the cue ball comes off a rail after striking the object ball. Always remember, never use english to make balls, only to play position on the next ball. Although english is extremely important in playing position, the pros

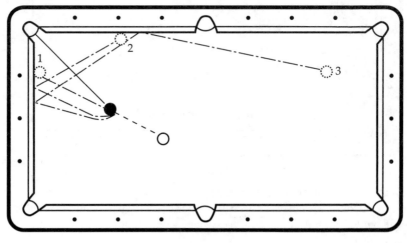

Diagram 5

will tell you: the less english you use, the less often you get in trouble (Diag. 4).

Follow Shots: Set up the balls as in Diagram 5. By stroking the cue ball between a tip and a tip and a half above center, the cue ball will follow to Position 1. Then,

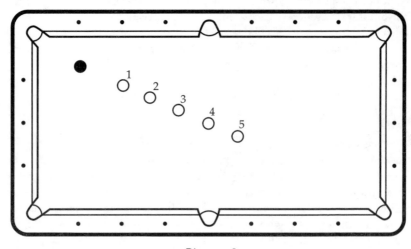

Diagram 6

set up the same shot and stroke the cue ball at the same height, add some power and see that the cue ball will end up in Position 2. Now stroke the cue ball again in the same position, but with an even firmer stroke to see the cue ball respond as in Position 3.

Stop Shots: Place the balls on the table as in Diagram 6. Strike the cue ball about a tip below center. Use a smooth stroke and practice stopping the cue ball as it contacts the object ball. Do this a few times to get the feel of how hard you shoot, then practice shooting this same shot a little lower on the cue ball with a little less speed and see if you can still get the same results. Then proceed to Position 2. This time, stroke the cue ball about a tip and a half below center and a little firmer than Position 1. By repeating this practice in a new position, you will learn how much force you need in order to stop the cue ball. Continue this practice with the cue ball in Positions 3 and 4, each time increasing the power of the stroke. If you have any difficulty at a particular position, repeat that practice until it feels comfortable. Remember, the lower you strike the cue ball, the less power is required to stop the cue ball on contact with the object ball.

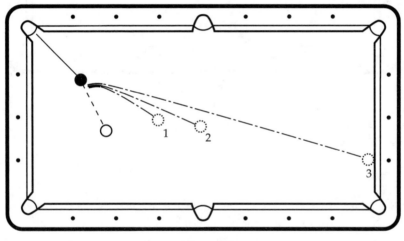

Diagram 7

Draw Shots: Place the balls as shown in Diagram 7. Notice there is a slight angle in the ball placement so that when you draw the cue ball it will move over to the right slightly and then come back past your cue. The reason for this is so that you can follow through the cue ball 4 to 6 inches to practice a good follow-through on each shot without worrying about the cue ball hitting your cue. With the balls in position, strike the cue ball about a tip and a half below center with a moderate stroke and notice that the cue ball travels a couple of inches to the right of your cue before it travels a short distance down the table to Position 1. By increasing the force of your stroke, you will be able to move the ball farther down the table toward Positions 2 and 3. It is important on all these exercises to be sure the cue tip follows through 4 to 6 inches. If you shoot the cue ball for any stop or draw shot, the cue ball is struck one to one and a half tips below center. When the pendulum motion of the arm is correct, the cue tip will follow through 4 to 6 inches past the cue ball, and continue in a slightly downward motion, ending up touching the cloth.

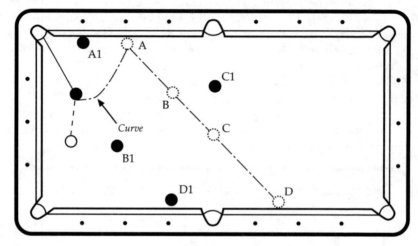

Diagram 8

Position Play: Players are forever trying to play position - that is, making an easy shot and making the cue ball arrive at a place on the table to have another easy shot. The two secrets of playing proper position are (1) memory and (2) speed control.

When a beginner is learning to play, he should repeat the same shots over and over. Not only do you watch the object ball being pocketed, but the path of the cue ball after contacting the object ball. If you are continually hitting the cue ball a little above center, the cue ball will always take virtually the same path. Fifty percent of position play is remembering where the cue ball went after that particular shot. The other 50 percent of position play is the speed control of the cue ball.

The most important and easiest way a beginner can learn position is to set up a shot (as in Diagram 8). When you set up a practice shot, mark the cloth with a chalk dot under the object ball and also the cue ball so you start at the same position each time. Pocket the object ball by hitting a little above center and watch where the cue ball hits the first rail and the direction it takes coming off that rail.

16

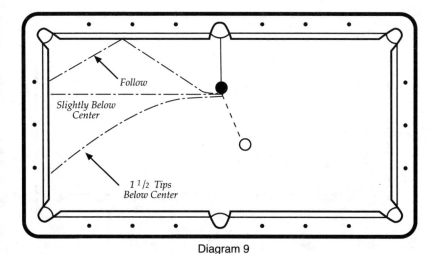

Diagram 9

By shooting this shot several times at different speeds, but striking the cue ball in the same spot each time, you will notice the path of the cue ball will follow in almost the same line each time you shoot. To improve your game, work on playing position on each of the shots in the diagram by varying the speed at which you strike the cue ball.

Now if you set the balls up in the same position and strike the cue ball a little below center, you will notice that the path of the cue ball will be completely different off the object ball. Repeat this several times, until you can make the cue ball go in the same direction, but travel farther down the table depending on the speed of your stroke. After setting up these shots and executing them by hitting the ball a little below center, set them up again and strike the cue ball even farther below center. This is a good exercise to learn the basics of what happens when you shoot the cue ball at different heights and speeds.

EXERCISES

Follow, Stop and Draw: This exercise is to show you the different ways the cue ball will react when it is cued at different levels. Set up the shot in Diagram 9. The object ball is about a diamond out and directly in line between the two side pockets. The cue ball is at a slight angle toward the diamond past the side pocket. When you hit the cue ball with follow, the cue ball will take a slight curve as shown in the path in the diagram. If you hit the cue ball slightly below center, it will go almost straight down the table. If the cue ball is hit about one and a half tips below center, it will curve back more toward the corner pocket.

Position Exercise: Learning Position Play is learning the easiest way to get the balls off the table. The best way to learn that is an exercise we call 3-Ball, Ball in

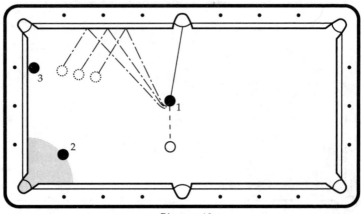

Diagram 10

Hand. This is one of the best exercises to improve your skill level in control and position. Put three balls on the table. In Diagram 10, we see balls 1, 2 and 3. This numeric order is the easiest way to play off these balls by placing the cue ball as shown. Striking the cue ball above center on the 1-ball, you can see by the path of the cue ball that it will follow into the rail and then head right toward the 2-ball. By going to the rail after pocketing the 1-ball and depending on your speed of stroke, you can end up in any of the three cue ball positions. It is very difficult to make a mistake. This is what pros look for: the easiest way to get position on their next ball. If you shoot the cue ball again above center and pocket the 2-ball, the cue ball ends up anywhere within the darkened circle around the 2-ball. Then the 3-ball is an easily pocketed shot.

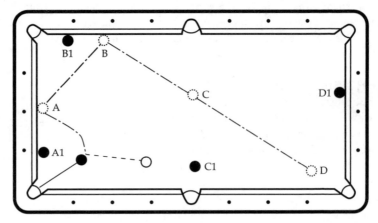

Diagram 11

One of the best ways of improving your game of pool is by repeating shots. Don't repeat long, difficult shots. The ones to repeat are the easy and semi-easy ones that are frequently missed. For the more proficient players, even if you make the object ball and fail to get position, repeat that same shot until you feel comfortable that you can make that ball and get position.

Most people think that if they could make tough shots, they would be better players. The reality is that games are not won by people who make the tough shots; games are lost by players who miss shots that are easy. Diagram 11 shows the many ways the speed of a stroke can be used to play position. By using a soft stroke, you can play shape to position A to play A1 for your next shot. A slightly harder stroke will go to position B for B1 as the next shot. Continue working on your speed of stroke until you can play position on shots C1 and D1.

EIGHT-BALL AND NINE-BALL, BALL IN HAND: Another great practice technique for beginners or stronger players is to play Eight-Ball or Nine-Ball with a rule change. When a person breaks and a ball is made on the break, he can take "ball in hand" anywhere on the table and shoot until missing. The incoming player also takes "ball in hand" and shoots until missing. The advantage of playing this way is that when you have ball in hand every time you come to the table, you start looking over the table. Even a beginner will start to see patterns of two or maybe three balls. The better player learns very quickly the easiest way to run the balls off. It trains you to see patterns and easier ways to go for a run out. By playing Ball in Hand pool, whether it is Eight-Ball or Nine-Ball, you learn in one hour the equivalent of what you would learn in about 15 hours of regular practice.

BALL IN HAND EQUAL OFFENSE: Another great practice game is a variation of Equal Offense (which is also in this book). In Equal Offense, each ball is one point and you can shoot at any ball. No balls count on the break. After the break, the same player who breaks gets ball in hand three times per rack. After each miss, he gets ball in hand again. Then he records how many balls he made that rack. A perfect score is 150 points in 10 racks. By playing this 3-miss way, a person learns to see and play simple patterns. When a person's score approaches 130 or more in 10 racks, then he progresses to the 2-miss level. Now he breaks the balls and after the break, he gets ball in hand twice per rack. When his score improves again to 130 or more in ten racks, then he is playing well enough to progress to the 1-miss level. Any player who shoots 130 points or more on the 1-miss level is a very good amateur player. This is a great practice game.

Throw Shots: (Diagrams 12-15) The object of a "throw" shot is to provide force or english that will move an object ball along an off-center path when two balls are frozen.

This situation often arises when the cue ball is touching (frozen to) an object ball. If the two are in alignment with a pocket, there is no problem. If not in alignment, it is still possible to pocket the object ball by using a "throw shot", which spins the object ball to the left or right. Diagram 12 shows how, by hitting the cue ball on the left side, the object ball is thrown to the right side. Diagram 13 illustrates that striking the cue ball on the right side moves the object ball to the left. Another version of the throw shot is when two object balls are frozen together. The cue ball is free, but not in position to pocket either ball easily. In this case, the cue ball (hit without english) strikes the closest object ball on either the right side (Diagram 14) or the left side (Diagram 15) to throw the second object ball in the opposite direction.

Kiss Shots: (Diagrams 16 & 17) The object of this exercise is to pocket one of the two balls that are frozen together without the use of english. When two balls are frozen together, an axis or center line is established by their relationship. A cue extended along this imaginary line will readily determine if the closest object ball, when struck on the back half, will follow the line into a pocket. If the cue does not point to a pocket, the object ball will not go into a pocket.

Diagram 16 shows how this kiss shot can be made from either side. Diagram 17 demonstrates that one object ball can be pocketed and the other cannot. Arrange two balls in various frozen positions and practice finding the center line. Then, mix throw shots with kiss shots to increase your options under these conditions.

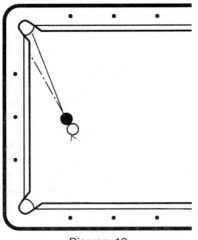

Diagram 12

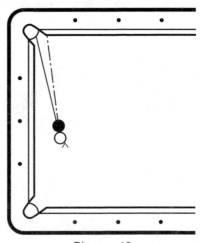

Diagram 13

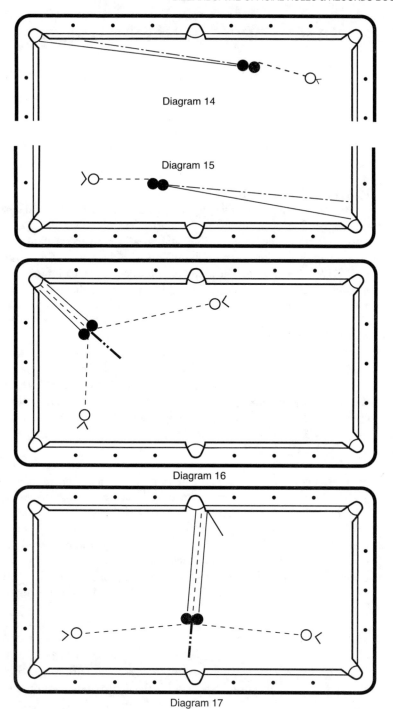

Diagram 14

Diagram 15

Diagram 16

Diagram 17

21

RULES FOR TOURNAMENT PLAY

The following rules concern the play, scoring, officiating and responsibilities for tournament competition in all pocket billiard games. However, the precepts and principles of these rules are to be considered part of the games' General Rules and should be applied as appropriate to all play, whether or not a formal tournament.

1.1 PLAYER RESPONSIBILITY

It is the player's responsibility to be aware of all rules, regulations and schedules applying to competition. While tournament officials will make every reasonable effort to have such information readily available to all players as appropriate, the ultimate responsibility rests with the player. (*For exceptions to this rule, see Rule 2.16*) The player has no recourse if such information is not volunteered; the responsibility for knowing the situation and/or the rules lies with the player.

1.2 ACCEPTANCE OF EQUIPMENT

Tournament players should assure themselves, prior to beginning play, that the balls and other equipment are standard and legal. Once they begin play of a match, they may no longer question the legality of the equipment in use (unless the opponent and tournament officials both agree with the objection and any available remedy proposed by the tournament officials).

1.3 USE OF EQUIPMENT

Players may not use equipment or accessory items for purposes or in a manner other than those for which the items were intended (*refer to rules 3.42 and 3.43*). For example, powder containers, chalk cubes, etc., may not be used to prop up a mechanical bridge (or natural hand bridge); no more than two mechanical bridges may be used at one time, nor may they be used to support anything other than the cue shaft. Extra or out-of-play balls may not be used by players to check clearance or for any other reason (except to lag for break); the triangle may be employed to ascertain whether a ball is in the rack when a match is unofficiated and the table has not been pencil marked around the triangle area. (*Also see rule 2.3*)

1.4 EQUIPMENT RESTRICTIONS

Players may use chalk, powder, mechanical bridge(s) and cue(s) of their choice or design. However, tournament officials may restrict a player if he attempts action that is disruptive of either the house equipment or normal competitive conditions. As examples, a player may: be restrained from using red chalk on green cloth; be advised not to use powder in such an excessive fashion as to unduly affect the balls or table cloth; and be barred from using a cue with a noise-making device that is clearly disruptive to other competitors. (*Also see Rule 2.15*)

1.5 MARKING OF TABLES

When racking the balls, a triangle must be used. Prior to competition, each table and the triangle to be used on it shall be marked so as to ensure that the same triangle will be used throughout the tournament on the same table.

An accurate and clearly visible pencil line must also be marked on the cloth: (1) around the outer edge of the triangle to ensure accurate and consistent placement to enable accurate judgement as to ball positions; (2) on the long string to enable accurate spotting of balls; and (3) on the head string to facilitate determinations of whether balls are behind the head string.

The head spot, center spot and foot spot must also be determined to be accurately marked, whether with discreet penciled "plus" marks, or with standard spots if being employed. In games which do not require them, the center and head spots do not need to be marked.

1.6 ADMINISTRATIVE DISCRETION

The management of each tournament shall reserve the right to set forth rules and procedures appropriate and reasonable for the particular tournament involved, such as may regard player' dress requirements, method of receiving entry fees, refund policy of entry fees, scheduling flexibility, pairing procedures, practice procedures, etc. However, for tournaments to receive a BCA sanction, certain requirements must be met, primarily with regard to safeguarding and ensuring proper distribution of the prize fund.

1.7 LATE START

A player must be ready to begin a match within 15 minutes of the start of the match, or the opponent wins by forfeit. The starting time is considered to be the scheduled time or the time the match is announced, whichever is later.

1.8 NO PRACTICE DURING MATCH

While a match is in progress, practice is not allowed. Taking a shot that is not part of that match is a foul. (*Refer to Rule 1.6*)

1.9 ASSISTANCE NOT ALLOWED

While a match is in progress, players are not allowed to ask for assistance in planning or executing shots. If a player asks for and receives assistance, he

23

loses the game. *Any person, except the opponent, who offers any significant assistance to a player, verbal or non-verbal, will be removed from the area. (Players refer to rule 2.28)*

1.10 FAILURE TO LEAVE THE TABLE

When a player's inning comes to an end, the player must discontinue shooting. Failure to do so is loss of game (*exception in 14.1 - ruled as "deliberate foul"*).

1.11 SLOW PLAY

If in the opinion of the referee a player is impeding the progress of the tournament or game with consistently slow play, the referee can warn the player and then at his discretion impose a time limit up to a maximum of 45 seconds that applies to both players between shots (*that is, both players are put on a shot-clock*). If the referee does impose a time limit and that limit is exceeded by a player who has received a 10 second "time" warning, a foul will be called and the incoming player is rewarded according to the rules applicable to the game being played.

During a player's inning, the shot-clock starts when the previous shot ends, and runs until tip-to-ball contact begins the next shot. The time while a shot is in progress is not counted. If a player begins with cue ball in hand, the shot-clock starts when he has possession of the cue ball, and any spotting or racking is finished.

If the player has not approached the shot, a warning with the announcement of "time" should be made 10 seconds prior to the time limit being reached. If a player exceeds the announced time limit, a foul will be called and the incoming player is rewarded according to the rules applicable to the game being played. In the case of a player down over a ball at the ten second mark prior to the time limit, no announcement is to be made and no penalty is to be imposed. In the event of the player standing up off the shot, "time" will be called at that point and normal shot clock procedure is followed. Each player may call for one extension per rack.

Extension period is identical to the time limit imposed. In the event of a tie score with only one game remaining, each player may utilize two extensions. The player must ensure that the referee/timekeeper is aware when an extension is called.

1.12 SUSPENDED PLAY

If a player shoots while play is suspended by the referee, he loses the game. Announcement of the suspension is considered sufficient warning. (*Also see Rule 2.27*)

1.13 TIME OUT

If time outs are allowed, a player is only allowed to take a time out during his/her turn at the table, between sets or games, or as permitted under administrative discretion. During a time out a sign or other designation should be placed on the table by the referee or tournament official, and no practice will be allowed on that table. In general, each player will be allowed one five (5) minute time out per match. (*Refer to Rule 1.6*)

1.14 CONCESSION

If a player concedes, he loses the *match. That is,* if a player attempts to unscrew his jointed playing cue stick while the opponent is at the table *and during the opponent's decisive game of a match,* it will be considered a concession of the match. No warning from the referee is required in the case of a concession. (*Refer to Rule 2.22*)

1.15 SCORING OF FORFEITS

Matches forfeited for any reason under these rules shall not result in any scores being included in the statistics of a tournament, regardless of whether any score had been reached prior to the declaration of forfeiture. For official records, no point scores should be recorded, but rather the notations "W(F)" and "L(F)" as appropriate should be employed. (*Matches lost through disqualification are considered forfeits for purposes of this rule.*)

If, however, the player awarded a match through the opponent's forfeiture has posted a high run (*or similar accomplishment for which an award is granted*) during play of the match prior to declaration of forfeiture, that high run or other mark shall be eligible for the tournament award or prize.

1.16 PLAYING WITHOUT A REFEREE

When a referee is not available, any dispute between the two players will be resolved by the Tournament Director or an appointed substitute.

1.16.1 CUE BALL FOULS ONLY

When a referee is presiding over a match, it is a foul for a player to touch any ball (*cue ball or object ball*) with the cue, clothing, body, mechanical bridge or chalk, before, during or after a shot. However, when a referee is not presiding over a game, it is not a foul to accidentally touch stationary balls located between the cue ball and the shooter while in the act of shooting. If such an accident occurs, the player should allow the Tournament Director to restore the object balls to their correct positions. If the player does not allow such a restoration, and a ball set in motion as a normal part of the shot touches such an unrestored ball, or passes partly into a region originally occupied by a disturbed ball, the shot is a foul. In short, if the accident has any effect on the outcome of the shot, it is a foul. In any case, the Tournament Director must be called upon to restore the positions of the disturbed balls as soon as possible, but not during the shot. It is a foul to play another shot before the Tournament Director has restored any accidentally moved balls.

At the non-shooting player's option, the disturbed balls will be left in their new positions. In this case, the balls are considered restored, and subsequent contact on them is not a foul. It is still a foul to make any contact with the cue ball whatsoever while it is in play, except for the normal tip-to-ball contact during a shot.

1.16.2 JUMP AND MASSÉ SHOT FOUL

If a match is not refereed, it will be considered a cue ball foul if during an attempt to jump, curve or massé the cue ball over or around an impeding numbered ball that is not a legal object ball, the impeding ball moves (*regardless of whether it was moved by a hand, cue stick follow-through or bridge*).

1.16.3 THIRD OPINION

When a shot comes up that seems likely to lead to controversy, either party may request a tournament official or a third party to judge the legality of the shot.

1.16.4 SPLIT HITS

If the cue ball strikes a legal object ball and a non-legal object ball at approximately the same instant, and it cannot be determined which ball was hit first, the judgement will go in favor of the shooter.

1.16.5 RACKING

The balls must be racked as tightly as possible, which means each ball should be touching its neighbor. Refrain from tapping object balls more than absolutely necessary; it is preferable to thoroughly brush the area of the rack to even out the cloth.

(Further instructions for Tournament Play are Included in the Next Section, "Instructions For Referees").

INSTRUCTIONS FOR REFEREES

2.1 TOURNAMENT OFFICIALS/REFEREES

Where these rules refer to a "referee", it should be noted that the referees' prerogatives and discretion also pertain to other tournament officials as appropriate.

2.2 REFEREE'S AUTHORITY

The referee will maintain order and enforce the rules of the game. The referee is the final judge in all matters of fact, and is in complete charge of the match. The referee may consult other tournament officials for rule interpretations, ball positions, etc. However, all matters of judgement are his and his alone; they cannot be appealed to higher tournament authority by players; only if the referee is in error on a rule or its application may higher tournament authority overrule him.

2.3 REFEREE'S RESPONSIVENESS

The referee shall be totally responsive to players' inquiries regarding objective data, such as whether a ball will be in the rack, if a ball is in the kitchen, what the count is, how many points are needed for a victory, if a player or his opponent is on a foul, what rule would apply if a certain shot is made, etc. When asked for a clarification of a rule, the referee will explain the applicable rule to the best of his ability, but any misstatement by the referee will not protect a player from enforcement of the actual rules. The referee must not offer or provide any subjective opinion that would affect play, such as whether a good hit can be made on a prospective shot, whether a combination can be made, or how the table seems to be playing, etc.

2.4 FINAL TOURNAMENT AUTHORITY

Though these rules attempt to cover the vast majority of situations that arise in competition, there still may be the occasional need for interpretation of the rules and their proper application under unusual circumstances. The Tournament Director or other official who assumes final responsibility for a tournament will make any such required decision (*other than referee's judgement calls*) at his discretion, and they shall be final.

2.5 WAGERING BY REFEREES

Referees are strictly prohibited from any wagering of any kind involving the games, players or tournament in any way. Any such wagering by a referee (*or other tournament official*) shall result in his immediate dismissal and the forfeiture of his entire financial compensation for the tournament.

2.6 EQUIPMENT PREPARATION

In general, the referee will have the table and balls cleaned as necessary. He will ensure that chalk, powder, and mechanical bridges are available. He will mark or have *marked*, spots, the head string, the long string, and the outer edge of the triangle, *directly on the playing surface*, when *required by specific game rules.*

2.7 RACKING

After the referee has racked the balls for a game, the player may examine the balls as racked but the referee shall be the sole authority regarding the suitability of the rack for play.

2.8 CALLING SHOTS

If a referee incorrectly calls a shot, where required by specific game rules, a player should correct him/her before completing the shot. If an incorrect call does occur for any reason, the shot shall be credited if, in the judgement of the referee, the player did legally execute the shot as intended.

2.9 CALLING FOULS

The referee will call fouls as soon as possible after they occur. No further play may occur until a decision regarding a foul has been rendered and both players informed. If the offending player continues to shoot after a foul is called, the referee may consider the action to be unsportsmanlike conduct, and the offending player loses the game (*or fifteen (15) points*) *if playing 14.1 Continuous*). The referee shall inform the incoming player of ball-in-hand where specific game rules apply and should pick up the cue ball and hand it to the incoming player. The referee may announce "Ball-in-hand".

2.10 SPLIT HITS

When the referee observes that the cue ball strikes a legal object ball and a non-legal object ball at approximately the same instant, and it cannot be determined which ball was hit first, the judgement will go in favor of the shooter.

2.11 CLEARING POCKETS

On tables which do not have ball return systems, the referee will remove pocketed object balls from full or nearly full pockets. It is the player's responsibility to see that this duty is performed; he has no recourse if a ball rebounds from a full pocket.

2.12 CLEANING BALLS

During a game a player may ask the referee to clean one or more balls. The referee will clean any visibly soiled ball.

2.13 SPOTTING BALLS

To avoid any unnecessary guidance to a player when spotting balls, the referee should position each ball so that the number is facing upward.

2.14 SOLICITING INFORMATION

If the referee does not have a clear view of a possible foul, he may form his decision by any means by which he feels comfortable.

2.15 INAPPROPRIATE USE OF EQUIPMENT

The referee should be alert for a player using equipment or accessory items for purposes or in a manner other than those for which they were intended, *or for the use of illegal equipment, as defined under "equipment specification".* Generally no penalty is applied. However, should a player persist in such activity or *use of such equipment, after having been advised that such activity or use is not permissible,* the referee or other tournament official may take action as appropriate under the provisions of "Unsportsmanlike Conduct" (*Also see Rules 1.3 and 1.4*)

2.16 MANDATORY WARNINGS

The referee must warn a player who is about to commit a serious foul (such as three (3) consecutive fouls, requesting coaching assistance, or failure to stop shooting after a foul has been called) whenever the referee has been given sufficient time to do so; otherwise any foul is considered to be a standard foul (except as specially noted). *For instance,* in games where the rule applies, the referee must inform a player who has two (2) consecutive fouls, otherwise the player is considered to have had only one foul prior to the shot; the referee must inform a player when an object ball is touching a rail, otherwise any contact on *that ball* is considered to have driven that ball to the rail. The referee should notify the player as soon as the corresponding situation arises and whenever enough time was given to issue the warning. *A warning issued just as a stroke occurs or is about to occur is not considered sufficient time for the shooter to react and the warning will be considered not to have been issued.*

2.17 RESTORING A POSITION

When necessary *for balls to be restored or cleaned*, the referee will restore disturbed balls to their original position to the best of his ability. *The players must accept the referees judgement as to placement.* The referee may ask for information for this purpose from whatever source deemed appropriate.

2.18 OUTSIDE INTERFERENCE

When outside interference occurs during a shot that has an effect on the outcome of that shot, the referee will restore the balls to the positions they had before the shot, and the shot will be replayed. If the interference had no effect on the shot, the referee will restore the disturbed balls and play will continue. If the balls cannot be restored to their original positions, the game should be replayed with the original player breaking.

2.19 ILLEGALLY CAUSING BALL TO MOVE

Any player who, in the referee's judgement, intentionally causes a ball to move by any illegal means (*pushing on bed cloth, bumping or slapping table, etc.*) will lose the game and/or match by forfeit. No preliminary warning from the referee is required. (*Referee's judgement and discretion under "Unsportsmanlike Conduct"*).

2.20 JUDGING DOUBLE HITS

When the distance between the cue ball and the object ball is less than the width of a chalk cube, (*See Diagram 18*) special attention from the referee is required. In such a situation, unless the referee can positively determine a legal shot has been performed, the following guidance may apply: if the cue ball follows through the object ball more than 1/2 ball, it is a foul.

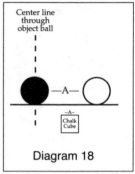

Diagram 18

2.21 OUT OF HEAD STRING WARNING

When a player has the cue ball in hand behind the head string, the referee shall warn him before he shoots if he has *placed the cue ball on or within 1/2 ball width outside of the head string. If the player then shoots from on or within the specified distance outside the head string, the stroke is a foul. If the shooter places the cue ball outside of the head string beyond the specified limit, no warning is required and the stroke is a foul.* (See specific game rule for penalty. Also refer to Rule 3.39)

2.22 REMAINING IN PLAYER'S CHAIR

Players are to remain in the chair designated for their use while the opponent is at the table. Should a player need to leave the playing area during a match, he must request and receive permission from the referee. *Should a player leave the playing area without the permission of the referee, it will be a concession and loss of game (or fifteen (15) points if in 14.1 Continuous).* The referee shall apply his good judgement to ensure that undue time is not being used or that a player is not abusing the privilege as a means of unsettling an opponent.

2.23 OUTSIDE ASSISTANCE PROHIBITED

Unless specifically permitted by the rules of a given tournament, players may not knowingly accept any form of playing advice during a match. A player may not engage in communication, either verbal or non-verbal, with persons other than the tournament officials or his opponent during play, or *during time-outs*. Should a player desire to so communicate, for example to obtain a beverage, get a piece of equipment, etc., he should either communicate through a tournament official or with the approval and observance of the referee.

If the referee has reason to believe that a player knowingly solicited or accepted outside assistance in any manner regarding the play of a game or match, he shall take steps appropriate under the provisions of "Unsportsmanlike Conduct". *In team or doubles play, communication rules may be altered by the appropriate organization as provided for under "Administrative Discretion".*

2.24 NON-PLAYER INTERFERENCE OR HARASSMENT

If a non-player *by any means* interferes with *either* or *both players, the referee should request the offending non-player or players be removed from the playing area for the duration of the match.*

2.25 SLOW PLAY

(*See Rule 1.11*)

2.26 PROTESTS

A player may request a rule interpretation or protest a failure to call a foul to the referee or appropriate tournament authority, but the request or protest must be made immediately and prior to any subsequent shot being taken, or it cannot be considered or honored. If the player fails to do so, the foul is considered not to have occurred. The referee is the final judge on all matters of fact. If either player thinks the referee is applying the rules incorrectly *or has made an interpretation incorrectly*, the referee must take the protest to the tournament director or his appointed substitute. The tournament director or his appointed substitute's interpretation of the rules is final. Play will be suspended until the protest is resolved. All players must honor an opponent's request that play be halted if an official is to be summoned or if a referee is to check or verify a rule question. Failure to honor such a request may result in disqualification or forfeiture of the game or match under the provisions of "Unsportsmanlike Conduct".

2.27 SUSPENDING PLAY

The referee has the authority to suspend play during protests by players and whenever he feels that conditions are unsuitable for play to continue. If a spectator is interfering with the game, play may be suspended until that spectator is removed from area. (*Also see Rule 1.12*)

2.28 UNSPORTSMANLIKE CONDUCT

The referee has the right and obligation to ensure that no player engages in any activity which, in his judgement, is unsportsmanlike in nature, embarrassing, disruptive or detrimental to other players, tournament officials or hosts, or the sport in general. The referee or other officials shall have the right to penalize or disqualify, with or without warning, any player who acts in an unsportsmanlike manner.

GENERAL RULES OF POCKET BILLIARDS

These general rules apply to all pocket billiard games, UNLESS specifically noted to the contrary in the individual game rules. To facilitate the use and understanding of these general rules, terms that may require definition are set in italics so that the reader may refer to the Glossary of Billiard Terms section for the exact meaning of the term.

3.1 TABLES, BALLS, EQUIPMENT

All games described in these rules are designed for tables, balls and equipment meeting the standards prescribed in the BCA Equipment Specifications.

3.2 RACKING THE BALLS

When racking the balls a triangle must be used, and the apex ball is to be spotted on the foot spot. All the balls must be lined up behind the apex ball and pressed together so that they all have contact with each other.

3.3 STRIKING CUE BALL

Legal shots require that the cue ball be struck only with the cue tip. Failure to meet this requirement is a foul.

3.4 CALLING SHOTS

For games of call shot, a player may shoot any ball he chooses, but before he shoots, must designate the called ball and called pocket. He need not indicate any detail such as kisses, caroms, combinations, or cushions (all of which are legal). "Any additionally pocketed ball(s) on a legal stroke is counted in the shooter's favor".

3.5 FAILURE TO POCKET A BALL

If a player fails to pocket a ball on a legal shot, then the player's inning is over, and it is the opponent's turn at the table.

3.6 LAG FOR BREAK

The following procedure is used for the lag for the opening break. Each player should use balls of equal size and weight (*preferably cue balls but, when not available, non-striped object balls*). With the balls in hand behind the head string, one player to the left and one to the right of the head spot, the balls are shot simultaneously to the foot cushion and back to the head end of the table. The player whose ball is the closest to the innermost edge of the head cushion wins the lag. The lagged ball must contact the foot cushion at least once. Other cushion contacts are immaterial, except as prohibited below. It is an automatic loss of the lag if:

(a) The ball crosses into the opponent's half of the table;
(b) The ball fails to contact the foot cushion;
(c) The ball drops into a pocket;
(d) The ball jumps off the table;
(e) The ball touches the long cushion;
(f) The ball rests within the corner pocket and past the nose of the head cushion, or;
(g) The ball contacts the foot rail more than once. If both players violate automatic-loss lag rules, or if the referee is unable to determine which ball is closer, the lag is a tie and is replayed.

3.7   OPENING BREAK SHOT

The opening break shot is determined by either lag or lot. (*The lag for break procedure is required for formal competition.*) The player winning the lag or lot has the choice of performing the opening break shot or assigning it to the opponent.

3.8   CUE BALL ON OPENING BREAK

The opening break shot is taken with cue ball in hand behind the head string. The object balls are positioned according to specific game rules. On the opening break, the game is considered to have commenced once the cue ball has been struck by the cue tip.

3.9   DEFLECTING THE CUE BALL ON THE GAME'S OPENING BREAK

On the break shot, stopping or deflecting the cue ball after it has crossed the head string and prior to hitting the racked balls is considered a foul and loss of turn. The opponent has the option of receiving cue ball in hand behind the head string or passing the cue ball in hand behind the head string back to the offending player. (*Exception: 9-Ball, see rule 5.4: "cue ball in hand anywhere on the table"*). A warning must be given that a second violation during the match will result in the loss of the match by forfeiture. (*See Rule 3.29*)

3.10   CUE BALL IN HAND BEHIND THE HEAD STRING

This situation applies in specific games whereby the opening break is administered or a player's scratching is penalized by the incoming player having cue ball in hand behind the head string. The incoming player may place the cue ball anywhere behind the head string. The shooting player may shoot at any object ball as long as the base of the object ball is on or below the head string. He may not shoot at any ball, the base of which is above the head string, unless he first shoots the cue ball below the head string and then by hitting a rail causes the cue ball to come back above the head string and hit the object ball. The base of the ball (the point of the ball touching the table) determines whether it is above or below the head string. If the incoming player inadvertently places the cue ball on or below the head string, the referee or the opposing player must inform the shooting player of improper positioning of the cue ball before the shot is made. If the opposing player does not so inform the shooting player before the shot is made, the shot is considered legal. If the shooting player is informed of improper positioning, he must then reposition the cue ball. If a player positions the cue ball completely and obviously outside the kitchen and shoots the cue ball, it is a foul. (*Refer to Rule 2.21*) When the cue ball is in hand behind the head string, it remains in hand (not in play) until the player drives the cue ball past the head string with his cue tip. The cue ball may be adjusted by the player's hand, cue, etc., so long as it remains in hand. Once the cue ball is in play per the above, it may not be impeded in any way by the player; to do so is to commit a foul. *Additionally, if the shot fails to contact a legal object ball or fails to drive the cue ball over the head string, the shot is a foul and the opposing player has ball in hand according to the specific game rules.*

3.11 POCKETED BALLS

A ball is considered pocketed if as a result of an otherwise legal shot, it drops off the bed of the table into the pocket and remains there. (*A ball that drops out of a ball return system onto the floor is not to be construed as a ball that has not remained pocketed.*) A ball that rebounds from a pocket back onto the table bed is not a pocketed ball.

3.12 POSITION OF BALLS

The position of a ball is judged by where its base (*or center*) rests.

3.13 FOOT ON FLOOR

Player must have at least one foot in contact with the floor at the moment the cue tip contacts the cue ball, or the shot is a foul. Foot attire must be normal in regard to size, shape and manner in which it is worn.

3.14 SHOOTING WITH BALLS IN MOTION

It is a foul if a player shoots while the cue ball or any object ball is in motion (*a spinning ball is in motion*).

3.15 COMPLETION OF STROKE

A stroke is not complete (*and therefore is not counted*) until all balls on the table have become motionless after the stroke (*a spinning ball is in motion*).

3.16 HEAD STRING DEFINED

The area behind the head string does not include the head string. Thus, an object ball that is dead center on the head string is playable when specific game rules require that a player must shoot at a ball past the head string. Likewise, the cue ball when being put in play behind the head string (*cue ball in hand behind the head string*), may not be placed directly on the head string; it must be behind it.

3.17 GENERAL RULE, ALL FOULS

Though the penalties for fouls differ from game to game, the following apply to all fouls:
  (a) Player's inning ends;
  (b) If on a stroke, the stroke is invalid and any pocketed balls are not counted to the shooter's credit, and;
  (c) Any ball(s) is respotted only if the rules of the specific game require it.

3.18 FAILURE TO CONTACT OBJECT BALL

It is a foul if on a stroke the cue ball fails to make contact with any legal object ball first. Playing away from a touching ball does not constitute having hit that ball.

3.19 LEGAL SHOT

Unless otherwise stated in a specific game rule, a player must cause the cue ball to contact a legal object ball and then:
  (a) Pocket a numbered ball, or;
  (b) Cause the cue ball or any numbered ball to contact a cushion or any part of the rail. Failure to meet these requirements is a foul.

3.20 CUE BALL SCRATCH

It is a foul (*scratch*) if on a stroke, the cue ball is pocketed. If the cue ball touches an object ball that was already pocketed (*for example, in a pocket full of object balls*), the shot is a foul.

3.21 FOULS BY TOUCHING BALLS

It is a foul to strike, touch or in any way make contact with the cue ball in play or any object balls in play with anything (*the body, clothing, chalk, mechanical bridge, cue shaft, etc.*) except the cue tip (*while attached to the cue shaft*), which may contact the cue ball in the execution of a legal shot. Whenever a referee is presiding over a match, any object ball moved during a standard foul must be returned as closely as possible to its original position as judged by the referee, and the incoming player does not have the option of restoration. (*Also see Rule 1.16.1*)

3.22 FOUL BY PLACEMENT

Touching any object ball with the cue ball while it is in hand is a foul.

3.23 FOULS BY DOUBLE HITS

If the cue ball is touching the required object ball prior to the shot, the player may shoot toward it, providing that any normal stroke is employed. If the cue stick strikes the cue ball more than once on a shot, or if the cue stick is in contact with the cue ball when or after the cue ball contacts an object ball, the shot is a foul (*See Rule 2.20 for judging this kind of shot*). If a third ball is close by, care should be taken not to foul that ball under the first part of this rule.

3.24 PUSH SHOT FOULS

It is a foul if the cue ball is pushed by the cue tip, with contact being maintained for more than the momentary time commensurate with a stroked shot. (*Such shots are usually referred to as push shots.*)

3.25 PLAYER RESPONSIBILITY FOULS

The player is responsible for chalk, bridges, files and any other items or equipment he brings to, uses at, or causes to approximate the table. If he drops a piece of chalk, or knocks off a mechanical bridge head, as examples, he is guilty of a foul should such an object make contact with any ball in play (*or the cue ball only if no referee is presiding over the match*).

3.26 ILLEGAL JUMPING OF BALL

It is a foul if a player strikes the cue ball below center (*"digs under" or "lofts" the cue ball*) and intentionally causes it to rise off the bed of the table in an effort to clear an obstructing ball. Such jumping action may occasionally occur accidentally, and such "jumps" are not to be considered fouls on their face; they may still be ruled foul strokes, if for example, the ferrule or cue shaft makes contact with the cue ball in the course of the shot.

3.27 JUMP SHOTS

Unless otherwise stated in rules for a specific game it is legal to cause the cue ball to rise off the bed of the table by elevating the cue stick on the shot, and forcing the cue ball to rebound from the bed of the table. Any miscue when executing a jump shot is a foul.

3.28 BALLS JUMPED OFF TABLE

Balls coming to rest other than on the bed of the table after a stroke (*on the cushion top, rail surface, floor, etc.*) are considered jumped balls. Balls may bounce on the cushion tops and rails of the table in play without being jumped balls if they return to the bed of the table under their own power and without touching anything not a part of the table. The table shall consist of the permanent part of the table proper. (*Balls that strike or touch anything not a part of the table, such as the light fixture, chalk on the rails and cushion tops, etc., shall be considered jumped balls even though they might return to the bed of the table after contacting items which are not parts of the table proper*). In all pocket billiard games, when a stroke results in the cue ball or any object ball being a jumped ball off the table, the stroke is a foul. All jumped object balls are spotted (except in 8 and 9-Ball) when all balls have stopped moving. See specific game rules for putting the cue ball in play after a jumped cue ball foul.

3.29 SPECIAL INTENTIONAL FOUL PENALTY

The cue ball in play shall not be intentionally struck with anything other than a cue's attached tip (*such as the ferrule, shaft, etc.*). While such contact is automatically a foul under the provisions of Rule 3.21, if the referee deems the contact to be intentional, he shall warn the player once during a match that a second violation during that match will result in the loss of the match by forfeiture. If a second violation does occur, the match must be forfeited.

3.30 ONE FOUL LIMIT

Unless specific game rules dictate otherwise, only one foul is assessed on a player in each inning; if different penalties can apply, the most severe penalty is the factor determining which foul is assessed.

3.31 BALLS MOVING SPONTANEOUSLY

If a ball shifts, settles, turns or otherwise moves "by itself", the ball shall remain in the position it assumed and play continues. A hanging ball that falls into a pocket "by itself" after being motionless for 5 seconds or longer shall be replaced as closely as possible to its position prior to falling, and play shall continue. If an object ball drops into a pocket "by itself" as a player shoots at it, so that the cue ball passes over the spot the ball had been on, unable to hit it, the cue ball and object ball are to be replaced to their positions prior to the stroke, and the player may shoot again. Any other object balls disturbed on the stroke are also to be replaced to their original positions before the shooter replays.

3.32 SPOTTING BALLS

When specific game rules call for spotting balls, they shall be replaced on the table on the long string after the stroke is complete. A single ball is placed on the foot spot; if more than one ball is to be spotted, they are placed on the long string in ascending numerical order, beginning on the foot spot and advancing toward the foot rail. When balls on or near the foot spot or long string interfere with the spotting of balls, the balls to be spotted are placed on the long string as close as possible to the foot spot without moving the interfering balls. Spotted balls are to be placed as close as possible or frozen (*at the referee's discretion*) to such interfering balls, except when the cue ball is interfering; balls to be spotted against the cue ball are placed as close as possible without

Spotting Balls

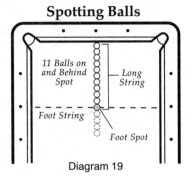

Diagram 19

being frozen. If there is insufficient room on the long string between the foot spot and the foot rail cushion for balls that must be spotted, such balls are then placed on the extension of the long string "in front" of the foot spot (*between the foot spot and the center spot*), as near as possible to the foot spot and in the same numerical order as if they were spotted "behind" the foot spot (*lowest numbered ball closest to the foot spot*).

3.33 JAWED BALLS

If two or more balls are locked between the jaws or sides of the pocket, with one or more suspended in air, the referee shall inspect the balls in position and follow this procedure: he shall visually (*or physically if he desires*) project each ball directly downward from its locked position; any ball that in his judgement would fall in the pocket if so moved directly downward is a pocketed ball, while any ball that would come to rest on the bed of the table is not pocketed. The balls are then placed according to the referee's assessment, and play continues according to specific game rules as if no locking or jawing of balls had occurred.

3.34 ADDITIONAL POCKETED BALLS

If extra balls are pocketed on a legal scoring stroke, they are counted in accord with the scoring rules for the particular game.

3.35 NON-PLAYER INTERFERENCE

If the balls are moved (*or a player bumped such that play is directly affected*) by a non-player during the match, the balls shall be replaced as near as possible to their original positions immediately prior to the incident, and play shall resume with no penalty on the player affected. If the match is officiated, the referee shall replace the balls. This rule also applies to "act of God" interferences, such as earthquakes, hurricanes, light fixture falling, power failures, etc. If the balls cannot be restored to their original positions, replay the game with the original player breaking. This rule is not applicable to 14.1 Continuous where the game consists of successive racks: the rack in progress will be discontinued and a completely new rack will be started with the requirements of the normal opening break (*players lag for break*). Scoring of points is to be resumed at the score as it stood at the moment of game disruption.

3.36 BREAKING SUBSEQUENT RACKS

In a match that consists of short rack games, the winner of each game breaks in the next. The following are common options that may be designated by tournament officials in advance:

(a) Players alternate break.

(b) Loser breaks.

(c) Player trailing in game count breaks the next game.

3.37 PLAY BY INNINGS

During the course of play, players alternate turns (*innings*) at the table, with a player's inning ending when he either fails to legally pocket a ball, or fouls. When an inning ends free of a foul, the incoming player accepts the table in position.

3.38 OBJECT BALL FROZEN TO CUSHION OR CUE BALL

This rule applies to any shot where the cue ball's first contact with a ball is with one that is frozen to a cushion or to the cue ball itself. After the cue ball makes contact with the frozen object ball, the shot must result in either:

(a) A ball being pocketed, or;

(b) The cue ball contacting a cushion, or;

(c) The frozen ball being caused to contact a cushion attached to a separate rail, or;

(d) Another object ball being caused to contact a cushion with which it was not already in contact. Failure to satisfy one of those four requirements is a foul. (*Note: 14.1 and other games specify additional requirements and applications of this rule; see specific game rules.*) A ball which is touching a cushion at the start of a shot and then is forced into a cushion attached to the same rail is not considered to have been driven to that cushion unless it leaves the cushion, contacts another ball, and then contacts the cushion again. An object ball is not considered frozen to a cushion unless it is examined and announced as such by either the referee or one of the players prior to that object ball being involved in a shot.

3.39 PLAYING FROM BEHIND THE STRING

When a player has the cue ball in hand behind the *head* string (in the kitchen), he must drive the cue ball to a point *across the head string* before it contacts either a cushion, an object ball, *or returns to the kitchen.* Failure to do so is a foul if a referee is presiding over a match. If no referee, the opponent has the option to call it either a foul or to require the offending player to replay the shot again with the balls restored to their positions prior to the shot (and with no foul penalty imposed). Exception: if an object ball lies on or outside the head string (and is thus playable) but so close that the cue ball contacts it before the cue ball is out of the kitchen, the ball can be legally played, *and will be considered to have crossed the head string.* If, with cue ball in hand behind the headstring and while the shooter is attempting a legitimate shot, the cue ball accidentally hits a ball behind the head string, and the cue ball crosses the line, it is a foul. If with cue ball in hand behind the head string, the shooter causes the cue ball to hit an object ball accidentally, and the cue ball does not cross the headstring, the following applies: the incoming player has the option of calling a foul and having cue ball in hand, or having the balls returned to their original position, and having the offending player replay the shot. If a player under the same conditions intentionally causes the cue ball to contact an object ball behind the headstring, it is unsportsmanlike conduct.

3.40 CUE BALL IN HAND FOUL

During cue ball in hand placement, the player may use his hand or any part of his cue (including the tip) to position the cue ball. When placing the cue ball in position, any forward stroke motion *of the cue stick* contacting the cue ball will be *considered a foul if not a legal shot.*

3.41 INTERFERENCE

If the non-shooting player distracts his opponent or interferes with his play, he has fouled. If a player shoots out of turn, or moves any ball except during his inning, it is considered to be interference.

3.42 DEVICES

Players are not allowed to use a ball, the triangle or any other width-measuring device to see if the cue ball or an object ball would travel through a gap, etc. Only the cue stick may be used as an aid to judge gaps *or as an aid to aligning a shot,* as long as the cue is held by the hand. To do so otherwise is a foul and unsportsmanlike conduct. (*Also see Rules 1.3., 1.4. and 2.15*)

3.43 ILLEGAL MARKING

If a player intentionally marks the table in any way (including the placement of chalk) to assist in executing the shot, it is a foul.

41

RULES FOR WHEELCHAIR COMPETITION

The International Stoke Mandeville Wheelchair Sports Federation (ISMWSF) is recognized by the World Pool-Billiard Association (WPA), the world governing body of pocket billiards, as governing all international competitions concerning wheelchair pocket billiards. The ISMWSF has adopted the rules of play within these pages except for the amendments, exceptions and alterations stipulated below.

CUE SPORTS CLASSIFICATION
There are two (2) categories or classes for those competing in wheelchairs:

1. Those players who meet the minimal disability and who are unable to make and sustain a functional bridge with their non-cueing hand.

2. All other players who meet the minimal disability who can make and sustain a functional bridge with the non-cueing hand.

DEFINITION OF MINIMAL DISABILITY:
1. Amputation above the ankle.

2. Decrease of muscle strength in one lower limb of at least 30 points.

3. Severe mobility problems comparable with handicaps under 1) and 2) of this section.

GENERAL RULES
1. Players must remain seated on the cushion or seat of the wheelchair when playing a shot. Should a players buttocks be clear of the cushion or seat when striking the cue ball, it will be deemed a foul.

2. Feet must be kept clear of the floor, should feet or foot-plates touch the floor when striking the cue ball, it will be deemed a foul.

3. Players in class 1 may request the Referee for assistance with rests and equipment etc.

4. Below the knee strapping is allowed to keep feet on foot-plates. Strapping above the waist is not allowed except for medical reasons.

TOURNAMENT POCKET BILLIARD GAMES

EIGHT-BALL
World-Standardized Rules
Except when clearly contradicted by these additional rules,
the General Rules of Pocket Billiards apply.

4.1 OBJECT OF THE GAME
Eight-Ball is a call shot game played with a cue ball and 15 object balls, numbered 1 through 15. One player must pocket balls of the group numbered 1 through 7 (*solid colors*), while the other player has 9 through 15 (*stripes*). **The player pocketing either group first, and then legally pocketing the 8-ball wins the game.**

4.2 CALL SHOT
In Call Shot, obvious balls and pockets do not have to be indicated. It is the opponent's right to ask which ball and pocket if he is unsure of the shot. Bank shots and combination shots are not considered obvious, and care should be taken in calling both the object ball and the intended pocket. When calling the shot, it is never necessary to indicate details such as the number of cushions, banks, kisses, caroms, etc. Any balls pocketed on a foul remain pocketed, regardless of whether they belong to the shooter or the opponent. The opening break is not a "called shot". Any player performing a break shot in 8-Ball may continue to shoot so long as any object ball is legally pocketed on the break.

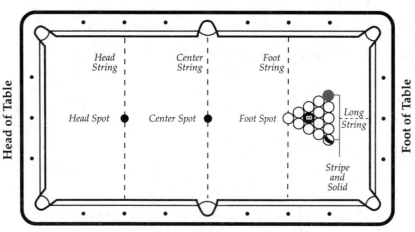

Diagram 20

4.3 RACKING THE BALLS

The balls are racked in a triangle at the foot of the table with the 8-ball in the center of the triangle, the first ball of the rack on the foot spot, a stripe ball in one corner of the rack and a solid ball in the other corner.

4.4 ORDER OF BREAK

Winner of the lag has the option to break. The winner of each game breaks in the next. The following are common options that may be designated by tournament officials in advance:

(a) Players alternate break.

(b) Loser breaks.

(c) Player trailing in game count breaks the next game.

4.5 LEGAL BREAK SHOT

(*Defined*) To execute a legal break, the breaker (*with the cue ball behind the head string*) must either (1) pocket a ball, or (2) drive at least four numbered balls to the rail. When the breaker fails to make a legal break, it is a foul, and the incoming player has the option of (1) accepting the table in position and shooting, or (2) having the balls reracked and having the option of shooting the opening break or allowing the offending player to rebreak.

4.6 SCRATCH ON A LEGAL BREAK

If a player scratches on a legal break shot, (1) all balls pocketed remain pocketed (*exception, the 8-ball: see rule 4.8*), (2) it is a foul, (3) the table is open. **Please Note:** The incoming player has cue ball in hand behind the head string and may not shoot an object ball that is behind the head string, unless he first shoots the cue ball past the head string and causes the cue ball to come back behind the head string and hit the object ball.

4.7 OBJECT BALLS JUMPED OFF TABLE ON THE BREAK

If a player jumps an object ball off the table on the break shot, it is a foul and the incoming player has the option of (1) accepting the table in position and shooting, or (2) taking cue ball in hand behind the head string and shooting.

4.8 8-BALL POCKETED ON THE BREAK

If the 8-ball is pocketed on the break, breaker may ask for a rerack or have the 8-ball spotted and continue shooting. If the breaker scratches while pocketing the 8-ball on the break, the incoming player has the option of a rerack or having the 8-ball spotted and begin shooting with ball in hand behind the head string.

4.9 OPEN TABLE

(Defined) The table is "open" when the choice of groups (stripes or solids) has not yet been determined. When the table is open, it is legal to hit a solid first to make a stripe or vice-versa. Note: The table is always open immediately after the break shot. When the table is open, it is legal to hit any solid or stripe first in the process of pocketing the called stripe or solid. However, when the table is open and the 8-ball is the first ball contacted, it is a foul and no stripe or solid may be scored in favor of the shooter. The shooter loses his turn; the incoming player is awarded cue ball in hand; any balls pocketed remain pocketed; and the incoming player addresses the balls with the table still open. On an open table, all illegally pocketed balls remain pocketed.

4.10 CHOICE OF GROUP

The choice of stripes or solids is not determined on the break even if balls are made from only one or both groups, because the table is always open immediately after the break shot. The choice of group is determined only when a player legally pockets a called object ball after the break shot.

4.11 LEGAL SHOT

(*Defined*) On all shots (*except on the break and when the table is open*), the shooter must hit one of his group of balls first and (1) pocket a numbered ball, or (2) cause the cue ball or any numbered ball to contact a rail. **Please Note**: It is permissible for the shooter to bank the cue ball off a rail before contacting the object ball; however, after contact with the object ball, an object ball must be pocketed, or the cue ball or any numbered ball must contact a rail. Failure to meet these requirements is a foul.

4.12 "SAFETY" SHOT

For tactical reasons, a player may choose to pocket an obvious object ball and also discontinue a turn at the table by declaring "safety" in advance. A safety shot is defined as a legal shot. If the shooting player intends to play safe by pocketing an obvious object ball, then prior to the shot, the shooter must declare a "safety" to the opponent. *It is the shooter's responsibility to make the opponent aware of the intended safety shot.* If this is not done, and one of the shooter's object balls is pocketed, the shooter will be required to shoot again. Any ball pocketed on a safety shot remains pocketed.

4.13 SCORING

A player is entitled to continue shooting until failing to legally pocket a ball of his group. After a player has legally pocketed all of his group of balls, he shoots to pocket the 8-ball.

45

4.14 FOUL PENALTY

Opposing player gets cue ball in hand. This means that the player can place the cue ball anywhere on the table (*does not have to be behind the headstring except on opening break*). This rule prevents a player from making intentional fouls which would put an opponent at a disadvantage. With "cue ball in hand", the player may use a hand or any part of a cue (*including the tip*) to position the cue ball. When placing the cue ball in position, any forward stroke motion contacting the cue ball will be a foul, if not a legal shot. (*Also see Rule 3.39*)

4.15 COMBINATION SHOTS

Combination shots are allowed; however, the 8-ball can't be used as a first ball in the combination unless it is the shooter's only remaining legal object ball on the table. Otherwise, *should such contact occur on the 8-ball, it is a foul.*

4.16 ILLEGALLY POCKETED BALLS

An object ball is considered to be illegally pocketed when (1) that object ball is pocketed on the same shot a foul is committed, or (2) the called ball did not go in the designated pocket, or (3) a safety is called prior to the shot. Illegally pocketed balls remain pocketed *and are scored in favor of the shooter controlling that specific group of balls, solids or stripes.*

4.17 OBJECT BALLS JUMPED OFF THE TABLE

If any object ball is jumped off the table, it is a foul and loss of turn, unless it is the 8-ball, which is a loss of game. Any jumped object balls are *not respotted.*

4.18 JUMP AND MASSÉ SHOT FOUL

While "cue ball fouls only" is the rule of play when a match is not presided over by a referee, a player should be aware that it will be considered a cue ball foul if during an attempt to jump, curve or massé the cue ball over or around an impeding numbered ball that is not a legal object ball, the impeding ball moves (*regardless of whether it was moved by a hand, cue stick follow-through or bridge*).

4.19 PLAYING THE 8-BALL

When the *8-ball is the legal object ball,* a scratch or foul is not loss of game if the 8-ball is not pocketed or jumped from the table. Incoming player has cue ball in hand. Note: A combination shot can never be used to legally pocket the 8-ball, *except when the 8-ball is the first ball contacted in the shot sequence.*

4.20 LOSS OF GAME

A player loses the game by committing any of the following infractions:
1. Fouls when pocketing the 8-ball (exception: see 8-Ball Pocketed On The Break).
2. Pockets the 8-ball on the same stroke as the last of his group of balls.
3. Jumps the 8-ball off the table at any time.
4. Pockets the 8-ball in a pocket other than the one designated.
5. Pockets the 8-ball when it is not the legal object ball.

Note: *All infractions must be called before another shot is taken, or else it will be deemed that no infraction occurred.*

4.21 STALEMATED GAME

If, after 3 consecutive turns at the table by each player (6 turns total), the referee judges that attempting to pocket or move an object ball will result in loss of game, the balls will be reracked with the original breaker of the stalemated game breaking again. The stalemate rule may *be applied regardless of the number of balls on the table*. **Please Note**: Three consecutive fouls by one player in 8-Ball is not a loss of game.

NINE-BALL
World-Standardized Rules
Except when clearly contradicted by these additional rules,
the General Rules of Pocket Billiards apply.

5.1 OBJECT OF THE GAME

Nine-Ball is played with nine object balls numbered one through nine and a cue ball. On each shot, the first ball the cue ball contacts must be the lowest numbered ball on the table, but the balls need not be pocketed in order. If a player pockets any ball on a legal shot, he remains at the table for another shot, and continues until missing, committing a foul, or winning the game by pocketing the 9-ball. After a miss, the incoming player must shoot from the position left by the previous player, but after any foul the incoming player may start with the cue ball anywhere on the table. Players are not required to call any shot. A match ends when one of the players has won the required number of games.

5.2 RACKING THE BALLS

The object balls are racked in a diamond shape, with the 1-ball at the top of the diamond and on the foot spot, the 9-ball in the center of the diamond, and the other balls in random order, racked as tightly as possible. The game begins with cue ball in hand behind the head string.

Pocket Billiards

5.3 ORDER OF BREAK

Winner of the lag has the option to break. In 9-Ball, the winner of each game breaks in the next, unless otherwise specified by the tournament organizer. The following are common options that may be designated by tournament officials in advance:

(a) Players alternate break.

(b) Loser breaks.

(c) Player trailing in game count breaks the next game.

Diamond Shaped Rack

1-Ball must be on the foot spot.
2-Ball must be in the center of the rack.

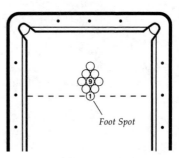

Foot Spot

Diagram 21

5.4 LEGAL BREAK SHOT

The rules governing the break shot are the same as for other shots except:

1. The breaker must strike the 1-ball first and either pocket a ball or drive at least four numbered balls to the rail.

2. If the cue ball is pocketed or driven off the table, or the requirements of the opening break are not met, it is a foul, and the incoming player has cue ball in hand anywhere on the table.

3. If on the break shot, the breaker causes an object ball to jump off the table, it is a foul and the incoming player has cue ball in hand anywhere on the table. The object ball is not respotted (*exception: if the object ball is the 9-ball, it is respotted*).

5.5 CONTINUING PLAY

On the shot immediately following a legal break, the shooter may play a "push out". (*See Rule 5.6*). If the breaker pockets one or more balls on a legal break, he continues to shoot until he misses, fouls, or wins the game. If the player misses or fouls, the other player begins an inning and shoots until missing, committing a foul, or winning. The game ends when the 9-ball is pocketed on a legal shot, or the game is forfeited for a serious infraction of the rules.

5.6 PUSH OUT

The player who shoots the shot immediately after a legal break may play a push out in an attempt to move the cue ball into a better position for the option that follows. On a push out, the cue ball is not required to contact any object ball nor any rail, but all other foul rules still apply. The player must announce the intention of playing a push out before the shot, or the shot is considered to be a normal shot. Any ball pocketed on a push out does not count and remains pocketed except the 9-ball. Following a legal push out, the incoming player is permitted to shoot from that position or to pass the shot back to the player who pushed out. A push out is not considered to be a foul as long as no rule (*except Rules 5.8 and 5.9*) is violated. An illegal push out is penalized according to the type of foul committed. After a player scratches on the break shot, the incoming player cannot play a push out.

5.7   FOULS

When a player commits a foul, he must relinquish his run at the table and no balls pocketed on the foul shot are respotted (*exception: if a pocketed ball is the 9-ball, it is respotted*). The incoming player is awarded ball in hand; prior to his first shot he may place the cue ball anywhere on the table. If a player commits several fouls on one shot, they are counted as only one foul.

5.8   BAD HIT

If the first object ball contacted by the cue ball is not the lowest numbered ball on the table, the shot is foul.

5.9   NO RAIL

If no object ball is pocketed, failure to drive the cue ball or any numbered ball to a rail after the cue ball contacts the object ball is a foul.

5.10   IN HAND

When the cue ball is in hand, the player may place the cue ball anywhere on the bed of the table, except in contact with an object ball. The player may continue to adjust the position of the cue ball until shooting.

5.11   OBJECT BALLS JUMPED OFF THE TABLE

An unpocketed ball is considered to be driven off the table if it comes to rest other than on the bed of the table. It is a foul to drive an object ball off the table. The jumped object ball(s) is not respotted (*exception: if the object ball is the 9-ball, it is respotted*) and play continues.

5.12   JUMP AND MASSÉ SHOT FOUL

If a match is not refereed, it will be considered a cue ball foul if during an attempt to jump, curve or massé the cue ball over or around an impeding numbered ball, the impeding ball moves (*regardless of whether it was moved by a hand, cue stick follow-through or bridge*).

5.13   THREE CONSECUTIVE FOULS

If a player fouls three consecutive times on three successive shots without making an intervening legal shot, the game is lost. The three fouls must occur in one game. The warning must be given between the second and

Pocket Billiards

third fouls. A player's inning begins when it is legal to take a shot and ends at the end of a shot on which he misses, fouls or wins, or when he fouls between shots.

5.14 END OF GAME

On the opening break, the game is considered to have commenced once the cue ball has been struck by the cue tip. The 1-ball must be legally contacted on the break shot. The game ends at the end of a legal shot which pockets the 9-ball, or when a player forfeits the game as the result of a foul.

14.1 CONTINUOUS
World-Standardized Rules
Except when clearly contradicted by these additional rules,
the General Rules of Pocket Billiards apply.

6.1 OBJECT OF THE GAME

14.1 is a nomination game. The player must nominate a ball and a pocket. The player is awarded one point for every correctly nominated and pocketed ball on a legal stroke, and is allowed to continue a turn until failure to pocket a nominated ball or commits a foul. The player can pocket the first 14 balls, but before continuing a turn by shooting at the 15th (*and last remaining*) ball on the table, the 14 pocketed balls are racked as before, except with the apex space vacant. The player then attempts to pocket the 15th ball in a manner so that the racked balls are disturbed and he can continue the run. The player who scores the predetermined point total for a game (*usually 150 in major tournament play or any agreed upon total in casual play*) prior to the opponent, wins the game.

6.2 PLAYERS

2, or 2 teams.

6.3 BALLS USED

Standard set of object balls numbered 1-15, plus the cue ball.

6.4 THE RACK

Standard triangle rack with the apex ball on the foot spot, 1-ball on the racker's right corner, 5-ball on left corner. Other balls are placed at random and must touch their neighbors.

6.5 SCORING

Any ball legally pocketed counts one point for the shooter.

6.6 OPENING BREAK

Starting player must either (1) designate a ball and a pocket into which that ball will be pocketed and accomplish the shot, or (2) cause the cue ball to contact a ball and then a cushion, plus cause two object balls to contact a cushion. Failure to meet at least one of the above requirements is a breaking violation. Offender's score is assessed a 2-point penalty for each breaking violation. In addition, the opponent has the choice of (1) accepting the table in position, or (2) having the balls reracked and requiring the offending player to repeat the opening break. That choice continues until the opening break is not a breaking violation, or until the opponent accepts the table in position. The three successive fouls rule does not apply to breaking violations. If the starting player scratches on a legal opening break, he is charged with a foul and assessed a one point penalty, which applies toward the "Successive Fouls Penalties". The incoming player is awarded cue ball in hand behind the head string, with object balls in position.

6.7 RULES OF PLAY

1. A legally pocketed ball entitles a shooter to continue at the table until he fails to legally pocket a called ball on a shot. A player may shoot any ball, but before the shot, must designate the called ball and called pocket. Details such as kisses, caroms, combinations or cushions (*all of which are legal*) need not be indicated. Any additionally pocketed ball(s) on a legal stroke is scored as one point for the shooter.

2. On all shots, a player must cause the cue ball to contact an object ball and then (1) pocket a numbered ball, or (2) cause the cue ball or any numbered ball to contact a cushion. Failure to meet these requirements is a foul. When an object ball is not frozen to a cushion, but is within a ball's width of a cushion (*referee to determine by measurement if necessary*), a player is permitted only two consecutive legal safeties on that ball using only the near rail. If such safety play is employed, that object ball is then considered frozen to the rail on the player's next inning. The General Rules of Pocket Billiards "Frozen Balls" requirements apply if the player chooses to make the first cue ball contact with that object ball on the third shot.

(**Note**: *If a player has committed a foul on the shot immediately before or the shot immediately after playing this ball, then he must immediately meet the requirements of the "Frozen Ball" rule when playing this object ball. Also, if he has committed two consecutive fouls, he must immediately meet the requirements of the Frozen Ball rule when playing this object ball. If such player fails to meet the requirements of the Frozen Ball rule, he is considered to have committed a third successive foul and the appropriate point penalty is assessed as well as one point for each of the previous fouls. All 15 balls are then reracked and the player committing the infraction is required to break, as at the beginning of the game.*)

51

3. When the 14th ball of a rack is pocketed, play stops momentarily with the 15th ball remaining in position on the table; the 14 pocketed balls are then racked (*with the space at the foot spot vacant in the triangle*). Player then continues, normally pocketing the 15th (*or "break" ball*) in such a manner as to have the cue ball carom into the rack and spread the balls to facilitate the continuance of his run. However, player is not compelled to shoot the 15th ball; he may shoot any ball he desires. See Diagram 22 if the 15th ball is pocketed on the same stroke as the 14th ball.

4. A player may call a safety rather than an object ball (*for defensive purposes*). Safety play is legal, but must comply with all applicable rules. The player's inning ends when a safety is played, and pocketed balls are not scored. Any object ball pocketed on a called safety is spotted.

5. A player may not catch, touch or in any way interfere with a ball as it travels toward a pocket or the rack area on a shot (*to include catching a ball as it enters a pocket by having a hand in the pocket*).
Doing so is a special "deliberate foul" and is penalized one point for the foul and an additional 15 point penalty, for a total of 16 points. The incoming player then has choice of (1) accepting the table in position with the cue ball in hand behind the head string, or (2) having all 15 balls reracked and requiring the offending player to shoot under the requirements of the opening break.

6. If the 15th (*unpocketed*) ball of a rack and/or the cue ball interferes with

Cue Ball Lies 15th Ball Lies	IN THE RACK	NOT IN THE RACK & NOT ON HEAD SPOT*	ON HEAD SPOT*
IN THE RACK	15th Ball: foot spot. Cue Ball: in kitchen.	15th Ball: head spot. Cue Ball: in position.	15th Ball: center spot. Cue Ball: in position.
POCKETED	15th Ball: foot spot. Cue Ball: in kitchen.	15th Ball: foot spot. Cue Ball: in position.	15th Ball: foot spot. Cue Ball: in position.
IN KITCHEN BUT NOT ON HEAD SPOT*	15th Ball: in position. Cue Ball: head spot.		
NOT IN KITCHEN & NOT IN THE RACK	15th Ball: in position. Cue Ball: in kitchen.		
ON HEAD SPOT*	15th Ball: in position. Cue Ball: center spot.		*On head spot means to interfere with spotting a ball on the head spot.

Diagram 22

the triangle being lowered straight down into position for racking, refer to the diagram, which indicates the proper manner of relocating balls. (*The gray boxes are those situations in which there is no interference, both balls remain in position.*)

7. When a player has the cue ball in hand behind the head string (*as after a scratch*) and all the object balls are behind the head string, the object ball

nearest the head string may be spotted upon request. If two or more balls are an equal distance from the head string, the player may designate which of the equidistant balls is to be spotted.

6.8   ILLEGALLY POCKETED BALLS
All spotted. No penalty.

6.9   OBJECT BALLS JUMPED OFF THE TABLE
The stroke is a foul. Any jumped ball(s) is spotted after the balls come to rest.

6.10   CUE BALL AFTER JUMPING OFF TABLE/SCRATCH
Incoming player has cue ball in hand behind the head string, unless the provision of Rule of Play 6.7.2, 6.7.5 or 6.12 apply to the offender's foul and dictate alternate choices or procedures.

6.11   PENALTIES FOR FOULS
One point deducted for each foul. Note: penalties are more severe for deliberate fouls (*Rule of Play 6.7.5*) and third "Successive Fouls" (*6.12*). Incoming player accepts cue ball in position unless foul was a jumped cue ball, pocket scratch, deliberate foul (*Rule of Play 6.7.5*) or third successive foul.

6.12   SUCCESSIVE FOUL PENALTIES
When a player commits a foul, penalization is one point (*or more as appropriate*) and a notation is made and posted by the scorer that the player is "on a foul". The player remains "on a foul" until the next shot attempt, at which time the foul may be removed by successfully pocketing a called ball, or completing a legal safety. If failing to meet these requirements on the next turn at the table, the player is penalized one point. The notation is changed to "on two fouls". If he fails to meet the requirements of successfully pocketing a called ball or completing a legal safety on the third consecutive turn at the table, penalization is one point and an additional penalty of 15 points is assessed (*a total of 18 points for three consecutive fouls equals -18 points*). The commission of a third successive foul automatically clears the offender's record of fouls. "The incoming player then has choice of 1) Accepting the table in position, or 2) having all 15 balls reracked and requiring the offending player to shoot under the requirements of the opening break".

It should be emphasized that successive fouls must be committed in successive turns (*or playing attempts*), not merely in successive innings. For example, if a player ends inning six with a foul, steps to the table for inning seven and fouls (*he is "on two fouls"*), and then starts inning eight with a legally pocketed ball before scratching on his second shot attempt of the inning, he has not committed three successive fouls, even though there were fouls in three successive innings. As soon as he legally pocketed the ball to start inning eight, he cleared the two fouls. He is, of course, "on one foul" when he plays the first stroke attempt of inning nine.

6.13 SCORING NOTE

The deduction of penalty points can result in negative scores. A running score can read "minus one", "minus two", "minus 15", etc. (*A player can win a game with a score of 150 while the opponent has scored but two fouls. The final score would read 150 to -2.*)

If a player fouls on a shot that has not pocketed a ball, the point penalty is deducted from his score at the end of the previous inning. If a player fouls and pockets a ball on the same shot, that ball is spotted (*not scored*) and the point penalty is deducted from his score at the end of the previous inning.

ONE POCKET
Except when clearly contradicted by these additional rules,
the General Rules of Pocket Billiards apply.

TYPE OF GAME
One Pocket is a unique game in which only two of the six pockets are employed for legal scoring. Any ball may be played and need not be called. What is required is that an object ball falls in the player's "target" pocket. It requires a wide variety of strokes, cue ball control, shot-making ability, patience and defensive strategy.

PLAYERS
2, or 2 teams.

BALLS USED
Standard set of object balls 1-15, plus cue ball.

THE RACK
Standard triangle rack; balls placed entirely at random.

OBJECT OF THE GAME
Score a total of eight object balls in a player's target pocket before opponent.

SELECTION OF POCKETS

Prior to the opening break shot, the starting player chooses one of the corner pockets on the foot end of the table as a target pocket; the opponent then has the other foot end corner as a target pocket.

SCORING

A legally pocketed ball is scored as one ball for shooter. Any ball pocketed in opponent's target pocket counts, unless the cue ball should scratch on the same shot. If the shot constitutes a foul other than a scratch, the opponent is allowed to keep the ball. A shooter's inning ends on a scratch or foul and any balls pocketed in the shooter's pocket don't count on a foul or scratch. In addition, the shooter is penalized one ball for a foul or scratch.

OPENING BREAK

Starting player must (1) legally pocket an object ball into his targeted pocket, or (2) cause the cue ball to contact an object ball and after contact, at least one object ball must contact a cushion. Failure to do so is a foul. Note: The cue ball does not have to strike a rail on the opening break.

RULES OF PLAY:

1. A legal shot requires that the cue ball contact an object ball and then (1) pocket a numbered ball, or (2) cause the cue ball or any numbered ball to contact a cushion. Failure to do so is a foul.

2. A legally pocketed ball in a target pocket entitles shooter to remain at the table until failing to pocket a ball in the target pocket on a legal shot. Player may choose to shoot any object ball, any ball pocketed in the target pocket on an otherwise legal stroke is a scored ball.

3. Balls pocketed in the four non-target pockets are "Illegally Pocketed Balls".

4. Balls pocketed by a shooter in an opponent's target pocket are scored for the opponent, even if the stroke was a foul, but would not count if the cue ball should scratch or jump the table. However, if the stroke is not a foul and the shooter pockets a ball(s) in both target pockets, the shooter's inning continues, with all legally pocketed balls scored to the appropriate player. If a shooter pockets a ball that brings the opponent's score to the number opponent needed to win the game, the shooter has lost unless the cue ball scratches or jumps off the table.

Pocket Billiards

5. When a player has the cue ball in hand behind the head string (*as after a scratch*) and all object balls are also behind the head string, the object ball nearest the head string may be spotted upon request. If two or more balls are an equal distance from the head string, the highest numbered ball is spotted.

6. Three successive fouls by the same player is loss of game.

ILLEGALLY POCKETED BALLS
All spotted. **Special spotting rules**: When a ball(s) is pocketed in a non-target pocket, spotting is delayed until the shooter's inning ends. Should a player legally score the last ball(s) on the table while any illegally pocketed balls are being held for delayed spotting, those balls are then spotted so the player may continue the inning.

OBJECT BALLS JUMPED OFF THE TABLE
All spotted. The stroke is a foul, and penalty for fouls is followed. The incoming player accepts the cue ball in position.

CUE BALL AFTER JUMPING OFF THE TABLE OR SCRATCH
Incoming player has cue ball in hand behind the head string.

PENALTY FOR FOULS
The player committing the foul must spot one of the previously scored object balls for each foul committed. If a player who fouls has no previously pocketed balls to spot up, the shooter "owes" for such fouls, and must spot balls after each scoring inning until all "owed" fouls are eliminated. After fouls other than jumped cue ball or cue ball scratch, incoming player accepts the cue ball in position.

THREE FOUL PENALTY
If a player fouls three consecutive times on three successive shots without making an intervening legal shot, he loses the game. The three fouls must occur in one game. The warning must be given between the second and third fouls. A player's inning begins when it is legal to take a shot and ends at the end of a shot on which he misses, fouls or wins, or when he fouls between shots.

BREAKING SUBSEQUENT RACKS
If a "race" or set of games is being played as a match, player's alternate the break shot in subsequent games.

SEVEN-BALL

Except when clearly contradicted by these additional rules,
the General Rules of Pocket Billiards apply.

TYPE OF GAME

Seven-Ball is a speedy rotational game. Averaging only about three minutes per game, contestants shoot at the same seven object balls, permitting players to show skills in making combination and carom shots, defensive shots and placement. At the same time, it is attractive to players of moderate skills, and readily adapts to handicapping by limiting the number of pockets in which the better contestant can legally pocket the game winning 7-ball.

PLAYERS

2, or 2 teams.

BALLS USED

Object balls numbered 1-7, plus cue ball.

THE RACK

Seven Ball Rack

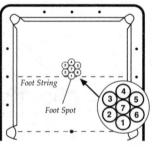

A special circular rack has been designed for this game. A standard diamond rack (*as used in Nine-Ball*) may also be used by turning it sideways.

The balls are racked in a circle on the foot spot, with the 1-ball at the apex (*12 o'clock*) and the balls increasing numerically 1-6 (clockwise in a circle) with the 7-ball in the middle of the circle. (*See Diagram 23*)

Diagram 23

OBJECT OF THE GAME

To legally pocket the 7-ball.

SCORING

The balls have no point value. The player legally pocketing the 7-ball is credited with a game won.

OPENING BREAK

The starting player must (1) make an open break, or (2) legally pocket an object ball. If not, the incoming player has choice of foul Penalty 1, or having the balls reracked and shooting the opening break shot. In subsequent games, players alternate the break shot.

57

RULES OF PLAY:

1. A legal shot requires that the cue ball's first contact be with the lowest numbered ball on the table. A player must then (1) pocket a numbered ball, or (2) cause the cue ball or any object ball to contact a cushion. Failure to meet these requirements is a foul and Penalty for Fouls (2) applies.

2. A legally pocketed ball entitles a shooter to remain at the table until failing to pocket a ball on a legal shot.

3. After a legal opening break, the opponent chooses which side of the table (*any of the three pockets on one side*) into which he will pocket the 7-ball. Balls 1-6 may be pocketed on either side of the table.

4. Pocketing the 7-ball on a fair opening break wins the game.

5. Any violation of General Rules results in Penalty for Fouls (2).

LOSS OF GAME

A player loses the game by committing any of the following infractions: (a) pockets the 7-ball in a non-assigned pocket after the break; (b) scratches when the 7-ball is the legal object ball; (c) pockets the 7-ball on an illegal shot; (d) misses when the 7-ball is the object ball (*optional-an alternative is to assess Foul Penalty 2*); (e) commits three successive fouls.

ILLEGALLY POCKETED OBJECT BALLS

All spotted; Penalty for Fouls (2) applies. (*Optional for coin-operated tables: all balls remain pocketed; Penalty for Fouls (2) applies.*)

OBJECT BALLS JUMPED OFF THE TABLE

All spotted. The stroke is a foul, and Penalty for Fouls (2) applies.

CUE BALL AFTER JUMP OR SCRATCH

Incoming player has cue ball in hand.

PENALTY FOR FOULS

No point penalty. (1) Incoming player has cue ball in hand behind the head string and object balls in position, but if the lowest numbered object ball is also behind head string it must be spotted. (2) Cue ball in hand anywhere on the table.

VARIATION

Players of unequal ability may be handicapped by assigning them more or less pockets in which they can play the 7-ball. It is suggested that more skilled players shoot the 7-ball into the side pocket on their side of the table. Players may also agree that the 7-ball can be pocketed anywhere on table.

TEN-BALL
Except when clearly contradicted by these additional rules,
the General Rules of Pocket Billiards apply.

TYPE OF GAME
Ten-Ball is a variation of Rotation in which a rack of just 10 object balls is employed. As you will discern from the following rules, it is virtually the same game as Nine-Ball, but with the extra ball adding both additional difficulty and generally fewer balls being pocketed on the opening break (*particularly the 10-ball, or game-ball*). Still, accomplished players turn it into a fast, action packed game!

PLAYERS
2 or more, though 2, 3, or 4 is generally preferred.

BALLS USED
Object balls 1-10, plus cue ball.

THE RACK
Triangle rack truncated by removal of the rear row of balls (*rows 1-2-3-4*) with the 1-ball on the foot spot, and the 10-ball in the center of the row-of-3; other balls may be placed entirely at random.

OBJECT OF THE GAME
To legally pocket the 10-ball.

SCORING
The balls have no point value. The player legally pocketing the 10-ball is credited with a game won.

OPENING BREAK
The starting player must either (1) make an open break, or (2) legally pocket an object ball. If failing to do so, the incoming player has choice of (1) cue ball in hand behind the head string and object balls in position, or (2) having the balls reracked and shooting the opening break shot.

RULES OF PLAY
1. A legal shot requires that the cue ball's first contact with a ball is with the lowest numbered ball on the table, and then either (1) pocket a numbered ball, or (2) cause the cue ball or any object ball to contact a cushion. Failure to meet this requirement is a foul.

59

2. A legally pocketed ball entitles the shooter to remain at the table until failing to pocket a ball on a legal shot.

3. When a player legally pockets a ball, he must shoot again. The player may not call a safety and spot a legally pocketed ball.

4. It is a loss of the game if a player commits three successive fouls.

ILLEGALLY POCKETED BALLS
All spotted, no penalty. (*Common option, coin-operated play: None spotted except the game-ball, no penalty.*)

OBJECT BALLS JUMPED OFF THE TABLE
All spotted. The stroke is a foul, and the incoming player has cue ball in hand, except after the break shot.

CUE BALL AFTER JUMPING OFF THE TABLE OR SCRATCH
Incoming player has cue ball in hand, except after the break shot.

PENALTY FOR FOULS
Incoming player is awarded cue ball in hand. (**Note:** *Rule of Play 4 calls for loss of game if the foul is a 3rd successive one.*)

ROTATION
Except when clearly contradicted by these additional rules,
the General Rules of Pocket Billiards apply.

Rotation requires that the cue ball contact the lowest numbered object ball first on each shot; any ball pocketed on a legal shot counts. It is not necessary to call balls or pockets. Rotation is a formidable test of a player's imagination, shot-making ability and repertoire. Few games require more exacting position play.

PLAYERS
2 or more.

BALLS USED
Standard set of object balls 1-15, plus cue ball.

THE RACK
Standard triangle rack with the 1-ball on the foot spot, 2-ball on the right rear corner, 3-ball on the left rear corner, and 15-ball in the center. All other balls placed entirely at random.

OBJECT OF THE GAME
To score balls of greater total point value than the opponent(s).

SCORING
Each legally pocketed object ball has a point value equal to its number. When a player's point total mathematically eliminates an opponent(s) from outscoring him (*61 points in a two-player game*), the game is ended. If two or more players tie for highest point total after all 15 object balls have been pocketed, the tied player who legally pocketed the last object ball is credited with an extra tie-breaking point and wins the game.

OPENING BREAK
The starting player must (1) make an open break, or (2) legally pocket an object ball. If failing to do so, the incoming player has the choice of (1) shooting with cue ball in hand behind the head string and object balls in position, or (2) having the balls reracked and shooting the opening break shot.

RULES OF PLAY
1. A legal shot requires that the cue ball's first contact be with the lowest numbered ball on the table. A player must then (1) pocket a numbered ball, or (2) cause the cue ball or any numbered ball to contact a cushion. Failure to do so is a foul.

2. A legally pocketed ball entitles a shooter to remain at the table until failing to pocket a ball on a legal shot. If necessary, a player is permitted only two legal safeties played by merely hitting that object ball (*only*) to the near cushion.

3. When a player legally pockets a ball, he must shoot again. The shooter can't call a safety and spot a legally pocketed object ball.

4. When a player has the cue ball in hand behind the head string (*as after a scratch*) and the legal object ball is also behind the head string, the object ball may be spotted on the foot spot upon request.

5. It is a loss of the game if a player commits three successive fouls. In more than a two player game, balls pocketed by disqualified players remain off the table.

ILLEGALLY POCKETED BALLS
All spotted.

OBJECT BALLS JUMPED OFF THE TABLE
All spotted. The stroke is a foul, and the penalty for fouls is followed.

CUE BALL AFTER JUMPING OFF THE TABLE OR SCRATCH
Incoming player has cue ball in hand behind the head string.

PENALTY FOR FOULS
No point penalty. Incoming player has the option of (1) accepting the balls in position, or (2) requiring offending player to shoot again with the table in position (*if cue ball is in hand behind the head string it is so for either player*). Rule of Play 5 takes precedence in the case of a third consecutive foul.

BANK POOL
Except when clearly contradicted by these additional rules,
the General Rules of Pocket Billiards apply.

TYPE OF GAME
In Bank Pool, each shot must be a bank of an object ball into at least one cushion before the ball is pocketed. "Straight-in" shots are not legal. It is by definition a demanding game, and fascinating to observe, particularly when the players are accomplished at the art of banking.

PLAYERS
2, 3, 4 or 5 players, though 2 players are generally preferred.

BALLS USED
Standard set of object balls 1-15, plus *cue ball* for long rack; or any nine balls racked in the shaped of a diamond, plus the *cue ball* for a short rack (*a popular form of competition*).

THE RACK
Standard triangle rack; balls placed entirely at random.

OBJECT OF THE GAME
To score a greater number of balls than the opponent(s).

SCORING
Each legally pocketed object ball is scored as one ball. In two-player games, the first player to score eight balls wins (*long rack*). In short rack the first player to score five balls wins. When 3, 4 or 5 players compete, long rack is generally played. In those contests, the first player to score five balls, four balls, and three balls respectively are considered winners.

OPENING BREAK

Starting player must make an open break. If failing to do so, the incoming player has choice of (1) accepting the table in position and shooting, or (2) having the balls reracked and shooting the opening break shot.

If any balls are pocketed on a legal opening break shot, the breaker continues shooting. Any balls pocketed on a legal break shot are spotted after the breaker completes his turn at the table.

RULES OF PLAY

1. A legal shot requires that the cue ball contact any numbered ball and then (1) pocket a numbered ball, or (2) cause the cue ball or any numbered ball to contact a cushion. Failure to do so is a foul.

2. A legally pocketed ball entitles shooter to remain at the table until failing to legally pocket a ball. Player may shoot any object ball, but must designate which ball, pocket and the cushion(s) that ball will contact. A legally pocketed ball must be driven into at least one cushion and rebounded into the called pocket.

3. A legally pocketed ball must be "cleanly" banked (*i.e., no kisses, combinations or caroms involving the object ball are permitted*). The cue ball may contact the object ball only once on a stroke.

4. On a legal scoring stroke, only the object ball is credited to the shooter. Any other balls pocketed on the same stroke do not count for the shooter, and may be subject to special spotting provisions regarding "Illegally Pocketed Balls".

5. When a player has the cue ball in hand behind the head string (*as after a scratch*) and all object balls are also behind the head string, the object ball nearest the head string may be spotted on the foot spot upon request. If two or more balls are an equal distance from the head string, the player may also designate which balls are to be spotted.

6. Cushion impact shall mean clear and distinct contact with a cushion by the object ball. Incidental contact with a cushion as the object ball approaches the called pocket shall not be considered an "extra" cushion(s) that would otherwise disqualify a legal shot. Rebounding of the object ball in the jaws of the pocket before dropping shall not be considered "extra" cushions unless otherwise designated by the player.

ILLEGALLY POCKETED BALLS

All spotted; no penalty. **Special spotting rule**: When in the course of a legal scoring stroke, an additional ball(s) is pocketed, spotting of the ball(s) is delayed until the shooter's inning ends. Should a player score the last ball on the table while any illegally pocketed balls are being held for delayed spotting, those balls are then spotted so the player may continue the inning.

OBJECT BALLS JUMPED OFF THE TABLE

All spotted. The stroke is a foul, and the penalty for fouls is followed. The incoming player accepts the cue ball in position.

CUE BALL AFTER JUMPING THE TABLE OR SCRATCH

Incoming player has cue ball in hand behind the head string.

PENALTY FOR FOULS

The player committing the foul must spot one of the previously scored object balls for each foul committed. If a player fouls when there are no previously pocketed balls to spot up, the shooter "owes" for such fouls, and must spot balls after each scoring inning until all "owed" fouls are eliminated. After fouls other than jumped cue ball or cue ball scratch, the incoming player accepts the cue ball in position.

OTHER POPULAR BILLIARD GAMES

BASEBALL POCKET BILLIARDS
Except when clearly contradicted by these additional rules,
the General Rules of Pocket Billiards apply.

TYPE OF GAME
The game is played with 21 object balls, numbered from 1-21, and a white cue ball. The object balls are racked at the foot spot (*in a 21-ball triangle*). The 1-ball is placed on the foot spot, which is called "home plate". The 2- and 3-balls, respectively, are placed at the left and right corners of the triangle. The 9-ball, called the "pitcher", is placed near the center of the rack. (*See Diagram 24*) Starting player has cue ball in hand.

SCORING
Players are credited with all balls legally pocketed. Each player has nine shots or innings at the table, which are played in succession. In other words, each player continues at the table until completing nine innings. An inning continues until a player misses or commits a foul, which results in a loss of turn.

The number of runs scored correspond to the number on the balls pocketed by the player. If a player scores the 12- and 13-balls in one inning, the player gets credit for 25 runs in that inning. Scores are posted by innings on a score sheet. The game ends when all players have completed nine innings of play. *The winner is the player with the most runs after all have played.*

Baseball Pocket Billiards

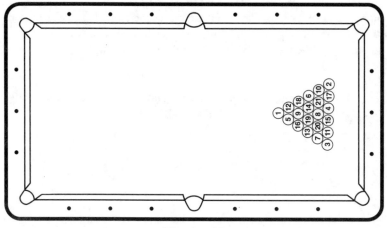

Diagram 24

START OF PLAY

Rotation of play may be determined by lag or lot. The starting player has the cue ball in hand within the string. The starting player is credited with all balls scored on the break shot. After the break, the player continues, but must "call shots"- ball and pocket.

SUBSEQUENT PLAY

Incoming players have balls racked and proceed as above, playing nine innings.

SPOTTING BALLS

If a player pockets a ball and makes a scratch, the object ball must be spotted on the "home plate" (*foot spot*). If home plate is occupied, balls are spotted according to general rules for spotting balls in pocket billiards.

SCRATCHES

If the player scratches, it completes the inning and an "O" is placed in that inning on the score sheet. He then plays the next inning. If the shooter scratches and no object ball is pocketed, it is still regarded as a scoreless inning. Scratches are penalized by forfeit of all balls pocketed on the foul stroke, plus the last called ball legally pocketed. If the player has no balls to his credit, he spots next called ball scored.

CALL SHOTS

If a player makes a called ball as designated, all other balls pocketed on the same stroke accrue to his credit. If failing to pocket the called ball, however, and other balls drop in the pockets, the pocketed balls are spotted, it counts as a scoreless inning and player continues, unless miss occurred in ninth inning.

NINE INNINGS

Any number of players may play baseball pocket billiards, but before the game is complete, all players must have nine innings at the table. If a player runs all the balls before completing nine innings of play, the balls are reracked and player continues until completing nine innings, and then the total score is posted.

GENERAL RULES

Unless conflicting with provisions for this game, the General Rules of Pocket Billiards apply to Baseball Pocket Billiards.

BASIC POCKET BILLIARDS

Except when clearly contradicted by these additional rules,
the General Rules of Pocket Billiards apply.

TYPE OF GAME

The game of Basic Pocket Billiards is a combination of the call shot aspects of 14.1 Continuous and the "anything goes" character of Fifteen Ball. It's a game well-suited for "mixed" (*beginners and accomplished players*) play, particularly in a team mode.

PLAYERS

2, or 2 teams.

BALLS USED

Standard set of object balls 1-15, plus *cue ball.*

THE RACK

Standard *triangle* rack; balls placed entirely at random.

OBJECT OF THE GAME

To score eight balls before the opponent.

SCORING

Any legally pocketed ball is scored as one ball.

OPENING BREAK

Starting player must:
1. legally pocket any numbered ball into a target pocket, or
2. cause the cue ball to contact any numbered ball and after contact, at least one numbered ball must contact a cushion. Failure to do so is a foul.

Note: The cue ball does not have to strike a rail on the opening break. Failure is a breaking violation; the opponent can accept the table in position and shoot, or require that the balls be reracked and the offending player repeat the opening break until the requirements are satisfied.

If a starting player pockets a ball on the opening break, it is a legally pocketed ball if no foul or other violation is committed, and continues at the table. On all subsequent shots, however, the shooter must comply with all the "Rules of Play".

RULES OF PLAY

1. A legally pocketed ball entitles the shooter to continue at the table until failing to pocket a ball on a legal shot. The player may choose and shoot any ball, but before shooting, must designate a single ball that will be pocketed; the shooter need not indicate *kisses, caroms, combinations or cushions (all of which are legal)*.

2. On all shots subsequent to the opening break, the player must cause the cue ball to contact an object ball, and then:
   (a) pocket an object ball, or;
   (b) cause an object ball or the cue ball to contact a cushion.
   Failure to do so is a foul.

3. When a player has the cue ball in hand behind the head string and all remaining object balls are behind the head string as well, the object ball nearest the head string may be spotted on the foot spot upon request. If two or more balls are an equal distance from the head string, the player may designate which of the equidistant balls should be spotted.

ILLEGALLY POCKETED BALLS

All *spotted*, no penalty.

OBJECT BALLS JUMPED OFF THE TABLE

All spotted. The stroke is a foul, and the penalty for fouls is followed.

CUE BALL AFTER JUMPING OFF THE TABLE OR SCRATCH

Incoming player has cue ball in hand behind the head string.

PENALTY FOR FOULS

One scored ball is returned to the table (*spotted*) by fouling player for each foul committed. If player who fouls has no previously pocketed balls to spot up, he "owes" for such fouls, and must spot balls after each scoring inning until his "owed" fouls are eliminated. After fouls other than cue ball jump or cue ball scratch, the incoming player accepts cue ball in position.

BOTTLE POOL

Except when clearly contradicted by these additional rules,
the General Rules of Pocket Billiards apply.

TYPE OF GAME

A unique pocket billiard game, Bottle Pool requires the use of an inexpensive but specially shaped and balanced leather or plastic container (*"bottle" or "shaker bottle"*), shaped much like some disposable beverage bottles. The play of

Bottle Pool

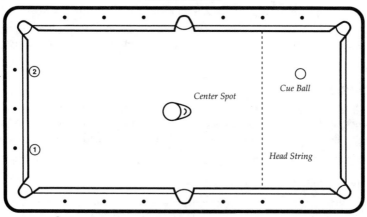

Diagram 25

Bottle Pool combines the ball pocketing abilities of pocket billiards with the carom-making requirements of carom games.

PLAYERS
2 or more.

BALLS USED
Object balls 1 and 2, plus cue ball.

THE RACK
No triangle needed; at the start of the game, the 1-ball is frozen to the *foot cushion*, centered on the first diamond in from the racker's right corner pocket; the 2-ball is also *frozen* to the foot cushion, centered on the first diamond in from the racker's left corner pocket; the bottle is placed open end down on the center spot. (*See Diagram 25*)

OBJECT OF THE GAME
To score exactly 31 points prior to opponent(s).

SCORING
There are five scoring possibilities. Executing a legal stroke scores as follows:
1. Pocketing the 1-ball: one point.
2. Pocketing the 2-ball: two points.
3. Carom of the cue ball on the two object balls: one point.
4. Carom of the cue ball from an object ball(s) to the bottle which knocks the bottle onto its side: five points.
5. Carom of the cue ball from an object ball(s) to the bottle which stands the bottle onto its base: automatic win of the game.

69

Should a player accomplish more than one scoring possibility on a shot, he scores for each; a single shot can result in a total of nine points scored. Since exactly 31 points must be scored for victory (*unless #5 above applies*), a player must not exceed 31; if he does, his inning ends and his score becomes only the total by which he exceeded 31.

OPENING BREAK

No "break shot" as such. Beginning with *cue ball in hand behind the head string*, starting player must cause the cue ball to contact either the 1-ball or the 2-ball. If failing to do so, the incoming player can require that offending player repeat the opening shot until that requirement is satisfied.

RULES OF PLAY

1. A legally executed scoring stroke entitles shooter to continue at the table until failing to legally score on a shot, exceeds 31 points on a shot, causes an object ball to contact the bottle before the cue ball contacts the bottle (*the entire shot is invalid and inning ends*), or causes the bottle to be forced off the table or into a pocket (*the entire shot is invalid and inning ends*).

2. On all shots, player must cause the cue ball to contact an object ball. Failure to do so is a foul.

3. Cue ball must contact an object ball before it contacts the bottle. Failure to do so is a foul.

4. If player causes the bottle to be upset, or upended by an object ball, the shot is a foul.

5. Player loses the game if he fouls in each of three consecutive innings at the table.

REPLACING UPSET BOTTLE

Whenever the bottle is upset, it is replaced on the table, open end down, with the open end as close as possible to its position when the bottle came to rest. It is, of course, replaced prior to the next shot.

When the bottle is forced off the table or into a pocket (*or into such position that the open end is over the pocket opening, making replacement as in the preceding paragraph impossible*), then bottle is replaced on the center spot. If occupied, then replace on the head spot; if occupied, use the foot spot; if occupied, hold out until center spot is vacant.

ILLEGALLY POCKETED BALLS
All spotted. The stroke is a foul, and the penalty for fouls is followed.

OBJECT BALLS JUMPED OFF THE TABLE
All spotted. The stroke is a foul, and the penalty for fouls is followed.

SPECIAL SPOTTING RULES
After each shot is completed, any pocketed object balls are spotted prior to the next shot. They are spotted in the positions as at the start of the game. If a ball or the bottle prevents the free placement of an object ball to be spotted, the object ball is spotted on the center spot; if that is also occupied, the object ball is then spotted on the head spot. If both object balls are being spotted, follow the above, first spotting the 1-ball, then the 2-ball.

CUE BALL AFTER JUMP OR SCRATCH
Incoming player has cue ball in hand behind the head string.

PENALTY FOR FOULS
One point is deducted from offender's score for each foul. Fouls other than cue ball jumped/scratched, incoming player accepts the cue ball in position.

Pocket Billiards

BOWLLIARDS
Except when clearly contradicted by these additional rules,
the General Rules of Pocket Billiards apply.

TYPE OF GAME
Bowlliards applies the scoring concepts of bowling to pocket billiards. It's one of the few games that can be quite interesting as a solitary exercise since, like bowling, there is a perfect game score to strive for, and a player can measure improvement quite easily over the course of time playing Bowlliards.

PLAYERS
Any number.

BALLS USED
Any ten objects balls, plus *cue ball.*

THE RACK
Standard triangle position (*front apex ball on foot spot*), using a 1-2-3-4 rack configuration.

OBJECT OF THE GAME
To score a perfect score of 300 points in 10 frames (*innings*) in solitary play. In competition, to score a higher point total in 10 innings than opponent(s).

71

SCORING

Each legally pocketed ball is scored as one point, regardless of ball number. The points scored per the "Rules of Play" below are treated exactly as is the pinfall in bowling.

OPENING BREAK

At the start of player's inning (frame), he has a free break (*no special balls-to-cushion or other requirements once break stroke commences, and a jumped or scratched cue ball is without penalty*). Any balls pocketed on the break are spotted, and player follows break by beginning scoring play with object balls in position and cue ball in hand behind the head string. (*The opening break takes place at the start of every inning.*)

RULES OF PLAY

1. A legally pocketed ball entitles the shooter to continue at the table until failing to pocket a *called ball* on a shot, or until scoring (10), the maximum total per inning possible. The player may choose and shoot any ball, but before shooting, must designate a single ball that will be pocketed and the pocket into which the ball will score; the shooter need not indicate *kisses, caroms, combinations or cushions* (*none of which are illegal*).

2. Player has two chances to pocket the 10 possible balls of each frame. If player legally pockets 10 consecutive balls on the first chance of a frame, that frame is completed and player scores the frame exactly as a strike in bowling. If player fails to pocket 10 consecutive balls on the first chance, the player takes a second chance immediately. If the shooter succeeds in legally pocketing the remaining balls of the 10 on the second chance, the frame is completed and player scores it exactly as a spare in bowling. If player fails to legally pocket all 10 balls in two chances, the frame is then completed and is scored just as in bowling; a "strike" in the 10th inning earns two extra shots, a spare one extra shot.

3. If players tie for high game total in competition, additional innings are played alternately by the tied players, with the first player posting a superior score to that of the opponent(s) being the winner (*"sudden death"*).

ILLEGALLY POCKETED BALLS

On the break, illegally pocketed balls are spotted prior to player beginning scoring play (*first chance of the frame*). During scoring play, illegally pocketed balls are spotted.

OBJECT BALLS JUMPED OFF THE TABLE

All spotted. The stroke is a foul, and the penalty for fouls is followed.

CUE BALL AFTER JUMP OR SCRATCH

Only applies if occurring as player's first foul of a frame, player has cue ball in hand behind the head string to begin a second chance of the frame.

PENALTY FOR FOULS

One point is deducted from offender's score for each foul. If a foul ends the player's first chance of a frame, he has cue ball in hand behind the head string to begin his second chance of the frame.

BUMPER POOL

Rules and Regulations (Reprinted with permission
of The Valley Company, Bay City, MI).

PLAYERS

Bumper Pool® is played by two players or by four as partners.

BALLS USED

Each side has five red balls or five white balls, one of each color being a marked cue ball.

THE RACK

To set up Bumper Pool, place two red balls on each side of the white cup (pocket) on markers, placing marked red ball directly in front of white cup. Place white balls in same position around the red cup (*pocket*).

Bumper Pool

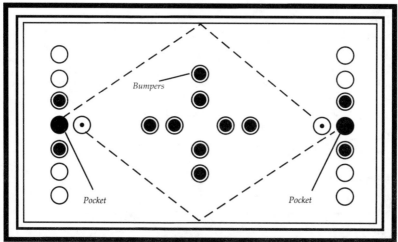

Diagram 26

OBJECT OF THE GAME

The first player or team to sink all five balls is the winner, except that player forfeits game if he shoots his last ball into his opponent's cup.

OPENING BREAK

Both players shoot the marked ball at the same time, hitting first the side-cushion, banking the ball into or near his color cup. The player who plays his ball into or nearest his cup shoots again.

RULES OF PLAY

1. Marked cue balls must be pocketed first. If a player sinks another ball before his marked ball is pocketed, his opponent may remove two of his own balls and drop them into his cup. In the event that both marked balls are pocketed on first shots, each player takes one of the remaining balls and spots it in front of cup and both shoot at same time, just as they did with marked balls. From there on they take turns, beginning with the player who pockets his ball or is nearest to his cup.

2. A player receives another shot upon sinking his own color ball in his own color cup.

3. In the event that a player causes a ball to leave the table, his opponent may place this ball anywhere he wishes, and in addition can remove two of his own balls and drop them into his cup as an additional bonus.

4. No player is allowed to jump his ball over balls or bumpers in making shots. Penalty for this will be the same as in "Penalty for Fouls".

5. The length of time that the winners may continue playing is governed by House Rule.

PENALTY FOR FOULS

If a player sinks one of an opponent's balls there is no penalty, but if sinking one of his own into an opponent's cup, or shooting one of the opponent's, the opponent may then drop two of his own balls into his cup.

COWBOY

Except when clearly contradicted by these additional rules,
the General Rules of Pocket Billiards apply.

TYPE OF GAME

Cowboy is another game that combines carom and pocket billiards skills, and employs a very unusual set of rules. It's certainly a change of pace game: how many games have you played in which the cue ball must be pocketed on a carom of the 1-ball on the last shot?

PLAYERS

Any number.

BALLS USED

Object balls 1, 3 and 5, plus the *cue ball.*

THE RACK

No triangle needed; the 1-ball is placed on the *head spot*, the 3-ball on the *foot spot*, and the 5-ball on the center spot.

OBJECT OF THE GAME

To score 101 points prior to opponent(s).

SCORING

The first ninety points exactly may be scored by any of these means on legal scoring strokes:

1. Pocketing any of the objects balls: points equal to the balls' numbers.
2. *Carom* of the cue ball off two of the object balls: one point.
3. *Carom* of the cue ball off the three object balls: two points.
   Points 91 through 100 (*exactly*) must, and may only, be scored by execution of carom shots 2 and 3 above.

Point 101 (*winning point*) must be scored by caroming the cue ball off the 1-ball into a called pocket without the cue ball contacting any other object ball. Should a player accomplish more than one scoring possibility permitted by these rules, he scores for each; thus a single shot can result in a total of 11 points scored.

OPENING BREAK

No "break shot" as such. Beginning with *cue ball in hand behind the head string*, starting player must cause the cue ball to contact the 3-ball first. If starting player fails to do so, incoming player has choice of

1. requiring starting player to repeat the opening shot, or
2. executing the opening shot.

75

Cowboy Pocket Billiards

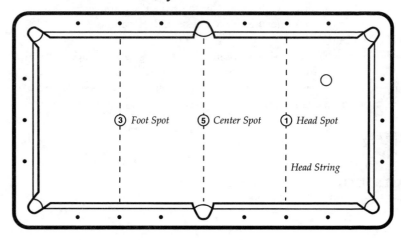

Diagram 27

RULES OF PLAY

1. A legally executed shot, conforming to the requirements of "Scoring", entitles the shooter to continue at the table until failing to legally execute and score on a shot.

2. On all shots, a player must cause the cue ball to contact an object ball, and then the cue ball or object ball must contact a *cushion*. Failure to do so is a *foul*.

3. At the completion of each shot, any pocketed object balls are *spotted* on their same positions as at the start of the game. If the appropriate position is occupied, the ball(s) in question remain off the table until the correct position is vacant after a shot. If, however, the 1-ball would be held out as a player with exactly 100 points is to shoot, the balls are all placed as at the start of the game, and the player shoots with cue ball in hand behind the head string.

4. When a player scores the 90th point, the shot must score the number of points exactly needed to reach 90; if the shot producing the 90th point also scores a point(s) in excess of 90 for the player, the shot is *a foul*.

5. When a player is playing for points 91 through 100 (*which must all be scored on caroms solely*), it is a foul to pocket an object ball on a shot.

6. When a player is playing for the 101st point, it is a foul if the cue ball is pocketed in a pocket other than the one called, or if the cue ball fails to contact the 1-ball, or if the cue ball contacts any other object ball.

7. When a player pockets the cue ball on an otherwise legal shot, and according to the special requirements given in "Scoring" for counting the 101st point, pocketing the cue ball on such a shot on the 101st point is not a foul.

8. The player loses the game when fouling in each of three consecutive plays at the table.

ILLEGALLY POCKETED BALLS
All spotted per the provision of Rule of Play 3, with no penalty, except in the special cases covered by the Rules of Play 4 and 5.

OBJECT BALLS JUMPED OFF THE TABLE
All spotted. The stroke is a foul, and the penalty for fouls is followed.

CUE BALL AFTER JUMP OR SCRATCH
Incoming player has cue ball in hand behind the head string.

PENALTY FOR FOULS
No point deduction, but any points scored on previous shots of the inning are not scored, and player's inning ends. After fouls other than cue ball jump or cue ball scratch, incoming player accepts the cue ball in position.

CRIBBAGE
Except when clearly contradicted by these additional rules,
the General Rules of Pocket Billiards apply.

TYPE OF GAME
Cribbage Pocket Billiards derives its name from the fact that a score can be made (*with two exceptions*) only by pocketing two consecutive balls which add up to 15; a similarity exists with the popular card game of Cribbage. In a sense, it represents a combination of a call-shot game and a set-order game, and is a bit different and quite interesting to play.

PLAYERS
2 players.

BALLS USED
Standard set of object balls 1-15 plus *cue ball*.

THE RACK
Standard *triangle* rack, with the 15-ball in the center; with the exception that no two of the three corner balls shall add up to a total of 15 points, all other balls may be placed entirely at random.

77

OBJECT OF THE GAME
To score five points (*cribbages*) out of a possible total of eight.

DEFINITION OF A CRIBBAGE
A cribbage is a pair of object balls, legally pocketed, numerically totaling 15. There are just these seven regular cribbages: 1-14, 2-13, 3-12, 4-11, 5-10, 6-9 and 7-8. No other ball combinations can be cribbages except that when all seven regular cribbages have been legally pocketed, the 15 ball becomes a legal cribbage by itself.

SCORING
Each legally pocketed cribbage counts one point for scoring player.

OPENING BREAK
Starting player must attempt an open break. Failure to do so is a breaking violation; opponent has the choice of:
1. requiring offending player to repeat the opening break (*until requirements are satisfied*), or;
2. playing the opening break shot. Starting player is not required to call the shot; if any balls are pocketed on the break shot, they accrue to him and he may continue at the table.

RULES OF PLAY
1. To legally pocket a cribbage, the two balls must be pocketed in the same inning. When a player has legally pocketed a single ball on a shot, he must legally pocket the appropriate companion ball on his next shot, or it is a *foul*.

2. If a player scores a legal cribbage, he can continue his inning and attempt to score more cribbages in the same inning.

3. When not "on a cribbage", if a player pockets two or more balls on a shot that do not constitute a cribbage, he may next pocket any of the proper companion balls as he chooses, but must successively pocket each of those companion balls if he is to continue at the table. If he fails, it is a foul. If, while satisfying the requirements of scoring companion balls, other ball(s) are incidentally pocketed, they likewise accrue to him; he must continue to complete one of the cribbages he is "on" on each successive stroke (*though in no special order*). Failure to do so is a foul; all balls of uncompleted cribbages are spotted.

4. When a ball is pocketed legally, but player fails to complete the cribbage legally during the same inning, the ball is spotted.

5. On all shots, the player must cause the cue ball to contact an object ball and then either:

(a) pocket a numbered ball, or;

(b) cause any numbered ball or the cue ball to contact a cushion.

Failure to do so is a foul.

6. A player loses the game if committing three successive fouls.

7. If the 15-ball is pocketed before all the other cribbages have been legally pocketed, it is an illegally pocketed ball and is spotted immediately following the stroke (*not inning*) on which it was pocketed. No penalty.

8. When a player has the *cue ball in hand behind the head string* (*as after a scratch*) and all the object balls are also behind the head string, the object ball nearest the head string may be spotted on the foot spot at his request. If two or more balls are an equal distance from the head string, the player may also designate which of the equidistant balls should be spotted.

ILLEGALLY POCKETED BALLS
All spotted; no penalty.

OBJECT BALLS JUMPED OFF THE TABLE
All spotted. The stroke is a foul, and the penalty for fouls is followed.

CUE BALL AFTER JUMPING OFF THE TABLE OR SCRATCH
Incoming player has cue ball in hand behind the head string.

PENALTY FOR FOULS
Inning ends; no point or ball penalty (*except per Rule of Play 6*). Incoming player has the option of:

1. accepting the table in position and shooting, or;
2. shooting with cue ball in hand behind the head string.

CUT-THROAT

Except when clearly contradicted by these additional rules,
the General Rules of Pocket Billiards apply.

TYPE OF GAME

Cut-Throat (*also known as Elimination*) is a very popular game in social situations, rather than for serious competitive play. It is very enjoyable to play - fast and with simple rules. A perfect game when an odd number of participants are available.

PLAYERS

3 or 5.

BALLS USED

Standard set of object balls 1-15 plus cue ball.

THE RACK

Standard *triangle* rack with the 1 ball on the foot spot, and the 6 and 11 balls on the two corners; all other balls placed at random.

DETERMINATION OF GROUPS

In three-player games, starting player has the group of balls 1-5; second 6-10; third player has balls 11-15. In five-player games, starting player 1-3; second player 4-6; third 7-9; fourth 10-12; and fifth 13-15.

OBJECT OF THE GAME

To legally pocket your opponents' balls before the opponents legally pocket your group of balls.

SCORING

Group balls have no point value. The player with a ball(s) still on the table, when all the other groups' balls are legally pocketed, wins the game.

OPENING BREAK

Starting player must make an *open break*. If failing to do so, incoming player may:
1. accept the *table in position* and shoot, or;
2. require that the balls be reracked and shoot the opening break himself. All balls pocketed on a legal break remain pocketed.

RULES OF PLAY

1. Players must decide prior to the game whether they are playing call shot or not.

2. A legal shot requires that the cue ball's first contact be with an opponents' object ball. On all shots, player must cause the cue ball to contact an object ball and then either

(a) pocket a numbered ball, or

(b) cause any numbered ball or the cue ball to contact a cushion. Failure to meet these requirements is a foul. Any legally pocketed ball entitles shooter to continue at the table until failing to pocket an object ball on a shot. (*Also see exception: Rule of Play 4.*)

3. If player pockets any opponents' balls on an illegal shot, they are spotted; but if he pockets his own group balls on an illegal shot, they remain pocketed. If player pockets the last ball of his own group, whether or not a legal shot, it remains pocketed and his inning ends.

4. When a player's last group ball is legally pocketed, he is eliminated from the shooting rotation. He remains eliminated for the duration of the game unless a foul is committed by a player still in the game; when a player is reinstated due to a foul, he resumes his normal position in the original order of play.

5. When a player has the *cue ball in hand behind the head string* (*as after a scratch*), and all balls of all opponents' groups are behind the head string, the object ball nearest the head string may, at the shooter's request, be spotted on the foot spot. If two or more balls are an equal distance from the head string, the player may designate which of the equidistant balls he desires to be spotted.

6. When successive games are played, the order of play for the next game is the same as the order of final elimination in the preceding game. (*First player eliminated breaks; winner shoots last; others in order of elimination.*)

ILLEGALLY POCKETED BALLS
Opponents' group balls are *spotted*; no penalty. Shooter's group balls remain pocketed, no penalty.

OBJECT BALLS JUMPED OFF THE TABLE
All spotted. The stroke is a foul, and the penalty for fouls is followed. The incoming player accepts the cue ball in position.

CUE BALL AFTER JUMPING OFF THE TABLE OR SCRATCH
Incoming player has cue ball in hand behind the head string.

PENALTY FOR FOULS
Shooter's inning ends. In addition, one ball from each of the opponents' groups that is off the table is brought back into play. Players who had been eliminated

can be reinstated at any time until the game is over. If a player's group has no pocketed balls at the time of a foul by one of his opponents, then the penalty has no effect on that group or player; the penalty is not carried forward.

EQUAL OFFENSE

Except when clearly contradicted by these additional rules,
the General Rules of Pocket Billiards apply.

TYPE OF GAME

Equal Offense is a game in which each player shoots until missing a shot, fouls or pockets the maximum amount of balls allowed for the inning. The winner is determined by the total inning score (*similar to bowling*). Based on 14.1 Continuous, the game is ideal for leagues, tournaments, handicapping and averaging; fair, fun and interesting for beginners as well as the advanced player. Although copyrighted by Billiard Congress of America Master Instructor Jerry Briesath, he has placed no restrictions on its use.

PLAYERS

Any number.

BALLS USED

Standard set of object balls 1-15, plus *cue ball*.

THE RACK

Standard *triangle* rack; balls placed entirely at random. The balls are racked at the beginning of each inning for each player.

OBJECT OF THE GAME

To score more total points than opponent(s) in a predetermined number of innings (*200 points in 10 innings maximum*).

SCORING

Any legally pocketed ball counts one point for shooter.

OPENING BREAK

At the start of each player's inning, he has a free break (*no special balls to cushion or other requirements once break stroke commences, and a jumped or scratched cue ball is without penalty*). Any balls pocketed on the break are spotted, and player then begins shooting with object balls in position and cue ball in hand behind the head string. The opening break takes place at the start of every inning of each player (*10 times per match in championship play for each player*).

RULES OF PLAY

1. Player may shoot any ball, but before shooting must designate an object ball and call a pocket. He need not indicate *kisses, caroms, combinations or cushions* (*none of which are illegal*). A legally pocketed ball entitles the shooter to continue at the table until failing to pocket a called ball, or until he has scored the maximum total per inning permissible (*20 points in championship play*).

2. Player is entitled to any additional balls pocketed on a shot, as long as he pockets his called ball.

3. Shooting order for subsequent innings is determined by the scoring results of preceding innings - player with the highest score shooting first. In the event of a tie inning, the order does not change.

4. If players are tied for high match total (*10 inning*) score, additional innings are played by each tied player with the first player posting a superior score to his opponent(s) in an equal number of innings being the winner (*"sudden death"*).

OBJECT BALLS JUMPED OFF THE TABLE
The stroke is a foul, and the penalty for fouls is followed.

CUE BALL AFTER JUMP OFF THE TABLE OR SCRATCH
This does not apply to Equal Offense, since a jumped or scratched cue ball ends player's inning, and all players' innings begin with the opening break.

PENALTY FOR FOULS
No point penalty; player's inning ends.

SOME VARIATIONS
For purposes of scheduling, handicapping, etc., variations can be made as follows:
1. A given number of misses or fouls may be allowed per inning (*use 14.1 Continuous rules for "Cue Ball After Jump or Scratch"*).
2. Maximum number of balls per inning permissible may be increased or decreased.
3. Number of innings constituting a *match* may be increased or decreased.
4. Each player's inning may be restricted by a time limit.
5. Combinations of any of the variations above may be utilized, and may be applied in a non-uniform manner as a means of handicapping players.
6. As an exercise for beginners to progress in finding patterns of play, three chances should be allowed (*two misses, cue ball in hand*) to reach a score of 15. An intermediate player should be allowed two chances. The 10-inning perfect score would thus be 150.
7. Third miss ends the player's inning.

Pocket Billiards

INTERNET EQUAL OFFENSE

Except when clearly contradicted by these additional rules,
the Rules of Equal Offense and the General Rules of Pocket Billiards apply.

TYPE OF GAME

Internet Equal Offense is the game of Equal Offense played using the Internet. Instead of players being on opposite sides of the table during the game, they can be, and are, on opposite sides of the world linked together via computer. Players' scores are typed into the computer and shared with participants via the Internet. Sven Davies of the USA and Jari Kokko of Finland pioneered this form of competition and direct regularly scheduled International Internet Equal Offense Tournaments each year.

PLAYERS

Two or more teams of five players each.

EQUIPMENT

In order to participate in scheduled Internet Equal Offense tournaments, you must have a computer dial-up or direct line connection to the Internet, or be a member of an online service that allows you to e-mail and telnet on the Internet. Your computer will need to be placed near one or more pocket billiard tables for play. All other equipment used is the same as in the game of Equal Offense.

COST

This form of international competition is very inexpensive; depending on your area and connection to the Internet, you will pay as little as a local phone call.

Because of the international appeal of the game and the fact that it's affordable, Internet Equal Offense is popular with colleges and universities around the world.

FOR MORE INFORMATION

For more information about Internet Equal Offense, please visit the official IEO website at http://www.tourboard.com/ieo/

FIFTEEN-BALL

Except when clearly contradicted by these additional rules,
the General Rules of Pocket Billiards apply.

TYPE OF GAME

Fifteen-Ball is a basic game variation that does not require calling balls or pockets, and yet rewards good shot selection because scoring is based on the numerical values of the balls (*numbers*) as in Rotation. It is a game well-suited for developing skills at beginning and intermediate player levels.

PLAYERS
2 or more, though 2 players are generally preferred.

BALLS USED
Standard set of object balls 1-15, plus *cue ball*.

THE RACK
Standard *triangle* rack with the 15-ball on the *foot spot*; other balls have no exact positions, but the higher numbered balls are placed at the front of the rack near the 15-ball, with the lower numbered balls near the back of the rack.

OBJECT OF THE GAME
To score balls of greater total point value than the opponent(s).

SCORING
Each legally pocketed object ball has a point value equal to its number. The game ends when a player's point total mathematically eliminates opponent(s) (*61 in a two player game*). If two or more players tie for highest point total, the tied player legally pocketing the last object ball is credited with the game.

OPENING BREAK
Starting player must either:
1. pocket a ball (*does not have to call either ball or pocket*), or
2. cause the cue ball to contact an object ball, and then the cue ball and two object balls must contact a cushion. If failing to do so, the incoming player has the choice of:
   (a) accepting the *table in position* and shooting, or;
   (b) having the balls reracked and shooting the opening break, or;
   (c) requiring offending player to repeat the opening break.

RULES OF PLAY
1. Any ball pocketed on a legal shot entitles shooter to continue at the table until failing to do so.

2. On all shots subsequent to the opening break, player must cause the cue ball to contact an object ball, and then either:
   (a) pocket an object ball, or;
   (b) cause an object ball or the cue ball to contact a cushion.
      Failure to do so is a foul.

3. When a player has the *cue ball in hand behind the head string* (*as after a scratch*) and all object balls are also behind the head string, the object ball nearest the head

Pocket Billiards

string may be spotted on the foot spot at his request. If two or more balls are an equal distance from the head string, the player may designate which of the equidistant balls should be spotted.

ILLEGALLY POCKETED BALLS
All spotted; no penalty.

OBJECT BALLS JUMPED OFF THE TABLE
All spotted. The stroke is a foul, and the penalty for fouls is followed.

CUE BALL AFTER JUMPING OFF TABLE OR SCRATCH
Incoming player has cue ball in hand behind the head string.

PENALTY FOR FOULS
Three points are deducted from the offender's score for each foul committed. After fouls other than jumped cue ball or cue ball *scratch*, incoming player accepts the table in position.

FORTY-ONE
Except when clearly contradicted by these additional rules,
the General Rules of Pocket Billiards apply.

TYPE OF GAME
Forty-One Pocket Billiards is another game that is well-suited for social play at parties or other gatherings where players of mixed abilities will take part. Since no one knows what number "pea" is held by the opponent(s), it is difficult to play defensively. In addition, the rules are designed to greatly equalize all the players' chances. An unusual and interesting game.

PLAYERS
2 to 15 (*though 3, 4, or 5 are generally preferred*).

BALLS USED
Standard set of object balls 1-15 plus cue ball. A set of 15 numbered peas (*or "pills"*) and a *shake bottle* are also used.

THE RACK
Standard triangle rack with balls placed entirely at random.

DETERMINING PRIVATE NUMBERS
After the balls are racked but before play begins, each player is given a pea from the shake bottle containing the peas numbered from 1-15. The number of the pea is the player's private number and is kept secret.

OBJECT OF THE GAME

To score points which, when added to the player's private number, total exactly 41.

SCORING

Each legally pocketed ball has a point value equal to its number.

OPENING BREAK

Starting player must make an *open break*. He is not obligated to pocket a ball on the break shot; but if he fails to make a legal *open break*, it is a foul.

RULES OF PLAY

1. Any ball(s) scored on a legal stroke count for the shooter. Players may shoot any ball and need not call ball, pocket or mode of shot.

2. A player is permitted only one shot or turn per inning, regardless of whether or not he scores.

3. An illegally pocketed ball is a foul, and does not score for the shooter.

4. On all shots, player must cause the cue ball to contact an object ball and then either
   (a) pocket an object ball, or
   (b) cause an object ball or the cue ball to contact a cushion.
   Failure to do so is a foul.

5. When a player has the *cue ball in hand behind the head string* (*as after a scratch*) and all object balls are also behind the head string, the object ball nearest the head string may be spotted on the foot spot at his request. If two or more balls are an equal distance from the head string, the player may designate which of the equidistant balls he desires to be spotted.

6. When player has a total count of 41, he must announce his victory and present his pea for confirmation before the next player shoots. If he fails to declare his 41 total until the next player has shot, he must wait until his next turn to so declare. If, in the meantime, another player succeeds in attaining a legal total count of 41 and properly declares, the latter player wins the game.

7. If a player totals more than 41 points, he has "burst" and must so declare immediately (*before the next player shoots*). All balls the burst player had pocketed are spotted, and the burst player may request a new pea prior to his next turn. Any player who bursts and does not declare it prior to the following player's shot is disqualified from further play in the game; if a two-player game, the opponent is automatically the winner.

8. If all balls are pocketed prior to any player attaining a total count of 41, the player whose count is closest to 41 wins the game. If two or more players are tied for nearest to 41 in this situation, the game is a tie.

ILLEGALLY POCKETED BALLS
All spotted; no penalty.

OBJECT BALLS JUMPED OFF THE TABLE
All spotted. The stroke is a foul, and the penalty for fouls is followed.

CUE BALL AFTER JUMPING OFF THE TABLE OR SCRATCH
Incoming player has cue ball in hand behind the head string.

PENALTY FOR FOULS
The player committing a foul must spot one of his previously scored object balls for each foul committed. If a player has no previously pocketed balls to his credit when he commits a foul, he is exempt from a penalty for that particular foul.

HONOLULU
Except when clearly contradicted by these additional rules,
the General Rules of Pocket Billiards apply.

TYPE OF GAME
Honolulu is a unique and fascinating pocket billiard game that confronts the player with an unending kaleidoscope of strategic and shot-making challenges.

Essentially, Honolulu is just a game of one-rack call shot. Call any ball in any pocket; score one point per legally pocketed ball; the first player to make eight points wins. (Said score, incidentally, being kept the same as in One Pocket: Put your balls in your bin [just pick a side] and respot out of your bin any time you scratch or foul.)

The major critical difference being - absolutely no "straight-in" shots are allowed. Each and every legally pocketed ball must be made by means of either (1) a bank, (2) a combination, (3) a carom, (4) a "kick" shot, or (5) some combination thereof.

PLAYERS
2, or 2 teams.

BALLS USED
Standard set of 15 object balls, plus *cue ball*.

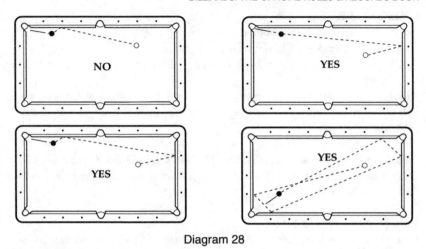

Diagram 28

THE RACK
Standard triangle; balls racked at random.

OBJECT OF THE GAME
Winner of game must score eight (8) points before opponent. (*Each legally pocketed ball scores one (1) point.*)

SCORING
Player must call ball and pocket. If called ball is made in designated pocket by means of either a bank, combination, carom or kick shot (*or any combination thereof*), it is considered a legally pocketed ball and scores one (1) point.

It is not necessary to call or specify kisses, caroms, rails, etc. Only called balls legally score. Any balls accidentally (*or illegally*) pocketed are re-spotted at the end of the inning. **Note:** 1985 Vaso Amendment may be implemented at player's option. To wit: Shooter may call any number of balls (two or more) on any one shot - as long as all balls called are pocketed as called - or none are scored. In other words, call all you want, but make all you call - or none qualify. Shooter calling two balls but pocketing only one (a) loses inning and (b) must respot pocketed ball.

KICK SHOTS
No short-rail kicks. Kick shots are legal only when cue ball is first banked off rail not connected with designated pocket (*or if cue ball is banked off any two, or more, rails before striking object ball*). (*See Diagram 28*)

Pocket Billiards

OPENING BREAK

On the opening break the shooter must either:

1. call and pocket a ball out of the rack, or;
2. cause two numbered balls plus the cue ball to hit the cushion after striking rack with cue ball.

Failure to do either is a foul. Penalty: One (1) point. Incoming player accepts cue ball where it lies. Breaker owes one (1) ball (*i.e., must respot first ball he legally pockets*).

All subsequent play is subject to standard BCA Pocket Billiard Regulations. (*Legal safety: Contact between cue ball and object ball, after which either cue ball - or object ball - or both - hit a cushion.*)

FOULS AND PENALTIES

One (1) point penalty (*one ball either re-spotted or owed*) per scratch or foul. Following scratch, incoming player has cue ball in hand in kitchen; following foul, incoming shooter accepts cue ball where it lies. The accidental touching or moving of any ball on the table is considered a foul. In Honolulu there is no three consecutive foul penalty.

ILLEGALLY POCKETED BALLS

Are all respotted at end of inning.

LINE-UP

Except when clearly contradicted by these additional rules,
the General Rules of Pocket Billiards apply.

TYPE OF GAME

Line-Up is a forerunner of 14.1 Continuous.

PLAYERS

2 players.

BALLS USED

Standard set of object balls numbered 1-15, plus *cue ball*.

THE RACK

Standard triangle rack with the front apex ball on the *foot spot*, 1-ball on the rack's right corner, 5-ball on left corner; other balls placed at random.

OBJECT OF THE GAME

To score the predetermined point total (*usually 150 in tournaments, or any agreed upon total*) for game prior to opponent.

SCORING
Any ball legally pocketed counts one point for shooter.

OPENING BREAK
Starting player must pocket a *called ball* or drive two object balls to a *cushion*. If he fails to do so, he is assessed a two point penalty. Incoming player may accept the *table in position* and shoot, or require that offender repeat the opening break until the requirements are satisfied. Each successive failure is a two point penalty for offending player.

RULES OF PLAY
1. A legally pocketed ball entitles shooter to continue at the table until failing to pocket a called ball on a shot. Player may shoot any ball he chooses, but before he shoots, must designate the ball he will pocket and the pocket into which the ball will score; he need indicate no other detail.

2. On all shots, player must cause the cue ball to contact an object ball and then either
   (a) pocket a numbered ball, or
   (b) cause the cue ball or any numbered ball to contact a cushion. Failure to do
      so is a *foul*.

3. A player may call a safety rather than an object ball if he so desires (*for defensive purposes*). Safety play is legal, but must comply with all applicable rules. Player's inning ends when safety is played, and pocketed balls are not scored. Any object ball pocketed on a called safety is spotted.

4. When the 15th ball of the rack has been pocketed, shooter records his scored balls from the rack. The balls are then spotted, and player continues shooting, playing the cue ball from where it came to rest after preceding shot, before the balls were spotted. (*If player misses or fouls during the rack, he records his score and incoming player shoots, accepting the table in position.*)

ILLEGALLY POCKETED BALLS
All spotted; no penalty.

OBJECT BALLS JUMPED OFF THE TABLE
All spotted. The stroke is a foul, and the penalty for fouls is followed.

CUE BALL AFTER JUMPING OFF THE TABLE OR SCRATCH
Incoming player has cue ball in hand behind the head string (*unless the foul was a third successive foul; see "Successive Fouls Penalty"*).

PENALTY FOR FOULS

One point is deducted from offender's score for each foul committed, unless the foul is a third *successive foul* (*see "Successive Fouls Penalty"*). After fouls other than cue ball jump, cue ball scratch, or third successive foul, incoming player accepts the table in position.

SUCCESSIVE FOULS PENALTY

If a player commits three successive fouls, he is penalized one point for each foul, and an additional deduction of 15 points. The balls are reracked and offending player is required to break the balls under the requirements of the opening break.

MR. AND MRS.

Except when clearly contradicted by these additional rules,
the General Rules of Pocket Billiards apply.

TYPE OF GAME

Mr. and Mrs. (*also called Boy Meets Girl*) is a game that combines the general forms of Rotation and Basic Pocket Billiards. The rules are different for players of widely differing skill levels.

PLAYERS

2 to 6.

BALLS USED

Standard set of object balls numbered 1-15, plus *cue ball*.

THE RACK

Standard *triangle* rack with the 1-ball on the *foot spot*, 2-ball on racker's right corner, 3-ball on left corner, 15-ball in the center. All other balls are placed at random.

OBJECT OF THE GAME

To score balls of greater total point value than opponent(s).

SCORING

Each legally pocketed object ball has a point value equal to its number. Game ends when a player's point total mathematically eliminates opponent(s) - 61 points in a two-player game. If two or more players tie for highest point total, the tied player that legally pocketed the last object ball is credited with a game won.

OPENING BREAK

Starting player must cause the cue ball's first contact to be with the 1-ball. If starting player fails to meet this requirement, incoming player has the choice of

(1) accepting the *table in position* and shooting, or (2) requiring that the balls be reracked and offending player repeat the *opening break*.

RULES OF PLAY

1. A legally pocketed ball entitles shooter to continue at the table until failing to legally pocket a ball.

2. On all shots, the more skilled player must cause the cue ball's first contact with a ball to be with the lowest numbered object ball on the table and then either
   (a) pocket a ball, or
   (b) cause the cue ball or any object ball to contact a *cushion*.
      Failure to do so is a foul.

3. The less skilled player may shoot any ball, regardless of number. He need not call ball, pocket or mode of shot. Any ball pocketed on a legal shot is a scored ball.

4. Player loses game if he commits three *successive fouls*. If more than a two-player game, balls previously pocketed by disqualified player remain off the table.

5. When a skilled player has the cue ball in hand behind the head string (as after a scratch) and the legal object ball is also behind the head string, the object ball may be spotted on the foot spot at his request.

6. When a less skilled player has the *cue ball in hand behind the head string* (*as after a scratch*) and all of the object balls are also behind the head string, the object ball nearest the head string may be spotted at his request. If two or more object balls are an equal distance from the head string, he may also designate which of the equidistant object balls should be spotted.

ILLEGALLY POCKETED BALLS
All spotted; no penalty.

OBJECT BALLS JUMPED OFF THE TABLE
All spotted. The stroke is a foul, and the player's inning ends. The penalty for fouls is followed.

CUE BALL AFTER JUMPING OFF THE TABLE OR SCRATCH
Incoming player has cue ball in hand behind the head string.

PENALTY FOR FOULS
No point penalty. If foul is other than jumped cue ball or cue ball scratch, incoming player accepts the cue ball in position. A third consecutive foul by the same player is loss of game.

PEA (KELLY) POOL

Except when clearly contradicted by these additional rules,
the General Rules of Pocket Billiards apply.

TYPE OF GAME

Pea (*or Kelly*) Pool is an old favorite among pocket billiard players who enjoy a group game in which the competitors play individually, and which entails a bit of luck (*not so much in the actual play but rather in the pea or pill each player receives during each game*). The game is very popular since it can accommodate players of widely differing levels of ability.

PLAYERS

4 to 6.

BALLS USED

Standard set of object balls numbered 1-15, plus cue ball. A set of 15 number peas (*or "pills"*) and a *shake bottle* are also used.

THE RACK

Standard triangle rack with 1-ball on the foot spot, 2-ball on racker's right corner, 3-ball on left corner. All other balls placed at random.

DETERMINING PRIVATE NUMBERS

After the balls are racked, but before play begins, each player is given a pea from the shake bottle (*containing the peas numbered 1-15*). The number of the pea is the player's private number and is kept secret.

OBJECT OF THE GAME

To legally pocket the object ball with the numerical value equivalent to the player's private number.

SCORING

No point value for object balls except the ball equivalent to pocketing player's private number; when a player legally pockets that object ball, he wins the game. Option: Game is played until a player legally pockets "his own" ball and wins, as above; he receives two points from each player for winning the game. In addition, when any player's "private number ball" is legally pocketed by any player other than himself, the pocketing player receives one point and the player whose ball was pocketed loses one point. Players whose private number balls have been pocketed by other players continue to shoot in the regular rotation, but if a player fails to announce that his object ball was pocketed by another player prior to a subsequent shot is being taken, the offending player is disqualified from further play during the game, and the forfeiture of points to the pocketing player is increased from one to two. If no player succeeds in pocketing his private number ball, the game ends when the last private number ball is pocketed, and another game is played with all point values doubled and player who pocketed the last private number ball being the starting player.

OPENING BREAK
Starting player must make an *open break*. If he fails to do so, incoming player has choice of either:
1. cue ball in hand behind the head string and table in position, or;
2. having the balls reracked and shooting the opening break shot.

RULES OF PLAY
1. A legally pocketed ball entitles shooter to continue at the table until he fails to legally pocket a ball.

2. On all shots, the cue ball's first contact must be with the lowest numbered object ball on the table and then must either
   (a) pocket a numbered ball, or
   (b) cause the cue ball or any object ball to contact a cushion.
      Failure to do so is a foul.

3. A player legally pocketing a ball must shoot again. He may not call a *safety* and *spot* a pocketed ball.

4. When a player has the *cue ball in hand behind the head string* (*as after a scratch*) and the legal object ball is also behind the head string, the object ball may be spotted on the foot spot at his request.

ILLEGALLY POCKETED BALLS
All spotted; no penalty.

OBJECT BALLS JUMPED OFF THE TABLE
All spotted. The stroke is a foul, and the penalty for fouls is followed.

CUE BALL AFTER JUMP OR SCRATCH
Incoming player has cue ball in hand behind the head string.

PENALTY FOR FOULS
No point penalty. Incoming player has choice of either:
1. accepting the table in position and shooting, or
2. requiring offending player to shoot again (*if cue ball is in hand behind the string, it is so for either player*).

95

POKER POCKET BILLIARDS

Except when clearly contradicted by these additional rules,
the General Rules of Pocket Billiards apply.

THE GAME

Poker Pocket Billiards is played with a white cue ball and a special set of 16 object balls. Fifteen of the object balls are numbered from 1 to 15, while the 16th ball has a "J" marked on two sides. Three of the numbered balls are also marked with a "J", which represents a "Jack", as in poker played with cards. Four of the numbered balls are marked with an "A" for ace; four are marked with a "K" for king, and the remaining four marked with a "Q" for queen.

START OF THE GAME

Rotation of play may be determined by lag or lot. The object balls are racked in any order on the foot spot in a 16-ball rectangle. (*See Diagram 29*) Starting player has cue ball in hand.

SCORING

The object of the game is to get a better poker hand than your opponents. The best hand is four of a kind - four aces, for example. The next best hand is a full house; then three of a kind; then two pairs; then a straight (*ace, king, queen, jack*) and finally a pair (*two of a kind*).

No player is allowed to score more than five balls in a single inning. Balls pocketed legally remain off the table.

THE BREAK

Starting player is credited with all balls scored on the break shot, providing he doesn't foul. If he counts, he continues shooting until he misses or pockets the limit of five balls allowed in one inning.

INCOMING PLAYER

Incoming player accepts balls in position and is limited to five scores in a single inning.

NUMBER OF PLAYERS

Two or more players can play.

GAME ENDS

Game ends when all the balls have been legally pocketed. For example, one player may have five balls to his credit. Another may have three scores. A third player may have four balls in his "hand". A fourth player may have two counts. In this event, two object balls remain on the table. The player with five balls to his cred-

Poker Pocket Billiards

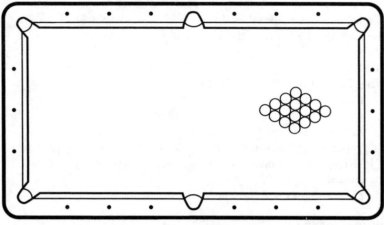

Diagram 29

it can continue to shoot in turn, spotting a ball from his hand each time he pockets a ball. He continues to pocket and spot balls in an attempt to better his hand, until he misses or scores the limit of five balls in an inning. The player with four counts to his credit, shooting in turn, can pocket a fifth ball and continue to shoot for the lone ball on the table in an effort to better his hand, spotting a ball each time he pockets one. He continues until he misses.

A player with three balls to his credit, however, with only two object balls on the table, ends the game if he pockets the two balls. In other words, he doesn't spot a ball after scoring, since he has only five counts to his credit.

ORDER OF FINISH
When all the balls are pocketed to end the game, players make the best poker hand out of the balls to their credit. A player with only three balls - if, for example, they are three kings - would win over a player who has five scores, but can get only two pairs out of this hand. A player with one ball to his credit defeats a player with no counts. A player with no balls to his credit finishes ahead of a player with no counts, who owes a ball as the result of a foul.

DELIBERATE MISS
It is obvious that if a player who has five balls to his credit can't better his hand by pocketing the balls on the table, he will miss deliberately rather than pocket a ball that will not better his hand. In making a deliberate miss, the player must drive an object ball to a cushion or cause the cue ball to hit a cushion after striking an object ball. Failure is a foul.

Pocket Billiards

PENALTIES

Players are penalized one ball for each foul. If a player fouls with no balls to his credit, he owes one to the table. If a player is forced to spot a ball from his hand as the result of a foul, he can choose the ball to be spotted.

FOULS

A player has fouled in Poker Pocket Billiards when:
1. Failing to hit an object ball.
2. Driving the cue ball or any object ball off the table.
3. Failing to have one foot on the floor when stroking.
4. Touching the cue ball except with the tip of the cue on a legitimate stroke or touching any object ball on the table, except on legal contact by the cue ball.
5. Fails to comply with rule on "deliberate miss".

GENERAL RULES

When not in conflict with specific game provisions, the rules of 14.1 Continuous Pocket Billiards apply.

WILD GAMES

1. By agreement, players can make the "J" ball "wild", players pocketing the "J's" designating them as any "card" they wish when the "hands are laid down" at the conclusion of the game. For example, a player with three "A" balls (aces) and a "J" ball (*jack, which is wild*) can call his hand "four aces".
2. Players may draw a ball from the shake bottle, the number of which is kept secret from all the players until the game is over. At the conclusion of the game, the secret number is revealed. If, for example, the number corresponds to a "K" ball, all the kings are wild, players holding kings thus having the advantage of a wild card in finally calling their hands.
3. Each player can draw a number from the shake bottle, which makes all balls he scores of that number wild.

SIX-BALL

Except when clearly contradicted by these additional rules,
the General Rules of Pocket Billiards apply.

TYPE OF GAME

Six-Ball is a variation of Rotation in which the lowest numbered ball on the table must always be the player's first cue ball contact. If a player complies, any pocketed ball counts. For example, if a player strikes the 1-ball legally, which then caroms into the 6-ball and causes it to be pocketed, that player wins the game. It's fast, and with only six object balls on the table, single inning racks are very common.

PLAYERS
2 or more, though 2 players are generally preferred.

BALLS USED
Object balls 1-6, plus *cue ball*.

THE RACK
Triangle rack (*rows of 1-2-3*) with the 1-ball on the foot spot, and the 6-ball in the center of the rear row. All other balls placed entirely at random.

OBJECT OF THE GAME
To legally pocket the 6-ball.

SCORING
The balls have no point value. The player legally pocketing the 6-ball is credited with a game won.

OPENING BREAK
The starting player must:
    1. make an *open break*, or;
    2. legally pocket an object ball. If failing to do so, the incoming player has choice of:
        (a) *cue ball in hand behind the head string* and object balls in position, or;
        (b) having balls reracked and shooting the opening break shot.

RULES OF PLAY
1. A legal shot requires that the cue ball's first contact be with the lowest numbered ball on the table. A player must then:
    (a) pocket a numbered ball, or;
    (b) cause the cue ball or any numbered ball to contact a cushion.
    Failure to do so is a foul.

2. A legally pocketed ball entitles a shooter to remain at the table until failure to pocket a ball on a legal shot.

3. When a player legally pockets a ball, he must shoot again. He may not call a safety and spot a legally pocketed object ball.

4. It is a loss of game if a player commits three *successive fouls*.

ILLEGALLY POCKETED BALLS
All spotted; no penalty, (*Common Option, coin-operated play: None spotted except game ball.*)

99

OBJECT BALLS JUMPED OFF THE TABLE
All spotted. The stroke is a foul, and the penalty for fouls is followed.

CUE BALL AFTER JUMPING OFF THE TABLE OR SCRATCH
Incoming player has *cue ball in hand.*

PENALTY FOR FOULS
Incoming player is awarded *cue ball in hand.* However, if a 3rd consecutive foul, Rule of Play 4 provides for a penalty of loss of game. The player's inning ends and no count can be scored.

SNOOKER GAMES

Pocket billiard games in America in the 1800s generally evolved from English Billiards (*with two cue balls and one red ball*), which was played on a 6' x 12' table with rails that sloped into the pocket openings. By 1860, New York table manufacturer, author and noted player Michael Phelan replaced the sloping sides of the pockets with straight corners, thus changing the direction of American pocket billiards from the English game from that time to the present.

English Billiards could only be played with two players, so eventually multi-player variations such as Life Pool and Pyramid Pool became popular in America, England, and territories in which English soldiers were stationed. Life Pool featured different colored balls used as both cue balls and/or object balls, depending on the situation and the number of players. Pyramid Pool featured 15 red balls racked on the Pyramid (*foot*) Spot, and each player received one point for each red ball legally potted. Black Pool was a form of Pyramid Pool which used the black ball from a Life Pool set so that a player could alternately pot a red and then attempt the black for extra points. Legend has it that in 1875, Sir Neville Chamberlain, an English regiment soldier stationed in Jubbulpore, India, was playing Black Pool with his fellow officers when he got the idea to add other colored balls to the game so that the variation eventually featured 15 red balls, a yellow, green, pink and black ball (*a blue and brown ball were added some years later*). In the course of play, one day a visiting military cadet remarked that first-year cadets at his particular academy were known as "snookers". When the cadet missed a particularly easy pot, Chamberlain exclaimed to him, "Why, you're a regular snooker!" After explaining the meaning of the word to his fellow peers, Chamberlain added that perhaps they were all snookers at the game. The term was adopted for this particular variation, and the game has been called snooker ever since.

Snooker spread to other posts, and soldiers returning to England introduced the game there. Champion player John Roberts, Jr. learned the rules of the game on one of his exhibition tours of India, and he may have had some influence in further popularizing the game in the U.K. When English Billiards started losing spectator interest at professional matches in England in the 1930s, champion billiardist Joe Davis recognized snooker as a more appealing alternative, and his cue prowess at the game eventually led to snooker being embraced as the more popular championship discipline in that country. Snooker has never gained as much popularity in the U.S., but its appeal to many American players, its rank as the #1 televised sport on English television, and the skillful variations it has bred around the world warrants the inclusion of three pertinent sets of rules in this section.

English Snooker – 6x12 Table

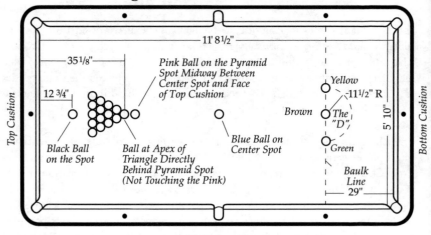

Diagram 30

INTERNATIONAL SNOOKER
World-Standardized Rules

The rules of Snooker as printed below are recognized by the International Billiards and Snooker Federation and the World Professional Billiards & Snooker Association as of September, 1995. The BCA is authorized to print these rules through the permission of the United States Snooker Association, the IBSF-recognized body governing the game and the rules in the United States.

EQUIPMENT (Section 1)
Measurements in parentheses state the metric
equivalent to the nearest millimeter.

THE STANDARD TABLE

DIMENSIONS
The playing area within the cushion faces shall measure 11' 8 1/2" x 5'10" (*3569 mm x 1778 mm*) with a tolerance on both dimensions of ± 1/2" (*±13 mm*).

HEIGHT
The height of the table from the floor to the top of the cushion rail shall be from 2' 9 1/2" to 2' 10 1/2" (*851 mm to 876 mm*).

POCKET OPENINGS
1. There shall be pockets at the corners (*two at the Spot end known as the top pockets and two at the Baulk end known as the bottom pockets*) and one each at the middle of the longer sides (*known as the center pockets*).

2. The pocket openings shall conform to the templates authorized by the World Professional Billiards and Snooker Association (WPBSA).
3. Corner Pocket: Mouth . . . . . 3 3/8" Minimum to 3 5/8" Maximum
   Side Pocket: Mouth . . . . . 4 1/16" Minimum to 4 5/16" Maximum

BAULK-LINE AND BAULK

A straight line drawn 29" (*737 mm*) from the face of the bottom cushion and parallel to it is called the Baulk-line, and that line and the intervening space is termed the Baulk.

THE "D"

The "D" is a semi-circle described in Baulk with its center at the middle of the Baulk-line and with a radius of 11 1/2" (*292 mm*).

SPOTS

Four spots are marked on the center longitudinal line of the table:

1. The Spot (*known as the Black Spot*), 12 3/4" (324 mm) from a point perpendicularly below the face of the top cushion.
2. The Center Spot (*known as the Blue Spot*), located midway between the faces of the top and bottom cushions.
3. The Pyramid Spot (*known as the Pink Spot*), located midway between the Center Spot and the face of the top cushion.
4. The Middle of the Baulk-line (*known as the Brown Spot*).
   Two other spots used are located at the corners of the "D". Viewed from the baulk end, the one on the right is known as the Yellow Spot and the one on the left as the Green Spot.

BALLS

The Balls shall be of an approved composition and shall each have a diameter of 52.5 mm with a tolerance of ± 0.05 mm and:

1. They shall be of equal weight within a tolerance of 3g per set
2. A ball or set of balls may be changed by agreement between the players or on a decision by the referee.

CUE

A cue shall be not less than 3'(*914 mm*) in length and shall show no substantial departure from the traditional and generally accepted shape and form.

ANCILLARY

Various cue rests, long cues (*called butts and half-butts according to length*), extensions and adapters may be used by players faced with difficult positions for cueing. These may form part of the equipment normally found at the table but also include equipment introduced by either player or the referee (*see also Section*

3 Use of Ancillary Equipment). All extensions, adapters and other devices to aid cueing must be of a design approved by the WPBSA.

DEFINITIONS (Section 2)
Standard definitions used throughout these Rules are hereinafter italicized.

FRAME
A frame of snooker is the period of play from the first stroke, with all the balls set as described in Section 3 *Position of Balls*, until the frame is completed by:
1. Concession by any player during a turn,
2. Claim by the striker when only the Black remains and there is more than seven points difference between the scores in his favor,
3. The final pot or foul when only the Black remains, or
4. Being awarded by the referee under Section 3 *Foul And A Miss* (3) or Section 4 *Unfair Conduct*.

GAME
A *game* is an agreed or stipulated number of *frames*.

MATCH
A *match* is an agreed or stipulated number of *games*.

BALLS
1. The White ball is the cue ball.
2. The 15 Reds and the 6 colors are the object balls.

STRIKER
The person about to play or in play is the striker and remains so until the referee has decided he has left the table at the end of his turn.

STROKE
1. A stroke is made when the striker strikes the cue ball with the tip of the cue.
2. A stroke is fair when no infringement of Rule is made.
3. A stroke is not completed until all balls have come to rest.
4. A stroke may be made directly or indirectly, thus:
   (a) a stroke is direct when the cue ball strikes an object ball without first striking a cushion.
   (b) a stroke is indirect when the cue ball strikes one or more cushions before striking an object ball.

POT

A pot is when an object ball, after contact with another ball and without any infringement of these Rules, enters a pocket. Causing a ball to be potted is known as potting.

BREAK

A break is a number of pots in successive strokes made in any one turn by a player during a frame.

In hand
1. The cue ball is in hand:
   (a) before the start of each frame,
   (b) when it has entered a pocket, or
   (c) when it has been forced off the table.
2. It remains in hand until:
   (a) it is played fairly from in hand, or
   (b) a foul is committed whilst the ball is on the table.
3. Striker is said to be in hand when the cue ball is in hand as above.

BALL IN PLAY

1. The cue ball is in play when it is not in hand.
2. Object balls are in play from the start of the frame until pocketed or forced off the table.
3. Colors become in play again when respotted.

BALL ON

Any ball which may be lawfully struck by the first impact of the cue ball, or any ball which may not be so struck but which may be potted, is said to be on.

NOMINATED BALL

1. A nominated ball is the object ball which the striker declares, or indicates to the satisfaction of the referee, he undertakes to hit with the first impact of the cue ball.
2. If requested by referee, the striker must declare which ball is on.

FREE BALL

A free ball is a ball which the striker nominates as the ball on when snookered after a foul (*see Section 3 Snookered After A Foul*).

FORCED OFF THE TABLE

A ball is forced off the table if it comes to rest other than on the bed of the table or in a pocket, or if it is picked up by the striker while it is in play except as provided for in Section 3 *Foul And A Miss* (8).

Snooker and Caroms

FOUL

A foul is any infringement of these Rules.

SNOOKERED

The cue ball is said to be snookered when a direct stroke in a straight line to every ball on is wholly or partially obstructed by a ball or balls not on. If one or more balls on can be struck at both extreme edges free of obstruction by any ball not on, the cue ball is not snookered.

1. If in hand, the cue ball is snookered if it is obstructed as described above from all possible positions on or within the lines of the "D".
2. If the cue ball is so obstructed from hitting a ball on by more than one ball not on:
   (a) The ball nearest to the cue ball is considered to be the effective snookering ball, and
   (b) Should more than one obstructing ball be equidistant from the cue ball, all such balls will be considered to be effective snookering balls.
3. When Red is the ball on, if the cue ball is obstructed from hitting different Reds by different balls not on, there is no effective snookering ball.
4. The striker is said to be snookered when the cue ball is snookered as above.
5. The cue ball cannot be snookered by a cushion. If the curved face of a cushion obstructs the cue ball and is closer to the cue ball than any obstructing ball not on, the cue ball is not snookered.

SPOT OCCUPIED

A spot is said to be occupied if a ball cannot be placed on it without that ball touching another ball.

PUSH STROKE

A push stroke is made when the tip of the cue remains in contact with the cue ball:

1. After the cue ball has commenced its forward motion, or
2. As the cue ball makes contact with an object ball except, where the cue ball and an object ball are almost touching, it shall not be deemed a push stroke if the cue ball hits a very fine edge of the object ball.

JUMP SHOT

A jump shot is made when the cue ball passes over any part of an object ball, whether touching it in the process or not, except:

1. When the cue ball first strikes one object ball and then jumps over another ball,
2. When the cue ball jumps and strikes and object ball, but does not land on the far side of that ball,

3. When, after striking an object ball lawfully, the cue ball jumps over that ball after hitting a cushion or another ball.

MISS

A miss is when the cue ball fails to first contact a ball on and the referee considers that the striker has not made a good enough attempt to hit a ball on.

THE GAME (Section 3)

DESCRIPTION

Snooker may be played by two or more players, either independently or as sides. The game can be summarized as follows:

1. Each player uses the same white cue ball and there are 21 object balls - 15 Reds each have a value of 1, and six colors: Yellow valued 2, Green 3, Brown 4, Blue 5, Pink 6 and Black 7.
2. Scoring strokes in a player's turn are made by potting Reds and colors alternately until all the Reds are off the table and the colors in the ascending order of their value.
3. Points awarded for scoring strokes are added to the score of striker.
4. Penalty points from fouls are added to the opponent's score.
5. A tactic employed at any time during a frame is to leave the cue ball behind a ball not on such that it is snookered for the next player. If a player or side is more points behind than are available from the balls left on the table, then the laying of snookers in the hope of gaining points from fouls becomes most important.
6. The winner of a frame is the player or side:
   (a) Making the highest score;
   (b) To whom the frame is conceded;
   (c) To whom it is awarded under Section 3 *Foul And A Miss*, or Section 4 *Unfair Conduct*.
7. The winner of a game is the player or side:
   (a) Winning most, or the required number of frames;
   (b) Making the greatest total where aggregate points are relevant, or
   (c) To whom the game is awarded under Section 4 *Unfair Conduct*.
8. The winner of a match is the player or side winning most games or, where aggregate points are relevant, with the greatest total.

POSITION OF BALLS

At the start of each frame the cue ball is in hand and the object balls are positioned on the table as follows:

1. The Reds in the form of a tightly-packed equilateral triangle, with the Red at the apex standing on the center line of the table, above the Pyramid Spot such that it will be as close to the Pink as possible without touching it, and the base of the triangle nearest to, and parallel with, the top cushion.

Snooker and Caroms

107

2. Yellow on the right-hand corner of the "D",
3. Green on the left-hand corner of the "D",
4. Brown on the Middle of the Baulk-line,
5. Blue on the Center Spot,
6. Pink on the Pyramid Spot, and
7. Black on the Spot.
   After a frame has started, a ball in play may only be cleaned by the referee upon reasonable request by the striker and:
8. The position of the ball, if not spotted, shall be marked by a suitable device prior to the ball being lifted for cleaning.
9. The device used to mark the position of a ball being cleaned shall be regarded as and acquire the value of the ball until such time as the ball has been cleaned and replaced. If any player other than the striker should touch or disturb the device, he shall be penalized as if he were the striker, without affecting the order of play. The referee shall return the device or ball being cleaned to its position, if necessary, to his satisfaction even if it was picked up.

MODE OF PLAY

The players shall determine the order of play by lot or in any mutually agreed manner.

1. The order of play thus determined must remain unaltered throughout the frame, except that a player may be asked by the next player to play again after any foul.
2. The player or side to strike first must alternate for each frame during a game.
3. The first player plays from in hand, the frame commencing when the cue ball has been placed on the table and contacted by the tip of the cue, either;
   (a) As a stroke is made, or
   (b) While addressing the cue ball.
4. For a stroke to be fair, none of the infringements described below in *Penalties*, must occur.
5. For the first stroke of each turn, until all Reds are off the table, Red or a free ball nominated as a Red is the ball on, and the value of each Red and any free ball nominated as a Red potted in the same stroke, is scored.
   (a) If a Red, or free ball nominated as a Red, is potted, the same player plays the next stroke and the next ball on is a color of the striker's choice which, if potted, is scored and the color is then spotted.
   (b) The break is continued by potting Reds and colors alternately until all Reds are off the table and, where applicable, a color has been played at following the potting of the last Red.
   (c) the colors then become on in the ascending order of their value as per

Section 3 *Description* (1) and when next potted remain off the table, except as provided for in *End Of Frame, Game Or Match* below, and the striker plays the next stroke at the next color on.

6. Reds are not replaced on the table once pocketed or forced off the table regardless of the fact that a player may thus benefit from a foul.

   Exceptions to this concept are provided for in Section 3 *Ball Of Position* (9), *Ball On Edge Of Pocket, Foul And A Miss* (6 & 8) and *Ball Moved By Other Than Striker*.

7. If the striker fails to score or commits a foul, his turn ends and the next player plays from where the cue ball comes to rest, or from in hand if the cue ball is off the table.

END OF FRAME, GAME OR MATCH

1. When only the Black is left, the first score or foul ends the frame excepting only if the following conditions both apply:
   (a) The scores are then equal, and
   (b) Aggregate scores are not relevant.
2. When both conditions in (1) above apply,
   (a) The Black is spotted;
   (b) The players draw lots for choice of playing;
   (c) The next player plays from in hand, and;
   (d) The next score or foul ends the frame.
3. When aggregate scores determine the winner of a game or match, and the aggregate scores are equal at the end of the last frame, the players in that frame shall follow the procedure for a respotted Black set out in (2) above.

PLAYING FROM IN HAND

To play from in hand, the cue ball must be struck from a position on or within the lines of the "D", but it may be played in any direction.

1. The referee will state, if asked, whether the cue ball is properly placed (*that is, not outside the lines of the "D"*).
2. If the tip of the cue should touch the cue ball while positioning it, and the referee is satisfied that the striker was not attempting to play a stroke, then the cue ball is not in play.

HITTING TWO BALLS SIMULTANEOUSLY

Two balls, other than two Reds or a free ball and a ball on, must not be struck simultaneously by the first impact of the cue ball.

SPOTTING COLORS

Any color pocketed or forced off the table shall be spotted before the next stroke is made, until finally potted under Section 3 *Mode Of Play* (5 *a and b*).

1. A player shall not be held responsible for any mistake by the referee in failing to spot any ball correctly.
2. If a color is spotted in error after being potted in ascending order as per Section 3 *Mode Of Play* (5c), it shall be removed from the table with out penalty when the error is discovered and play shall continue.
3. If a stroke is made with a ball or balls not correctly spotted, they will be considered to be correctly spotted for subsequent strokes. Any color incorrectly missing from the table will be spotted:
   (a) without penalty when discovered if missing due to previous oversight
   (b) subject to penalty if the striker played before the referee was able to effect the spotting.
4. If a color has to be spotted and its own spot is occupied, it shall be placed on the highest value spot available.
5. If there is more than one color to be spotted and their own spots are occupied, the highest value ball shall take precedence in order of spotting.
6. If all spots are occupied, the color shall be placed as near its own spot as possible, between that spot and the nearest part of the top cushion.
7. In the case of Pink and Black, if all spots are occupied and there is no available space between the relevant spot and the nearest part of the top cushion, the color shall be placed as near to its own spot as possible on the center line of the table below the spot.
8. In all cases, the color when spotted must not be touching another ball.
9. A color, to be properly spotted, must be placed by hand on the spot designated in these Rules.

TOUCHING BALL

1. If the cue ball comes to rest touching another ball or balls that are, or could be, on, the referee shall state TOUCHING BALL and indicate which ball or balls on the cue ball is touching.
2. When a touching ball has been called, the striker must play the cue ball away from that ball without moving it or it is a push stroke.
3. Providing the striker does not cause the object ball to move, there shall be no penalty if:
   (a) The ball is on:
   (b) The ball could be on and the striker declares he is on it, or
   (c) The ball could be on and the striker declares, and first hits, another ball that could be on.
4. If the cue ball comes to rest touching or nearly touching a ball that is not on, the referee, if asked whether it is touching, will answer YES or NO. The striker must play away without disturbing it as above but must first hit a ball that is on.
5. When the cue ball is touching both a ball on and a ball not on, the referee shall only indicate the ball on as touching. If the striker should ask

the referee whether the cue ball is also touching the ball not on, he is entitled to be told.

6. If the referee is satisfied that any movement of a touching ball at the moment of striking was not caused by the striker, he will not call a foul.

7. If a stationary object ball, not touching the cue ball when examined by the referee, is later seen to be in contact with the cue ball before a stroke has been made, the balls shall be repositioned by the referee to his satisfaction.

BALL ON EDGE OF POCKET

1. If a ball falls into a pocket without being hit by another ball, and being no part of any stroke in progress, it shall be replaced and any points scored shall count.

2. If it would have been hit by any ball involved in a stroke:

   (a) with no infringement of these Rules, all balls will be replaced and the same stroke played again or a different stroke maybe played at his discretion, by the same striker.

   (b) if a foul is committed, the striker incurs the penalty prescribed, all balls will be replaced and the next player has the usual options after a foul.

3. If a ball balances momentarily on the edge of a pocket and then falls in, it shall count as in the pocket and not be replaced.

SNOOKERED AFTER A FOUL

After a foul, if the cue ball is snookered, the referee shall state FREE BALL (*see Section 2, Snookered*).

1. If the player next in turn elects to play the next stroke,

   (a) he may nominate any ball as the ball on, and

   (b) any nominated ball shall be regarded as, and acquire the value of, the ball on except that, if potted, it shall then be spotted.

2. It is a foul if the cue ball should

   (a) fail to hit the nominated ball first, or first simultaneously with the ball on, or

   (b) be snookered on all Reds, or the ball on, by the free ball thus nominated, except when Pink and Black are the only object balls remaining on the table.

3. If the free ball is potted, it is spotted and the value of the ball on is scored.

4. If a ball on is potted, after the cue ball struck the nominated ball first, or first simultaneously with a ball on, the ball on is scored and remains off the table.

5. If both the nominated ball and a ball on are potted, only the ball on is scored unless it was a Red, when each ball potted is scored. The free ball is then spotted and the ball on remains off the table.

6. If the offender is asked to play again, the free ball call becomes void.

FOULS

If a foul is committed, the referee shall immediately state FOUL:

1. If the striker has not made a stroke, his turn ends immediately and the referee shall announce the penalty.
2. If a stroke has been made, the referee will wait until completion of the stroke before announcing the penalty.
3. If a foul is neither awarded by the referee, nor successfully claimed by the non-striker before the next stroke is made, it is condoned.
4. Any color not correctly spotted shall remain where positioned except that if off the table it shall be correctly spotted.
5. All points scored in a break before a foul is awarded are allowed but the striker shall not score any points for any ball pocketed in a stroke called foul.
6. The next stroke is played from where the cue ball comes to rest or, if the cue ball is off the table, from in hand.
7. If more than one foul is committed in the same stroke, the highest value penalty shall be incurred.
8. The player who committed the foul
   (a) incurs the penalty described in *Penalties* below, and
   (b) has to play the next stroke if requested by the next player.

PENALTIES

All fouls will incur a penalty of four points unless a higher one is indicated in paragraphs 1 to 4 below. Penalties are:

1. Value of the ball on by:
   (a) Striking the cue ball more than once;
   (b) Striking when both feet are off the floor;
   (c) Playing out of turn;
   (d) Playing improperly from in hand, including at the opening stroke;
   (e) Causing the cue ball to miss all object balls;
   (f) Causing the cue ball to enter a pocket;
   (g) Playing a snooker behind a free ball;
   (h) Playing a jump shot;
   (i) Playing with a non-standard cue, or;
   (j) Conferring with a partner contrary to Section 3 *Four-Handed Snooker* (5).
2. Value of the ball on or ball concerned, whichever is higher, by:
   (a) Striking when any ball is not at rest;
   (b) Striking before referee has completed the spotting of a color;
   (c) Causing a ball not on to enter a pocket;
   (d) Causing the cue ball to first hit a ball not on;
   (e) Making a push stroke;
   (f) Touching a ball in play, other than the cue ball with the tip of the

cue as a stroke is made, or;

(g) Causing a ball to be forced off the table.

3. Value of the ball on or higher value of the two balls concerned by causing the cue ball to first hit simultaneously two balls, other than two reds or a free ball and a ball on.

4. A penalty of seven points is incurred if the striker:

(a) Uses a ball off the table for any purpose;

(b) Uses any object to measure gaps or distance;

(c) Plays at Reds, or a free ball followed by a Red, in successive strokes;

(d) Uses any ball other than White as the cue ball for any stroke once the frame has started;

(e) Fails to declare which ball he is on when requested to do so by the referee, or;

(f) After potting a Red or free ball nominated as a Red, commits a foul before nominating a color.

PLAY AGAIN

Once a player has requested an opponent to play again after a foul, such request cannot be withdrawn. The offender, having been asked to play again, is entitled to:

1. Change his mind as to

(a) Which stroke he will play, and

(b) Which ball on he will attempt to hit.

2. Score points for any ball or balls he may pot.

FOUL AND A MISS

The striker shall, to the best of his ability, endeavor to hit the ball on. If the referee considers the Rule infringed, he shall call FOUL AND A MISS unless only the Black remains on the table, or a situation exists where it is impossible to hit the ball on. In the latter case it must be assumed the striker is attempting to hit the ball on provided that he plays, directly or indirectly, in the direction of the ball on with sufficient strength, in the referee's opinion, to have reached the ball on but for the obstructing ball or balls.

1. After a foul and a miss has been called, the next player may request the offender to play again from the position left or, at his discretion, from the original position, in which latter case the ball on shall be the same as it was prior to the last stroke made, namely:

(a) Any Red, where Red was the ball on,

(b) The color on, where all Reds were off the table, or

(c) A color of the striker's choice, where the ball on was a color after a Red had been potted.

2. If the striker, in making a stroke, fails to first hit a ball on when there is a clear path in a straight line from the cue ball to any part of any ball that is

or could be on, the referee shall call FOUL AND A MISS unless either player needed snookers before, or as a result of, the stroke played and the referee is satisfied that the miss was not intentional.

3. After a miss has been called under paragraph (2) above when there was a clear path in a straight line from the cue ball to a ball that was on or that could have been on, such that central, full ball, contact was available (*in the case of Reds, this to be taken as a full diameter of any Red that is not obstructed by a color*), then:

   (a) a further failure to first hit a ball on in making a stroke from the same position shall be called as a FOUL AND A MISS regardless of the difference in scores, and

   (b) if asked to play again from the original position, the offender shall be warned by the referee that a third failure will result in the *frame* being awarded to his opponent.

4. After the cue ball has been replaced under this Rule, when there is a clear path in a straight line from the cue ball to any part of any ball that is or could be on, and the striker fouls any ball, including the cue ball while preparing to play a stroke, a miss will not be called if a stroke has not been played. In this case the appropriate penalty will be imposed and:

   (a) the next player may elect to play the stroke or ask the offender to play again from the position left, or;

   (b) the next player may ask the referee to replace all balls moved to their original position and have the offender play again from there, and;

   (c) If the above situation arises during a sequence of miss calls, any warning concerning the possible awarding of the frame to his opponent shall remain in effect.

5. All other misses will be called at the discretion of the referee.

6. After a miss and a request by the next player to replace the cue ball, any object balls disturbed will remain where they are unless the referee considers the offending player would or could gain an advantage. In the latter case, any or all disturbed balls may be replaced to the referee's satisfaction and in either case, colors incorrectly off the table will be spotted or replaced as appropriate.

7. When any ball is being replaced after a miss, both the offender and the next player will be consulted as to its position, after which the referee's decision shall be final.

8. During such consultation, if either player should touch any ball in play, he shall be penalized as if he were the striker, without affecting the order of play. The ball touched shall be replaced by the referee, to his satisfaction, if necessary, even if it was picked up.

9. The next player may ask if the referee intends to replace balls other than the cue ball in the event that he should ask for the stroke to be played from the original position, and the referee shall state his intentions.

BALL MOVED BY OTHER THAN STRIKER

If a ball, stationary or moving, is disturbed other than by the striker, it shall be repositioned by the referee to the place he judges the ball was, or would have finished, without penalty.

1. This rule shall include cases where another occurrence or person, other than the striker's partner, causes the striker to move a ball.
2. No player shall be penalized for any disturbance of balls by the referee.

STALEMATE

If the referee thinks a position of stalemate exists, or is being approached, he shall offer the players the immediate option of restarting the frame. If any player objects, the referee shall allow play to continue with the provision that the situation must change within a stated period, usually after three more strokes to each side but at the referee's discretion. If the situation remains basically unchanged after the stated period has expired, the referee shall nullify all scores and reset all balls as for the start of a frame and

(a) The same player shall again make the opening stroke.

(b) The same order of play shall be maintained.

FOUR-HANDED SNOOKER

1. In a four-handed game, each side shall open alternate frames and the order of play shall be determined at the start of each frame and, when so determined, must be maintained throughout that frame.
2. Players may change the order of play at the start of each new frame.
3. If a foul is committed and a request to play again is made, the player who committed the foul plays again, even if the foul was made out of turn, and the original order of play is maintained, such that the offender's partner may lose a turn.
4. When a frame ends in a tie, Section 3 *End Of Frame, Game Or Match* applies. If a respotted Black is necessary, the pair who play the first stroke have the choice of which player will make that stroke. The order of play must then continue as in the frame.
5. Partners may confer during a frame but not:
   (a) While one is the striker and at the table, nor
   (b) After the first stroke of the striker's turn until the break ends.

USE OF ANCILLARY EQUIPMENT

It is the responsibility of the striker to both place and remove any equipment to be used at the table.

1. The striker is responsible for all items including, but not limited to, rests and extensions brought to the table, whether owned by him or borrowed (*except from the referee*) and he will be penalized for any fouls made by him when using this equipment.

Snooker and Caroms

115

2. Equipment normally found at the table which has been provided by another party, including the referee, is not the responsibility of the striker. Should this equipment prove to be faulty and thereby cause the striker to touch a ball or balls, no foul will be called. The referee will, if necessary, reposition any balls in accordance with *Ball Moved By Other Than Striker* (*above*) and the striker, if in a break, will be allowed to continue without penalty.

INTERPRETATION

1. Throughout these Rules and Definitions, words implying the male gender shall equally apply to and include the female gender.
2. Circumstances may necessitate adjustment in how Rules are applied for persons with physical handicaps. In particular and for example:
   (a) Section 3 *Penalties* (1b) cannot be applied to players in wheelchairs, and
   (b) a player, upon request to the referee, shall be told the color of a ball if he is unable to differentiate between colors as, for example, red and green.
3. When there is no referee, the opposing player or side will be regarded as such for the purpose of these Rules.

THE PLAYERS (Section 4)

TIME WASTING

If the referee considers that a player is taking an abnormal amount of time over a stroke or the selection of a stroke, he shall warn the player that he is liable to have the frame awarded to his opponent.

UNFAIR CONDUCT

For refusing to continue a frame, or for conduct which, in the opinion of the referee is wilfully or persistently unfair, including continued time wasting after being warned under *Time Wasting* (above) or ungentlemanly conduct, a player shall lose the frame and the referee shall issue a warning that if such conduct continues, he shall lose the game.

PENALTY

1. If a frame is forfeited under this Section, the offender shall
   (a) lose the frame, and
   (b) forfeit all points scored and the non-offender shall receive a number of points equivalent to the value of the balls remaining on the table, with each Red counting as eight points and any color incorrectly off the table being counted as if spotted.
2. If a game is forfeited under this section, the offender shall
   (a) lose the frame in progress as in (1), and
   (b) additionally lose the required number of unplayed frames to complete the game where frames are relevant, or

(c) additionally lose the remaining frames, each valued at 147 points, where aggregate points apply.

NON-STRIKER
The non-striker shall, when the striker is playing, avoid standing or moving in the line of sight of the striker. He shall sit or stand at a reasonable distance from the table.

ABSENCE
In the case of his absence from the room, the non-striker may appoint a deputy to watch his interests and claim a foul if necessary. Such appointment must be made known to the referee prior to departure.

CONCEDING
1. A player may only concede when he is the striker. The opponent has the right to accept or refuse the concession, which becomes null and void if the opponent chooses to play on.
2. When aggregate scores apply and a frame is conceded, the value of any balls remaining on the table is added to the score of the other side. In such case, Reds shall count as eight points each and any color incorrectly off the table shall be counted as if spotted.

THE OFFICIALS (Section 5)

THE REFEREE
1. The referee shall:
   (a) Be the sole judge of fair and unfair play;
   (b) Be free to make a decision in the interests of fair play for any situation not covered adequately by Rule;
   (c) Be responsible for the proper conduct of the game under these Rules;
   (d) Intervene if he sees any infringement of these Rules;
   (e) Tell a player the color of a ball if requested, and;
   (f) Clean any ball upon reasonable request by a player.
2. The referee shall not:
   (a) Answer any questions not authorized in these Rules;
   (b) Give any indication that player is about to make a foul stroke;
   (c) Give any advice or opinion on points affecting play, nor;
   (d) Answer any questions regarding the difference in scores,
3. If the referee has failed to notice any incident, he may take the evidence of the marker or other officials or spectators best placed for observation to assist his decision.

THE MARKER

The marker shall keep the score on the scoreboard and assist the referee in carrying out his duties. He shall also act as recorder if necessary.

THE RECORDER

The recorder shall maintain a record of each stroke played, showing fouls where appropriate and how many points are scored by each player or side as required. He shall also make note of break totals.

ASSISTANCE BY OFFICIALS

1. At the striker's request, the referee or marker shall move and hold in position any lighting apparatus that interferes with the action of the striker in making a stroke.
2. It is permissible for the referee or marker to give necessary assistance to handicapped players according to their circumstances.

AMERICAN SNOOKER

TYPE OF GAME

American Snooker is a cousin of Snooker as it is played widely around the world, the rules giving it a distinct orientation toward the structure of many American pocket billiard games. It is generally played on either 4 1/2 x 9', 5 x 10' or 6 x 12' Snooker tables, with cushions that are more narrow than other pocket billiard tables, and curve smoothly into the pocket openings. The balls used are either 2 1/16" or 2 1/8" diameter. (*See BCA Specifications.*)

PLAYERS

2.

BALLS USED

Set of Snooker balls: 15 object balls that are not numbered and are solid red (*called reds*), six object balls that may or may not be numbered (*called colors*) and a cue ball. Point values for object balls: red-1, yellow-2, green-3, brown-4, blue-5, pink-6, black-7.

THE RACK

Play begins with balls placed as in Diagram 31.

OBJECT OF THE GAME

To score a greater number of points than opponent.

SCORING

Points are scored in two ways: players are awarded points for fouls by the opponent (*see "Penalty For Foul" below*), and by legally pocketing reds or colors.

Each legally pocketed red ball has a point value of one; each legally pocketed color ball has a point value as indicated (*"Balls Used" above*). Game ends when all balls have been pocketed, following the Rules of Play; if, however, only the black 7-ball is left on the table, the game ends with the first score or foul.

If the players' scores are equal after that scoring, the black ball is spotted on its original position and the players lag for the choice of shooting at, or assigning opponent to shoot at the black ball with the cue ball in hand within the D; the first score or foul then ends the game.

American Snooker-5x10 Table

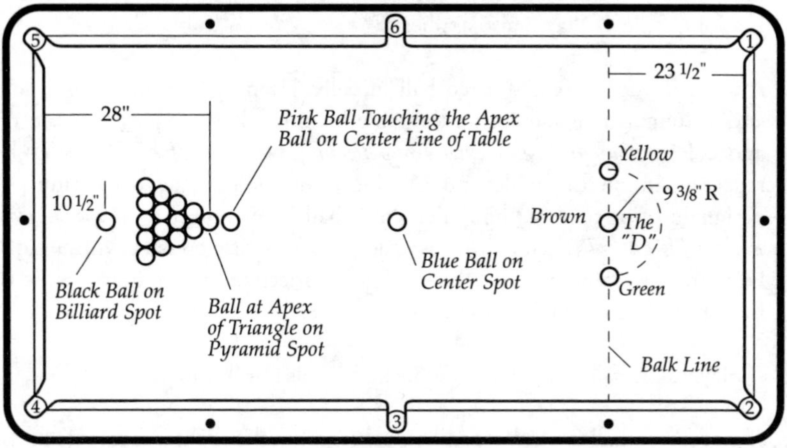

Diagram 31

OPENING BREAK

Starting player has cue ball in hand within the "D". He must:

1. Cause the cue ball to contact a red ball prior to contacting a color, and
2. Cause a red ball to contact a cushion or drop into a pocket, and
3. Cause the cue ball to contact a cushion after it contacts a red ball. Failure to meet these requirements is a foul and a breaking violation. A foul is scored and incoming player has the choice of:
   (a) Accepting the table and shooting, or;
   (b) Requiring offender to break again.

RULES OF PLAY

1. A legally pocketed ball entitles the shooter to continue at the table until failing to legally pocket a ball.

2. On all shots, player must comply with the appropriate requirements of Rules of Play 5 and 6, plus cause the cue ball or an object ball to

119

contact a cushion or drop in a pocket after the cue ball has contacted a legal object ball (*on ball*). Failure to do so is a foul.

3. As long as reds are on the table, an incoming player (*player taking his first shot of an inning*) always has a red as his legal object ball (*on ball*).

4. Any red balls pocketed on a legal shot are legally pocketed balls; player need not call any particular red ball(s), pocket(s) or mode of pocketing.

5. When a player has a red ball as his "on ball" (*required legal object ball*), he must cause the cue ball's first contact to be with a red ball. Failure to do so is a foul. Rule of Play 2 also applies.

6. After a player has scored a red ball initially, his next legal object is a color, and as long as reds remain on the table he must alternate play between reds and colors (*though within each group he may play ball of his choice*). When reds remain on the table and a color is his object, the player must (a) designate prior to shooting which color ball is his object (*that specific color is then his "on ball"*), and (b) cause the cue ball's first contact with a ball to be with that color ball. If a player fails to meet these requirements, it is a foul. Rule 2 requirements also apply.

7. If player's on ball is a red and he pockets a color, it is a foul.

8. If player's on ball is a color and he pockets any other ball, it is a foul.

9. It is a foul if a player intentionally causes the cue ball to jump (*rise from the bed of the table*) by any means, if the jump is an effort to clear an obstructing ball.

10. While reds remain on the table, each pocketed color ball is spotted prior to the next stroke. (*See "Spotting Balls" below for spotting rules.*) If a player shooting after a color has been spotted plays while that ball is incorrectly spotted (*and opponent or referee calls it before two such shots have been taken*), the shot taken is a foul. If such shooting player shoots twice after such error without its being announced by opponent or referee, he is free of penalty and continues shooting and scoring normally as though the spotting error simply had not occurred.

11. If a player fouls and the incoming player is blocked from seeing any part of a ball on, the player may remove the impeding ball (*mark the spot*) and shoot

the ball on. The player cannot score by pocketing this ball on that had been blocked, and the next player returns to the table when the stroke is completed.

12. When no reds remain on the table, player's on balls become the colors, in ascending numerical order (2, 3, 4, 5, 6, 7). These legally pocketed colors are not spotted after each is pocketed; they remain off the table (*the seven-ball is an exception in the case of a tie score; see "Scoring".*)

ILLEGALLY POCKETED BALL
Reds illegally pocketed are not spotted; they remain off the table. Colors illegally pocketed are spotted (*See "Spotting Balls".*)

OBJECT BALLS JUMPED OFF THE TABLE
Reds jumped off the table are not spotted. Colors jumped off the table are spotted. The stroke is a foul, and the penalty for fouls is followed.

SPOTTING BALLS
Reds are never spotted. Colors to be spotted are placed at the start of the game. If a color's spot is occupied (*to mean that to spot it would make it touch a ball*), it is placed on the spot of the highest value color that is unoccupied. If all spots are occupied, the color is spotted as close as possible to its original spot on a straight line between its spot and the nearest point on the foot cushion.

CUE BALL AFTER JUMPING OFF THE TABLE OR SCRATCH
Incoming player has cue ball in hand within the D. When cue ball is in hand within the D (*except on the opening break*), there is no restriction (*based on position of reds or colors*) as to what balls may be played; player may play at an on ball regardless of where it is on the table.

PENALTY FOR FOULS
Seven points are added to non-fouling player's score for each foul committed (*no deduction from offender's score*). Incoming (non-offending) player has the choice of either

1. accepting the table in position and shooting, or
2. requiring the offending player to shoot again. If the foul is a cue ball jumped off the table or a cue ball scratch, the cue ball is in hand within the D for either player. If the foul is other than cue ball jumped off the table or scratch, the cue ball remains in position. If a player pockets a ball and fouls, the player is not credited with any points.

GOLF

TYPE OF GAME

In many sections of the United States the most popular game on a snooker table is Golf. It is usually played on a 4 1/2' x 9', 5 x 10' or 6 x 12' snooker table with either 2 1/8" or 2 1/16" diameter snooker balls. (*See BCA Specifications.*)

PLAYERS

2 or more, with a game often including 4 players or more.

BALLS USED

The numbered group of snooker balls (*2-yellow through 7-black*) and a white snooker cue ball.

THE RACK

Starting player's object ball is spotted on the foot (*pyramid*) spot.

OBJECT OF THE GAME

For a player to successfully pocket his object ball in each of the six pockets in numerical pocket order (*Diagram 31*) before his opponent(s) does.

DETERMINING ORDER OF PLAY

Players draw lots (or numbered peas) from a shake bottle. Lowest drawn number goes first with the remainder of the order corresponding to the ascending draw of peas for each player. Starting player's object ball throughout the game is the 2-ball (*yellow*); the next player - the 3-ball (*green*); the next player - the 4-ball (*brown*); etc.

SCORING

The balls have no numerical value for scoring. The first player to follow the rules of play and legally pocket his object ball in the #6 (*side*) pocket wins the game. Players keep track of the number of fouls (*known as hickeys*) each competitor accrues throughout the game. A hickey may be assigned any value, and players must determine the differences in the totals of hickeys due at the end of each game. For example, if the winning Player A has 6 hickeys, Player B has 4 hickeys, and Player C has 10 hickeys, Player A's hickeys are irrelevant. Player B owes Player A the value of 4 hickeys and Player C owes Player A the value of 10 hickeys. Usually the game itself has a value and Player A receives that value from each player for winning the game.

OPENING BREAK

Starting player begins play with the cue ball on or within the D and his object ball (*for the starting player - the yellow 2-ball*) on the foot spot. His objective is to pocket his ball in pocket #1. If the first player misses, the second player takes the cue ball in hand within the D positions his object ball (3 - *the green*) on the foot spot and attempts to pocket it in pocket #1. If the second player misses, the third player takes cue ball in hand within the D, positions his object ball (4 - *the brown*) on the foot spot, and attempts to pocket it in pocket #1. Subsequent players follow the same procedure to enter the game. If a player pockets his first shot into pocket #1, his object ball is respotted on the foot spot and the player shoots again to pocket his object ball in pocket #2 from wherever the cue ball comes to rest. Once his inning is complete, the next player entering the game takes cue ball in hand within the D and starts play as described above.

SUBSEQUENT HOLES

After all players have entered the game (*unless a player runs out the game from his break*) the cue ball is played from wherever it comes to rest after each player's shot for the remainder of the game (*See below if jumped or scratched.*) Once a player pockets his object ball in pocket #1, the object ball is respotted on the foot spot, and the player continues shooting for pocket. When he misses, the next player shoots at his object ball. A player must successfully complete all six holes, playing in order, in this manner. The player who completes this pattern first wins the game.

RULES OF PLAY

1. It is a foul to pocket the object ball in any pocket other than the one in which the player is attempting to score.

2. On all shots it is necessary for the player to hit the object ball first.

3. To be a legal shot, a player is required to either send the cue ball to a rail and then hit the object ball first, and pocket it, or hit the object ball first and send any ball to a cushion.

4. It's a foul to strike, touch or make contact with the cue ball in play or any object balls in play with anything (*the body, clothing, chalk, mechanical bridge, cue shaft, etc.*) except the cue tip (*while attached to the cue shaft*), which may contact the cue ball in the execution of a legal shot.

5. It's a foul to hit another player's object ball first. If a player hits an opponent's object ball first, the player loses his turn, is credited with a hickey, and the opponent has the choice of returning the object ball to its original position.

6. If a player has a clear shot at his full object ball and misses the entire ball, it is a foul (*hickey*), he loses his turn, and the object ball is spotted on the foot spot.

123

7. If a player commits a foul and the incoming player is snookered from seeing the entire ball, that player may mark the position(s) of the offending ball(s), remove the obstacle ball(s) from the table, shoot at the object ball, and replace the removed ball(s) to original position(s) immediately after the stroke.

ILLEGALLY POCKETED BALLS
All are spotted on the foot spot, unless an opponent's ball was struck first. Then the opponent may choose to return his object ball to its original position. The stroke is a foul and the offending player receives a hickey.

OBJECT BALLS JUMPED OFF THE TABLE
An object ball that jumps off the table is a foul, and the offending player loses his turn and receives a hickey. The object ball is spotted on the foot spot unless an opponent's ball was struck first. In that case the opponent may choose to return his object ball to its original position.

CUE BALL AFTER JUMPING OFF THE TABLE OR SCRATCH
The offending player fouls, loses his turn, and receives a hickey. The incoming player has cue ball in hand on or within the D, may shoot in any direction, and may shoot at his object ball if it is in the D as well. Any object balls pocketed on the foul stroke are respotted on the foot spot in numerical order unless an opponent's ball was struck first. In that case the opponent may choose to return his object ball to its original position.

SPOTTING BALLS
After each player has completed his opening break shot, if a player is required to spot a ball on the foot spot, he must do so immediately after the resulting stroke. If the ball cannot be spotted without touching another ball, the ball is spotted as close to it as possible without touching (*if the obstacle ball is the cue ball*) and frozen to the ball (*if the obstacle ball is an object ball*), and on the direct line between the foot spot and the foot rail.

GENERAL RULES OF CAROM BILLIARDS

The rules in this section apply generally to all the specific forms and varieties of carom billiard games included in this rule book. Certain games, however, do have exceptions that supersede or modify the General Rules; these exceptions are flagged with a parenthetical notation, referencing the particular game or variation in which the general rule might be either modified or non-applicable. Thus, unless specifically noted otherwise, the General Rules apply to all carom billiard games.

To facilitate the use and understanding of the General Rules, many terms that may require definition for some readers are set in italic in their first appearance, so that the reader may refer to the Glossary of Billiard Terms section for the exact meaning of the term.

Although most references in these rules are to a "player" or "players"; since most carom billiard games can be adapted to team play, the reader should interpret the rules as equally applicable to a team of teams when appropriate.

The United States Billiard Association today sanctions most U.S. play of the popular carom game of Three-Cushion Billiards. In the individual game rules for Three-Cushion, the U.S.B.A. official rules have been reprinted exactly as published by that group, resulting in some duplication of General Rules from this section within U.S.B.A.'s rules.

The Carom Table

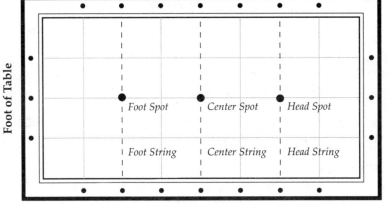

Diagram 32

TABLES, BALL, EQUIPMENT
All games are contested on tables, and with balls and equipment, meeting the standards prescribed in the *BCA Specifications*.

BALLS DEFINED
Two white balls and a red; each player has a white ball that is a cue ball when he is shooting, while the red is never a cue ball. One of the white balls has two or three small colored spots to differentiate it from the other. (**Note:** *Four Ball is played with a fourth ball as well; see Four Ball rules.*)

STRIKING CUE BALL
Legal shots require that the *cue ball* only be struck with the cue tip only.

DETERMINING FIRST PLAYER
The player to perform the opening break shot is determined by either *lag for break or lot.* (*The lag-for-break procedure is required for formal competition.*) The player winning the lag or lot has the choice of performing the opening break shot or assigning it to the opposition.

LAG FOR BREAK
Red ball is spotted on *foot spot* (*except in Four-Ball*). With the *cue balls in hand* behind the head string, one player to the right and one to the left of the head spot, the balls are shot to the foot cushion and back to the head end of the table. The player whose ball ends up closest to the head cushion wins the lag, subject to the following qualifications:

The lagged ball must contact the foot cushion at least once; other cushion contacts are immaterial except as prohibited below. It is an automatic loss of the lag if:
1. the ball crosses into the opponent's half of the table, or;
2. the ball fails to contact the foot cushion, or;
3. the ball jumps the table, or;
4. the ball hits the red ball.

If both players violate automatic-loss lag rules as above, or if the referee is unable to determine which ball is closer, the lag is a tie and is replayed.

The lag for opening break is performed by both players simultaneously, although they need not stroke the lag shots in unison.

CHOICE OF CUE BALLS
The winner of the lag has the choice of cue balls, either the all-white "clear" or the color-marked "spot", which is then used throughout the game. If an odd number of players are competing, the same cue ball is not played throughout the game.

Rather, the incoming player always plays the cue ball that was not used by the player who immediately preceded him (*Exception: Four-Ball Caroms*).

BALL POSITIONS - OPENING BREAK

The red ball is spotted on the foot spot. Non-breaking player's cue ball is spotted on the head spot. Breaking player's cue ball is placed on the head string within six inches (*measured to the ball's center*) of the head spot. (**Note:** *Four-Ball uses a different opening break position.*)

The Break Shot

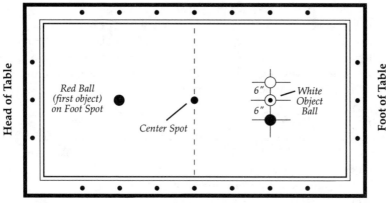

Diagram 33

RED BALL FIRST OBJECT

Player making opening break shot must contact the red ball first, rather than the opponent's cue ball. If the cue ball on the opening break strikes the other white ball first rather than the red ball, it is an error and ends his inning; no score is valid. (*Exception: Four-Ball Caroms.*) On all subsequent shots, players may make either the red or the white (*or "pink" in Four Ball*) ball his first object (*first ball struck by the cue ball*). (*Exception: Red Ball.*)

FOOT ON FLOOR

It is a foul if a player shoots when at least one foot is not in contact with the floor. Foot attire must be normal in regard to size, shape and the manner in which it is worn.

SHOOTING WITH BALLS IN MOTION

It is a foul if a player shoots while the cue ball or any object ball is in motion. (*A spinning ball is in motion.*)

COMPLETION OF STROKE

A stroke is not complete (*and therefore is not counted*) until all balls on the table have become motionless after the stroke.

FOULS BY TOUCHING BALLS

It is a foul to strike, touch or in any way make contact with the cue ball in play or any object balls in play with anything (*the body, clothing, chalk, mechanical bridge, cue shaft, etc.*) except the cue tip (*while attached to the cue shaft*), which may contact the cue ball once in the execution of a shot.

FOULS BY DOUBLE HITS

It is a foul if the cue ball is struck more than once on a shot by the cue tip. If, in the referee's judgement, the cue ball has left initial contact with the cue tip and then is struck a second time in the course of the same stroke, it shall be a foul. If the referee judges, by virtue of sound, ball position and action, and stroke used, that there were two separate contacts of the cue ball by the cue tip on a stroke, the stroke is a foul and must be called.

PUSH SHOT FOULS

It is a foul if the cue ball is pushed or shoved by the cue tip, with contact being maintained for more than the momentary time necessary for a stroked shot. If the referee judges that the player put the cue tip against the cue ball and then pushed or shoved on into the shot, maintaining contact beyond the normal momentary split-second, the stroke is a foul and must be called.

JUMPED CUE BALL

When a stroke results in the cue ball being a jumped ball, the stroke is a foul. (**Note:** *jumped object balls may or may not be fouls; see specific game rules.*)

GENERAL RULE, ALL FOULS

Though the penalties for fouls differ from game to game, the following applies to all fouls:

1. player's inning ends, and
2. if on a stroke, the stroke is invalid and cannot be a scoring stroke.

ILLEGAL JUMPING OF BALL

It is a foul if a player strikes the cue ball below center (*"digs under" it*) and intentionally causes it to rise off the bed of the table (*usually in an effort to clear an obstructing ball*). Such jumping action may occur accidentally on occasion, and such "jumps" are not necessarily considered fouls. They may still be ruled foul strokes however, if for example, the ferrule or cue shaft makes contact with the cue ball in the course of the shot.

SPECIAL INTENTIONAL FOUL PENALTY

The cue ball in play shall not be intentionally struck with anything other than a cue's attached tip (*such as the ferrule, shaft, etc.*). While such contact is automatically a foul under the provisions of "Fouls By Touching Balls", if the referee deems the contact to be intentional, he shall warn the player once during a match that a second violation during that match will result in the loss of the match by forfeiture. If a second violation does occur, the match must be forfeited.

BALLS MOVING SPONTANEOUSLY

If a ball shifts, settles, turns or otherwise moves "by itself," the ball shall remain in the position it assumed and play continues.

PLAYER RESPONSIBILITY FOULS

The player is responsible for chalk, bridges, files and any other items or equipment he brings to, uses at, or causes to approximate the table. If he drops a pen or a piece of chalk, or knocks off a mechanical bridge head, as examples, he is guilty of a foul should such an object make contact with a ball in play.

JUMPED BALLS DEFINED

Balls coming to rest other than on the bed *of the table* after a stroke (*on the cushion top, rail surface, floor, etc.*) are considered jumped balls. Balls may bounce on the cushion tops, rails or light fixtures of the table in play without being jumped balls if they return to the bed of the table under their own power and without touching anything not a part of the table equipment. The table equipment shall consist of its light fixture, and any permanent parts of the table proper. (*Balls that strike or touch anything not a part of the table equipment shall be considered jumped balls even though they might return to the bed of the table after contact with the non-equipment item[s]*). All jumped balls are spotted when all balls have stopped moving. (*See "Spotting Jumped Balls"*).

OUTSIDE INTERFERENCE

If the balls are moved (*or a player bumped such that play is directly affected*) by a non-player during a match, the balls shall be replaced as near as possible to their original positions immediately prior to the incident, and play shall resume with no penalty on the player affected. If the match is officiated, the referee shall replace the balls. This rule shall also apply to "act of God" interference, such as earthquake, hurricane, light fixture falling, power failure, etc.

DEFINITION OF LEGAL SAFETY

Player must drive an object ball to a cushion or cause the cue ball to contact a cushion after striking an object ball. Failure to do so is a foul. (**Note:** *U.S.B.A. Three-Cushion rules prohibit all intentional safeties*).

129

LIMIT ON SAFETY PLAY

Player may not play safety in consecutive innings. When a player's last shot was a safety, he cannot play another safety on his next shot. If he does so, it is a foul. (**Note**: *does not apply in U.S.B.A. Three-Cushion play.*)

PLAYING FROM SAFETY

When a player has either fouled or played an intentional safety on his last shot, he comes to the table for his next shot "playing from safety".

The player must make an obvious and legal attempt to score. If he again resorts to safety play, whether or not the effort meets the requirements of a legal safety, he has fouled. (**Note**: *"Playing From Safety" does not apply in Three-Cushion*).

SPOTTING JUMPED BALLS

1. If the cue ball is jumped off the table (*foul*), is spotted on the head spot (*if occupied, the foot spot; if that is also occupied; the center spot*).
2. If the white object ball is jumped, it is spotted on the head spot (*if occupied, the foot spot; if that is also occupied, the center spot*).
3. If the red object ball is jumped, it is spotted on the foot spot (*if occupied, the head spot; if that is also occupied, the center spot*). If the cue ball and an object ball are both jumped, the cue ball is spotted first, then the object ball following the appropriate spotting order above.
4. If both object balls are jumped, they are spotted as above. If the cue ball occupies either of the object balls' primary spot locations, spot first the ball that spots freely; then the other according to the appropriate alternative spotting order above.

CUSHION CAROMS

Except when clearly contradicted by these additional rules,
the General Rules of Carom Billiards apply.

PLAYERS

2 or 3.

BALLS USED

Standard set of one white clear, one white spot, and one red.

OBJECT OF THE GAME

Score the predetermined number of points (*may be 30-60 in tournament play, or any agreed upon number*) for game prior to opponent(s).

SCORING
Each legal count is scored as one point for the shooter.

DEFINITION OF A COUNT
A shot is a count if not in violation of any "Rules of Play" or General Rules of Carom Billiards, and the cue ball contacts both object balls.

OPENING BREAK
General Rules of Carom Billiards regarding opening break apply, as well as "Rule of Play 2" below. Failure to comply is a violation; player's inning ends and no count can be scored.

RULES OF PLAY
1. A legal counting stroke entitles the shooter to continue at the table until failing to legally count on a shot.

2. On all shots, the player must cause the cue ball to contact one or more cushions before it contacts either of the two object balls (*red ball only on opening break*). Failure to comply is a violation; the player's inning ends and no count can be scored on the violating stroke.

PENALTY FOR FOULS
One point is deducted from offender's score for each foul.

FOUR-BALL CAROMS
Except when clearly contradicted by these additional rules,
the General Rules of Carom Billiards apply.

PLAYERS
2.

BALLS USED
Standard set of one white clear, one white spot and one red, plus one light red (pink).

OBJECT OF THE GAME
Score the predetermined number of points for game prior to opponent.

SCORING
Each legal two-ball carom count is scored as one point for shooter; each legal three-ball carom count is scored as two points for shooter.

DEFINITION OF A COUNT

If not in violation of any "Rules of Play" or General Rules of Carom Billiards, a shot is: a two-ball carom count if the cue ball contacts any two of the three object balls, or a three-ball carom *count* if the *cue ball* contacts all three of the object balls.

BALL POSITIONS - OPENING BREAK

The light red (*pink*) ball is spotted on the *foot spot*. The red ball is *spotted* on the head spot. Both balls are in position before the lag for break.

OPENING BREAK

The lag for break is actually part of the *opening break*. With the red and pink balls spotted as immediately above, players select cue balls and lag for break as in General Rules of Carom Billiards (automatic loss of lag applying to contact with the pink ball as well as the red). When lag is completed, both players' cue balls remain in position; the first shot of the game is from this position (*if cue ball[s] contacted either red and/or pink object balls - which were spotted - on lag, they are respotted prior to first shot of game*). Winner of lag has choice of shooting first or assigning first shot to opponent; in either case, cue balls are played from the position following lag for break, and each player's cue ball is the one used for the lag for break. The starting player (*first shooter after lag for break*) must cause the cue ball's first contact with a ball to be with the pink object ball (*on the foot spot*). Failure to comply is a violation; player's inning ends and no count can be scored.

RULES OF PLAY

1. On all shots subsequent to the first shot following the lag, shooter may make his first object (*first balls contacted by the cue ball*) any of the three object balls.

2. A legal counting stroke entitles shooter to continue at the table until he fails to legally count on a shot.

SPOTTING JUMPED BALLS

(*Differs from General Rules of Carom Billiards*)
1. If the red ball is jumped off the table, it is spotted on the head spot. If the head spot is occupied (*spotting a ball on it would result in contact with another ball*), the red ball is held off the table until the first time the head spot is vacant at the completion of a shot.
2. If the pink ball is jumped, it is spotted on the foot spot. If the foot spot is occupied (spotting a ball on it would result in contact with another ball), the pink ball is held off the table until the first time the foot spot is vacant at the completion of a shot.
3. If the white object ball is jumped, it is spotted on the head spot. If the head spot is occupied, the white object ball is held off the table until the first

time the head spot is vacant at the completion of a shot. Should the head spot be occupied after each shot until such time as the white object ball is required as incoming player's cue ball, that ball shall then be spotted on the foot spot; if the foot spot is also occupied, it shall be spotted on the center spot; if the center spot is also occupied, incoming player may place the ball anywhere on the head string, not *frozen* to a ball.

4. If the white cue ball is jumped, the same rule (#3) applies.

5. If the red ball and the pink balls are jumped on a shot, spot the pink ball first, then the red ball, according to spotting rules for those balls. If neither can be spotted per those rules, spot the pink ball on the center spot and continue holding the red ball off the table until the head spot is vacant per the red spotting ball rule.

6. If either one of the white balls and one or both of the red balls are jumped on a shot, first spot the white ball per appropriate rule above, then the red ball per appropriate rule (*or if both reds, the immediately preceding paragraph*).

7. If both of the white balls and one of the red balls is jumped, spot all balls that will spot directly (*beginning with the white object ball, then the white cue ball, then the red*). If all jumped balls cannot be spotted directly, spot remaining balls per appropriate rule above.

8. If all four balls are jumped on a shot, the jumper's cue ball is spotted on the center spot, the red ball on the head spot, the pink on the foot spot, and the incoming player may place his cue ball anywhere on the head string not frozen to the red ball.

9. Jumped balls result in no penalty unless the player's cue ball is jumped. If a player does jump his cue ball off the table, the stroke is invalid and is a foul.

PENALTY FOR FOULS
One point is deducted from offender's score for each foul.

STRAIGHT RAIL
Except when clearly contradicted by these additional rules,
the General Rules of Carom Billiards apply.

PLAYERS
2 or 3.

BALLS USED
Standard set of one white clear, one white spot and one red.

OBJECT OF THE GAME
Score the predetermined number of points for game prior to opponent(s).

SCORING
Each *legal count* is scored as one point for shooter.

DEFINITION OF A COUNT
A shot is a count if not in violation of any "Rules of Play" or General Rules of Carom Billiards and the *cue ball* contacts both object balls.

OPENING BREAK
General Rules of Carom Billiards regarding *opening break* apply. Failure to comply is a violation; player's inning ends and no count can be scored.

RULES OF PLAY
1. A legal counting stroke entitles shooter to continue at the table until he fails to legally count on a shot.

2. When the object balls are in a *crotch*, player may score no more than three successive counts with the balls remaining in the crotch. If three successive in-crotch counts are made, player must, on his next shot, drive at least one object ball out of the crotch. Failure to do so is a violation; player's inning ends and no count can be scored.

PENALTY FOR FOULS
One point is deducted from offender's score for each foul.

UNITED STATES BILLIARD ASSOCIATION
THREE-CUSHION RULES

1. USBA-sanctioned tournaments will be governed by the rules that follow. Any exception must be stated in the tournament notice, or discussed and approved by a majority of the players present before the start of any USBA tournament.

2. A three-cushion billiard is valid and is a count of one in any of the following cases:
   (a) cue ball strikes an object ball and then strikes three or more cushions before striking the second object ball;
   (b) cue ball strikes three or more cushions and then strikes the two object balls;
   (c) cue ball strikes a cushion, then strikes one object ball, and then strikes two or more cushions before striking the second object ball;
   (d) cue ball strikes two cushions, then strikes first object ball, and then strikes one or more cushions before striking the second object ball.

3. Three cushions means three impacts. The number of cushions does not mean three different ones; a valid count may be executed on one cushion, if they are the result of the overspin or underspin on the ball.

4. **LAGGING FOR THE BREAK**

(a) The two players select a cue ball, which is placed on the table within the head string, and stroke the ball to the foot of the table and return. The side rails may be touched by the ball in lagging, though it is not required.

(b) Player whose ball comes to rest nearest to the head rail wins the lag.

(c) The winner of the lag has the right to shoot the first shot or assign the break shot to the opponent.

(d) Winner of the lag has the choice of cue balls, which is then used for the duration of the game.

5. **BREAK SHOT**

(a) Opponent's ball is placed on the head spot. Starting player's cue ball is placed within eight inches to the right or left of the head spot. Red ball is placed on the foot spot.

(b) Starting player must contact red ball first. Failure to contact red ball first is an error and ends the starting player's inning.

(c) On subsequent shots, either red ball or cue ball can be the first object ball.

6. **FOULS WHICH END A PLAYER'S TURN**

(a) Jumped balls (*Rule 11*).

(b) Starting play while balls are in motion.

(c) Touching any of the balls by hand, part of clothing, cue or any other object such as chalk or pen. The balls shall remain in position to which they were thus moved.

(d) Push or shove shot (*Rule 15*).

(e) Double stroke (*Rule 15*).

(f) When, at moment of shooting, neither foot is touching the floor.

(g) Wrong ball (*Rule 8*).

(h) Touching ball with cue during warm-up (*Rule 18*).

(i) Player interference (*Rule 20*).

7. Any foul caused by outside interference is not to be charged as a penalty to the player with shot in progress. If the balls are displaced by the disturbance, they will be restored to their original position as precisely as possible, and the player will continue shooting.

8. **WRONG BALL**

(a) Shooting with a wrong ball is a foul, and ends player's inning.

(b) The opponent or the referee may call this foul; opponent may call before or after the shot, while referee calls it only after the shot.

(c) Such a foul can be called at any time during a run, but the shooter shall be entitled to all points made previous to the stroke in which error was detected.

(d) The incoming shooter shall play the balls as left after error was called.

135

9. **FROZEN BALLS**

   (a) If during the course of an inning the shooter's ball comes to rest in contact with the opponent's ball, or if the shooter's ball comes to rest in contact with the red ball, the shooter has the option of playing away from the ball with which he is in contact, or elect to have the balls in contact spotted.

   (b) If an inning ends with the shooter's ball in contact with the next shooter's ball, or the red ball in contact with the next shooter's ball, the incoming player has the option of playing away from the ball in contact, or may elect to have the two balls which are in contact spotted.

   (c) Only those balls which are in contact are to be spotted. The loose or unfrozen ball is not to be touched. The red ball is spotted on the foot spot, the player's cue ball on the head spot, and the opponent's cue ball on the center spot.

   (d) If the spot reserved for the ball to be spotted is hidden by another ball, the ball to be spotted is placed on the spot usually reserved for the hiding ball.

   (e) The same rules apply when a ball or balls jump the table.

10. When a cue ball is frozen to a cushion, a player may shoot into (*play against*) that cushion, but the first contact shall not count. Subsequent contacts with the same cushion are valid.

11. When a player's cue ball, the opponent's ball, or the red ball jumps the table, it is a foul and the player's inning ends. Spot balls by Rule 9 (*c and d*).

12. No shot can be started while balls are still in motion, or are still spinning. If a player disregards this rule, it's a foul and inning ends.

13. When the cue ball bounces and rides the top of the rail and returns to the table, the ball is in play. It shall count as one cushion. If it rides two or more rails, each rail will count as a cushion. If ball remains on top of the rail, it is considered a jumped ball, which is a foul, and player's inning ends.

14. If in playing a shot the cue ball leaves the playing surface and rides the rail or cushion, regardless of the number of impacts on that cushion, only one impact will be allowed.

15. If a player has pushed or shoved the cue ball with his cue, it is a foul and player's inning ends. A push shot is one in which the cue tip remains in contact with the cue ball after cue ball strikes an object ball, or when cue tip again contacts the cue ball after cue ball strikes the object ball. Double stroke is similar and occurs when player's tip or cue shaft hits cue ball twice. If a billiard is made, it shall not count, and the player's inning ends.

16. All kiss shots are fair, whether they deprive a player of an imminent score, or whether they assist in a score.

17. Miscues shall not end the player's inning, unless it is construed that the player's ferrule or shaft also touched the cue ball. Not all miscues are fouls, and if a billiard is completed in the miscue stroke, it shall be counted and turn continues.

18. If a player during the "warm-up" stroking should touch the cue ball, it is a foul and inning ends.

19. A game is official when a player scores the number of points designated as constituting a game, even though the opponent has had one less turn at the table. If a scorekeeper is used, the game becomes official after the score sheet is signed by the players. The referee and the scorekeeper should also sign the sheet. After the losing player signs the score sheet, no protest can be made.

20. If a player at the table is responsible for interference in any manner, it is a foul, and the inning ends. Incoming player must accept balls in position. A player not at the table must not distract the opponent with undue motions or noise. The referee or tournament official may issue a warning or disqualify the player for unsportsmanlike conduct.

21. If, for reasons beyond his control, a player cannot start a game as scheduled, the game may be postponed if the tournament director so decides. If a player is unable to finish a game, he forfeits, unless the opponent waives the forfeiture and agrees to finish the game at a time convenient to the tournament management. If a player is unable to return to the tournament, all his games are nullified as they would be in disqualification.

22. If a player is disqualified in a game, he loses that game and gets no points. The opponent is credited with a game won and is given the number of points he would have scored had he won the game. If a player is disqualified from a tournament, all his games are nullified (*that is, games played and games remaining on the schedule*). Tournament continues as though one less player started when tournament opened.

23. If, for reasons beyond his control, a player cannot start a game, he must notify the tournament manager in time to allow for a substitute player, or for another pair of players. All tournament contestants are subject to immediate call if a substitute is necessary.

24. If a referee is officiating and considers a player to be taking an abnormal amount of time between strokes or in determining the choice of shots with the intention of upsetting an opponent, the referee shall warn the player that he runs the risk of disqualification if he pursues these tactics. Continued disregard of warning shall be proper grounds to disqualify the player. If no referee is officiating, the tournament manager shall have the right to invoke this rule.

25. Deliberate safeties are not allowed. If played, the incoming player may accept balls as they are, or set up a break shot.

Snooker and Caroms

26. At any tournament sanctioned by the USBA, the tournament director plus some other member of the USBA who is not playing in the tournament shall constitute a grievance committee to whom unsportsmanlike conduct during the tournament may be reported. Before commencement of the tournament, the players shall designate two of the players to serve on such a committee to protect the interests of the players. The two persons representing the USBA and the two persons representing the players shall jointly consider any evidence or reports of unsportsmanlike conduct. If this grievance committee is unable to resolve the complaint, the representatives shall submit a written report to the USBA for consideration by the Board of Directors. The two player representatives may indicate their concurrence in the findings of the USBA representatives or may submit dissenting views to the Board of Directors. At the next regular meeting or special meeting of the Board of Directors, these reports shall be considered and the action recommended by a majority shall be binding on the accused member of the USBA.

THE DIAMOND SYSTEM

There are various systems in billiards which make use of the spots, or diamonds, inset in the rails. Numerical values assigned to the diamonds enable players to plan shots, particularly banks shots, with the help of simple arithmetic. Some world-class players don't use diamond systems, some use them only to check their instinct or judgment, and some use them at every opportunity. The fact is, on

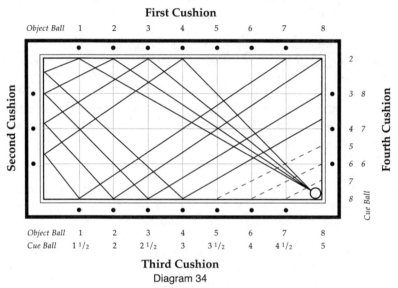

First Cushion

Third Cushion
Diagram 34

many shots in three-cushion billiards, diamond systems greatly reduce the need for guesswork. What follows is a description of the most widely-used system, the "Corner 5", also called "The Diamond System", or simply "The System".

A cue ball hit with slight running english that strikes the third rail at diamond No. 1 will travel back to diamond No. 7 on the first cushion. If it strikes diamond No. 2 on the third rail it will travel back to diamond No. 8 on the first rail (*or corner*). Diamond No. 3 on the third rail connects with diamond No. 3 (object ball number) on the lower rail. The various diamonds connect as illustrated in the diagram. A player must memorize these connections to use the diamond system, since he must know the path the ball will travel after it comes off the third rail.

Playing the diamond system, a player studies his shot backwards - that is, he must find out where he will come off the third cushion to score. Say, for example, that both object balls lie in the upper right corner of the diagram, with the cue ball in the lower right corner as shown.

The player, having memorized the connecting diamonds, knows that the cue ball must come off diamond No. 2 on the third rail to bank the shot in that corner.

Note that there are object ball markings on the third cushion. They start from No. 1 at the first diamond and go up to 8 which is the corner. If the player has to come off the second diamond, his object ball number is 2.

Note that there are cue ball numbers on the third cushion. They start with 1 1/2 on the first diamond and go up to 5, which is the corner. The cue ball numbers also continue on the lower rail, as 6, 7, and 8 (*See Diagram* 34).

The player is still playing the bank shot with the two object balls in the upper right hand corner. He knows up to this time that he must come off diamond No. 2 on the third rail to count.

He must figure out where he will hit on the first cushion to bring the cue ball back to diamond No. 2 on the third cushion. In the diagram the cue ball lies at cue ball No. 5, which is the corner. Thus, knowing the object ball number (2) and the cue ball number (5), he subtracts the object ball number (2) from the cue ball number (5) and gets 3, which is the diamond he must hit on the first rail. If he wants to get to diamond No. 1 on the third rail, with the cue ball still at 5, he subtracts 1 from 5 and gets 4, the diamond he must hit on the first rail. If he wants to get to 3 on the third rail, he subtracts 3 from 5 and gets 2.

If he wants to get 2 on the third rail and finds the cue ball is at 6 on the lower rail, he subtracts 2 from 6 and gets 4, which is where he will hit on the first rail. If the cue ball lies at 3 1/2 as a cue ball number and he wants to get to 2 on the third rail, he subtracts 2 from 3 1/2 and gets 1 1/2, which he must hit on the first rail.

Note that when a ball lies at cue ball position No. 5 (*See Diagram 35*) and the player is playing to come off the cushion at 2 on the third rail, player must hit 3 on the first cushion. The diagram shows a line running from cue ball position 5 to the 3 diamond on the first cushion.

That line is cue ball position 5, no matter where the cue ball rests on that line. If the ball is in the corner it is 5. If the cue ball is on the line and four inches from the first cushion, it is still cue ball number 5.

Our discussion to this point covers only bank shots. The system can also be used when a ball is hit first. Consider the position in the second diagram (*Diagram 35*). In shots of this type, the first object ball gives the player his cue ball number. Suppose the first object ball lies on the line of cue ball position 5 we discussed

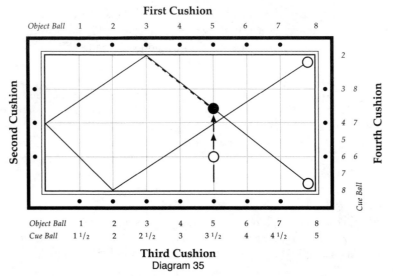

First Cushion

Diagram 35

immediately above. If the player drove the object ball on cue ball line 5 into the first cushion at diamond No. 3, he would hit the third cushion at No. 2 and travel to the lower right hand corner; assuming the second object ball is in that corner.

However, the player cannot drive the object ball with his cue. So, knowing the first object ball rests on cue ball line 5, he must drive the cue ball from the first object ball into the first cushion at diamond No. 3 to come off the third rail at diamond No. 2 and make the shot on the second object ball in the lower right hand corner. Here, the ability to make caroms reveals its importance.

The most important thing in 3-cushion billiards is being able to drive the cue ball from the first object ball into the first cushion at the point desired. In other words, unless the player can make the simple carom of driving the cue ball from the first object ball into the desired point of the first cushion, his chances of making the count are minimized.

If the first object ball lies on cue ball track (*or line*) 4 1/2 and the player wants to come off diamond No. 2 on the third cushion, he subtracts 2 from 4 1/2 and then proceeds to drive his cue ball off the first object ball into 2 1/2 on the first cushion (*which is 2 from 4 1/2*).

Many players refuse to learn the diamond system, because written explanations of it are somewhat complicated and require studious attention. However, if the player will follow the instructions above and test them out on a table, the system is comparatively simple. Oral explanations from a player who knows the system make for easier understanding, of course.

The diamond system is not infallible, but on bank shots particularly, it serves a player better than his instinct. If you watch players in world's tournaments study bank shots, they will determine first from what point they must come off the third rail to score.

Say a player must come off diamond 2 1/2 on the third rail. He then determines his cue ball number. Say it is 4 1/2. By subtracting 2 1/2 from 4 1/2 he knows he must hit diamond No. 2 on the first rail to get back to diamond No. 2 1/2 on the third rail. The system tells him exactly where to hit. His instinct may have given him the general location of the desired point on the first cushion, but if he hit 1 3/4 or 2 1/4 on the first rail, chances are he would miss the shot.

When using the diamond system, strike the cue ball above center with running english, following through on your stroke. If you stab the cue ball with a jerky stroke you will shorten the angle. If you slam the cue ball too hard you are likely to shorten the angle. Use a stroke of medium force and follow through.

If the balls do not lie exactly on the object ball and cue ball tracks, you may parallel or figure the diamonds in fractions. For example, if the object ball number is 1 1/4 and the cue ball number is 3 1/2, your subtraction gives you point 2 1/4 on the first rail. The diamond system does not apply to all shots on the table. It is confined almost entirely to natural angle shots.

You may find that in using the diamond system on a certain table that your cue ball "comes short". If this happens, you allow for it in your calculations, moving up higher on the first rail. Thus, instead of hitting 2 (*assuming your calculations tell you to hit 2*) you move down to 1 3/4 or maybe 1 1/2. Make sure first, however, that you are stroking your cue ball with running english and are following through before you decide the table runs "short".

When using the diamond system, aim at the diamond through the cushion - that is, at an angle through the cushion to the diamond, which is set back on the rail. Do not aim at a point at the edge of the cushion which is directly opposite the diamond.

See pages 143-144 for Three-Cushion practice shots.

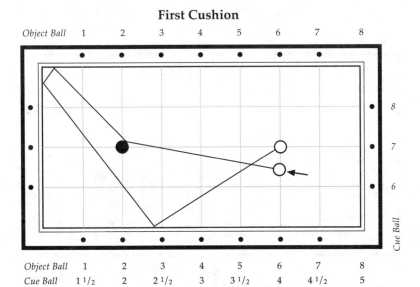

First Cushion

| Object Ball | 1 | 2 | 3 | 4 | 5 | 6 | 7 | 8 |

| Object Ball | 1 | 2 | 3 | 4 | 5 | 6 | 7 | 8 |
| Cue Ball | 1 1/2 | 2 | 2 1/2 | 3 | 3 1/2 | 4 | 4 1/2 | 5 |

Diagram 36 - Three-Cushion Shot
Hold cue level. Hit object ball 1/3 right. Strike cue ball center, slight english left. Use 7" bridge with moderate stroke.

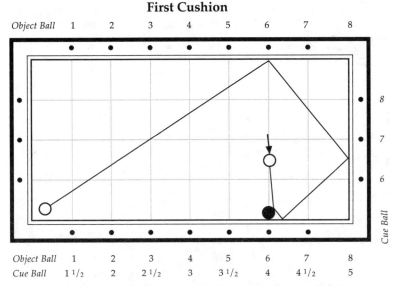

First Cushion

| Object Ball | 1 | 2 | 3 | 4 | 5 | 6 | 7 | 8 |

| Object Ball | 1 | 2 | 3 | 4 | 5 | 6 | 7 | 8 |
| Cue Ball | 1 1/2 | 2 | 2 1/2 | 3 | 3 1/2 | 4 | 4 1/2 | 5 |

Diagram 37 - Three or Four Cushion Shot
Hold cue level. Hit object ball 1/4 left. Strike cue ball center, english left. Use 6" bridge. Use moderate stroke.

Snooker and Caroms

First Cushion

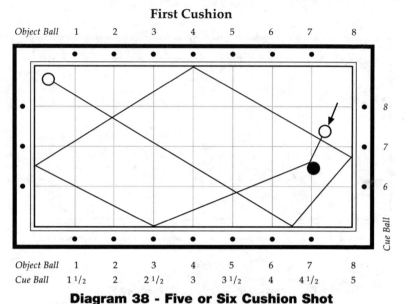

Diagram 38 - Five or Six Cushion Shot

Hold cue level. Hit object ball thin. Strike cue ball center, english right. Use 8" bridge. Use hard stroke.

First Cushion

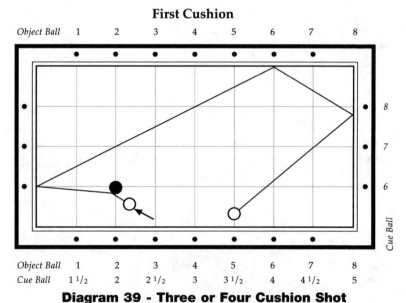

Diagram 39 - Three or Four Cushion Shot

Hold cue level. Hit object ball 1/4 left. Strike cue ball center, english right. Use 7" bridge. Use moderate stroke.

BCA HALL OF FAME

The purpose of the Billiard Congress of America Hall of Fame is to honor outstanding persons of the international billiard community who, through their competitive skill and/or dedication, have enriched the sport of billiards.

Two categories have been established in the BCA's Hall of Fame. The *Greatest Player* category is reserved for persons who have competed professionally for at least 20 years and have won at least one national or world cue sport title recognized by the BCA or other sanctioning body of which the BCA is a member.

The *Meritorious Service* category is reserved for persons who have made lasting, memorable and important contributions to billiards, even though they may not have distinguished themselves as competitors. Pictured on the following pages are those who have the distinct honor of membership in the Billiard Congress of America Hall of Fame.

RALPH GREENLEAF possessed all the flash and flair of a natural showman, as he won the World Championship title on 20 separate occasions during 14 years. With his beautiful wife, Princess Nai Tai Tai, the handsome Greenleaf put together a sparkling trick-shot performance and toured the Vaudeville circuit in the 20s and 30s. The audiences watched him perform his spectacular shots by looking at a huge mirror suspended on stage over the playing table. Greenleaf won his first Pocket Billiard championship in 1919 and his last one in 1937.

Ralph Greenleaf
1899-1950
Inducted 1966

WILLIE HOPPE, whose brilliant career was one of the longest in the annals of the sport, is considered by many to be the greatest all-around billiard player of any era. In 1906, at the tender age of 18, Hoppe won his first world's title by defeating the renowned French champion, Maurice Vignaux, at 18.1 Balkline in a memorable match in Paris. He went on to win the 18.2 Balkline and Cushion Carom titles and years later, between 1936 and 1952, held the Three-Cushion title 11 times.

William F. Hoppe
1887-1959
Inducted 1966

Charles C. Peterson
1880-1962
Inducted 1966

CHARLIE PETERSON earned the title "Missionary of Billiards" for his untiring efforts to promote the game throughout the United States. In addition to being the world's fancy-shot champion and, for years, holder of the Red Ball title, Peterson made scores of personal appearances at colleges and universities across the country and was the guiding spirit of the Intercollegiate and Boys' Club of America tournaments. Peterson died at the age of 83, after a life devoted to winning friends for the sport of billiards.

Welker Cochran
1896-1959
Inducted 1967

WELKER COCHRAN, a champion who trained for his billiard matches with the same intensity as a professional boxer, won his first of two 18.2 Balkline titles in 1927. He later went on to become the Three-Cushion champion five times in the 30's and 40's. Like many stars of the sport, Cochran learned the game in his father's billiard establishment, and he became the protege of Frank Gotch, the wrestler, who sent young Cochran to Chicago to hone his playing talents.

Alfredo DeOro
1862-1948
Inducted 1967

ALFREDO DeORO lived the life of a distinguished Spanish champion. His career encompassed both three-cushion and pocket billiards and spanned the closing of the 19th and the opening of the 20th century. DeOro, who served in his country's diplomatic corps, first gained the Pocket Billiard crown in 1887. He was to repeat the achievement 31 more times over the next 25 years. DeOro held the Three-Cushion title 10 times from 1908 through 1919. In 1934, at the age of 71, DeOro came out of retirement for a championship tournament, winning two dramatic victories from defending champion Welker Cochran and the ultimate winner of the tournament, Johnny Layton.

Ben Nartzik
1895-1963
Inducted 1967

BEN NARTZIK will always be remembered for his tireless crusade to revive billiards from its severe doldrums in the 1950's. Nartzik deserves a lion's share of the credit for ridding the game of its "pool hall" image and reestablishing its status as a "gentleman's sport". Under his leadership, the BCA was able to help both the Boys' Club of America and the Association of College Unions organize billiard programs and run successful annual tournaments. Nartzik recognized the potential of the industry and bought the National Billiard Chalk Co. of Chicago.

Willie Mosconi
1913-1993
Inducted 1968

WILLIE MOSCONI is a name that, to most people, is synonymous with Pocket Billiards. Rightly so, since from 1941 to 1956 Mosconi had a near-stranglehold on the world title, winning it 19 times in that period. Born in Philadelphia in 1913, Mosconi was a prodigy with the cue by the age of 7. At 20, he embarked on a hectic cross-country exhibition tour with his idol, Ralph Greenleaf, then world champion at the height of his game. The result: 57 wins for Greenleaf and an amazing 50 wins for the young Mosconi. One of the most astounding of Mosconi's many records is his yet-unbroken exhibition high run of 526 balls.

Jake Schaefer, Sr.
1855-1910
Inducted 1968

JAKE SCHAEFER, SR., "A player whose super-brilliance with a billiard cue won for him the sobriquet of 'Wizard'". So ran the lead of a 1909 newspaper article singing the praises of Jake Schaefer, Sr. From the last quarter of the 19th century through the first decade of the 20th, Schaefer, Sr. was one of the most feared names in Balkline Billiards. Derivations of the game were invented just to stymie his genius - all unsuccessfully. He traveled throughout the world winning matches and gathering fans. On March 11, 1908, though desperately ill, he successfully defended his title in his final match for the 18.1 championship against Willie Hoppe by a score of 500 to 423.

Hall of Fame

147

Jake Schaefer, Jr.
1894-1975
Inducted 1968

JAKE SCHAEFER, JR. is generally ranked by billiard historians as one of the greatest American Balkline players. He was the world champion at 18.2 in 1921, 1925, 1926, 1927, and 1929-1933. He held the 18.1 honors in 1926-1927 and the 28.2 title in 1937-1938. At the 18.2 game, he holds four records which have never been equaled in this country: best game average, 400 (from the break); grand average, tournament, 57.14; grand average, match 93.25; high run, match, 432.

Herman Rambow
1881-1967
Inducted 1969

HERMAN RAMBOW crafted custom cues for the greatest players in billiards over the course of a 65-year career. Those who knew him called him the "Stradivari" of his trade. Captains of industry and celebrities of the entertainment world also beat a path to his door to have the privilege of paying from $50 to $300 for one of his perfectly balanced "Rambow Specials". It was Rambow who perfected the jointed cue by inserting a countersunk screw in the recessed butt end, making an extra sturdy connection. Only death at age 86 stopped the craftsman from his labor of love. To billiard cognoscenti the world over, there will never be another Rambow.

Harold Worst
1929-1966
Inducted 1972

HAROLD WORST of Grand Rapids, MI was only 19 years old when he played the great Willie Hoppe, winner of 51 major billiard championships, in a demonstration game in Detroit in 1949. Hoppe soon took an interest in Worst's playing potential, and under his guidance, Worst won the world title for Three-Cushion billiards in Argentina in 1954, the youngest player to compete in world competition. He successfully defended this title for many years. Equally skilled at pocket billiards, Worst dominated play to win the All-Around titles in both the 1965 Johnston City, IL and 1965 Stardust Open Championships.

John Wesley Hyatt
1837-1920
Inducted 1972

JOHN WESLEY HYATT, known as the father of the American plastic industry, was an inventor rather than a player, but his invention of the celluloid plastic billiard ball in 1868 revolutionized the billiard industry. Hyatt began his search for a suitable synthetic billiard ball material when a New York billiards firm offered a $10,000 prize for a substitute for ivory. Hyatt's earlier attempts involved shellacking a paper pulp sphere and a ball made of layers of cloth.

Johnny Layton
1887-1956
Inducted 1974

JOHNNY LAYTON, born in Sedalia, MO., won the world's Three-Cushion Championship 12 times, defeating such champions as Willie Hoppe, Welker Cochran, Jake Schaefer, Jr. and Augie Kieckhefer in the 1920's and 1930's. Layton recorded the high Three-Cushion game mark of 50 points in 23 innings, a record which still stands today. He was credited with originating the method of using the diamond system, using table markers to indicate direction of ball rebounds, a style that he perfected through the application of his highly developed mathematical mind.

Frank Taberski
1889-1941
Inducted 1975

FRANK TABERSKI grew up in Schenectady, NY. At the age of 26, he attended a pocket billiard championship in New York City, and came home convinced he played as well as the champions. The next year, he entered and placed third behind Johnny Layton. From then on, he was almost invincible. In those days, 450-point challenge matches were the means of competition; the prize a ruby and diamond studded gold medal with the provision that any one who won 10 consecutive challenge matches could keep it. Alfredo DeOro had come closest with five straight defenses. By 1918, Taberski had accomplished the impossible and the medal was his.

Hall of Fame

149

James Caras
1908-2002
Inducted 1977

JIMMY CARAS was born in Scranton, PA., and started playing billiards at the age of five. At the age of 17, he defeated Ralph Greenleaf in an exhibition match to become known as the Boy Wonder of The World. Nine years later, in 1936, he won his first world championship. He won again in 1938, 1939 and in 1949. Eighteen years later, in 1967, he won the U.S. Open in a field of 48 players. His record of "most balls", "most games won" and "fewest innings by a champion" still stand in the record book for that size field.

Irving Crane
1913-2001
Inducted 1978

IRVING CRANE was born in Livonia, NY. His love for the game started as a child, when he was given a toy billiard table. Although he played steadily as a teenager, he did not enter tournament play until the age of 23. He won his first world title in 1942. Since then, he has won almost two dozen major championships, including the world crown in 1946, 1955, 1966, 1968, 1970, 1972, plus the International Round-Robin championship in 1968. Crane was the victor in the 1978 World Series of Billiards (a combination of 14.1 and Nine-Ball) against a strong field of outstanding competitors. His greatest triumph, however, was his victory in the 1966 U.S. Open, when he won the championship in a never-to-be-excelled record run of 150 and out.

Steve Mizerak
1944-Present
Inducted 1980

STEVE MIZERAK, was born in Perth Amboy, NJ., and to date, is the youngest inductee to the BCA Hall of Fame. In the brief span of his career, he has been four time champion of the U.S. Open, winning the title in 1970, 1971, 1972, and 1973. Mizerak also captured the PPPA World Open title in 1982 and 1983. Mizerak continued to finish near the top in several national tournaments each year.

DOROTHY WISE was born in Spokane, WA. In her early years, there were very few national tournaments for women. Since she was in many local and state tournaments, she became the self-proclaimed World Champion. When the BCA staged the first National Tournament for women in 1967, she immediately entered. For the next five years, she proved herself most worthy as she won five consecutive U.S. Open titles.

Dorothy Wise
1914-1995
Inducted 1981

JOE BALSIS was born in Minnersville, PA. He couldn't resist knocking the balls around one of the pool tables at his father's recreation room. By the time he was 11, Balsis was playing exhibitions against the likes of Andrew Ponzi and Erwin Rudolph. He won junior titles four consecutive years. During pool's doldrum years, Balsis left the game and it wasn't until 1944 that Balsis, a boat machinist in the Coast Guard, won his next title; Armed Services Champ. In 1964 "the Meatman", as Balsis is known because of his family's meat business, returned to competitive pool. Between 1965 and 1975, Balsis competed in the finals of the U.S. Open five times, winning twice (1968 & 1974). He won the prestigious Billiard Room Proprietor's Association tournament in 1965, then captured the World All-Around Championship in Johnston City, IL., in 1966. He won the Jansco brothers' Stardust Open All-Around title back-to-back in 1968 and 1969.

Joseph Balsis
1921-1995
Inducted 1982

Hall of Fame

Luther Lassiter
1919-1988
Inducted 1983

LUTHER LASSITER was considered by many to be the finest Nine-Ball player ever. Lassiter earned his nickname "Wimpy" for all the hotdogs and Orange Crushes he could pack away as a youngster hanging around the local pool hall in Elizabeth City, NC. By the time he was 17, "Wimpy" was packing away his share of opponents. Lassiter's biggest years in tournament play came in the 1960's. In the 11 years of the Jansco brothers' All-Around Championships in Johnston City, IL. (1962-1972) Lassiter won the straight pool title five times, the Nine-Ball title four times and the One Pocket title once. On three occasions, Lassiter went on to capture the All-Around title (1962, 1963, and 1967). He also won the BCA U.S. Open in 1969 and the Stardust World All-Around Championships in 1971.

Rudolph Wanderone
1913-1996
Inducted 1984

RUDOLPH WANDERONE, more commonly known as "Minnesota Fats", is perhaps the most recognizable figure in the history of pool. Wanderone was elected to the BCA Hall of Fame for Meritorious Service. Although he never actually won a designated "World Championship", the game's leading comic, orator and publicity generator has probably done more for the game in terms of sheer exposure than any other player. Initially nicknamed "Brooklyn Fats", and "New York Fats", Wanderone dubbed himself "Minnesota Fats" after the film version of "*The Hustler*" hit movie screens around the country in the early 1960's. Since that time, he became known around the world as pool's foremost sideshow. "Fats", whose exact age was a mystery, hosted a national television show, "Celebrity Billiards", during the 1960's. He stopped playing in tournaments around that time.

Jean Balukas
1959-Present
Inducted 1985

JEAN BALUKAS is the second woman inducted into the BCA Hall of Fame. She was born in Brooklyn, NY. An excellent all-around athlete, Jean competed in her first BCA U.S. Open when she was nine years old, finishing seventh. She won her first BCA crown when she was 12. Since then Jean has collected seven BCA U.S. Open 14.1 titles, six World Open titles and countless Nine-Ball and straight pool crowns. She has been named Player of the Year five times.

Lou Butera
1938-Present
Inducted 1986

LOU BUTERA was born in Pittston, PA. He learned to play at his father's pool room in the small coal-mining town. After watching BCA Hall of Famer Erwin Rudolph in an exhibition, 14-year-old Lou decided to devote his life to pool. He was runner-up to Irving Crane in the 1972 World Championship in Los Angeles. In 1973 he defeated Crane in the finals of the same event to win his first World Championship. Nicknamed "Machine Gun Lou" for his rapid-fire style, Lou recorded a 150-ball run against Allen Hopkins in just 21 minutes in 1973. Butera has since won numerous titles.

Erwin Rudolph
1894-1957
Inducted 1987

ERWIN RUDOLPH participated in his first world 14.1 Championship at the age of 24. Five years later, in 1926, he gained national acclaim by ending Ralph Greenleaf's six-year reign as World Champion in a challenge match. After losing his world title to Thomas Hueston, Rudolph reclaimed it by winning the 1933 World Championship. At the age of 47, he captured his fourth and final world title by defeating a young Irving Crane in the finals of the 1941 World Championship. At the time of his death in 1957, he held the record for the fastest game in a world tournament, scoring 125 points in just 32 minutes.

Hall of Fame

Andrew Ponzi
1903-1950
Inducted 1988

ANDREW PONZI was born Andrew D'Allesandro in Philadelphia. He acquired the name Ponzi after a witness to his cue prowess compared the likelihood of beating D'Allesandro with beating the infamous "Ponzi Scheme", an early version of the pyramid game. A dazzling offensive player, Ponzi competed in the game's Golden Era, the 1930's and 1940's, against the likes of Mosconi, Crane, Caras, Rudolph and Greenleaf. Despite that stiff competition, Ponzi captured World 14.1 titles in 1934, 1940 and 1943.

Michael Sigel
1953-Present
Inducted 1989

MIKE SIGEL, at 35, became the youngest male elected to the BCA Hall of Fame. Born in Rochester, NY. Sigel began playing pool at 13, and turned professional when he was 20. A natural right-hander who shoots left-handed, Sigel won his first major tournament, the U.S. Open Nine-Ball Championship, in 1975. His career blossomed quickly, and Sigel was perhaps the game's dominant player in the 1980's. He amassed 38 major 14.1 and Nine-Ball championships in that decade. Sigel has won three World 14.1 Crowns (1979, 1981 and 1985) and one World Nine-Ball title (1985) as well as numerous national titles.

John Brunswick
1819-1886
Inducted 1990

JOHN BRUNSWICK was a Swiss immigrant woodworker who founded what has become the Brunswick Corporation, one of the largest pool table manufacturers in the United States. Producing his first billiard table in 1845, Brunswick went on to develop an American market for billiard equipment. He is credited with the rapid growth of billiards in the late 19th century.

Walter Tevis
1928-1984
Inducted 1991

WALTER TEVIS is best remembered as the author of two popular novels about pool, *The Hustler* and *The Color of Money*. Both books were made into enormously successful movies starring Paul Newman. *The Hustler* documented pool culture in the United States in the late 1950's and *The Color of Money* followed up on the same theme 25 years later. Both movies were directly responsible for igniting strong uptrends in pocket billiards during the years immediately following their releases. Tevis also wrote numerous short stories and several other novels including *The Man Who Fell To Earth* (a science fiction thriller) and *The Queen's Gambit* (a portrait of a female chess master). He was a Milton scholar and held two masters degrees (from the University of Kentucky and the Writers' Workshop at the University of Iowa). He taught creative writing at Ohio University from 1965 to 1978. His works have been translated into many languages and are popular all over the world.

Nick Varner
1948-Present
Inducted 1992

NICK VARNER learned the basics of pool at an early age from his father in his hometown of Owensboro, Kentucky. Varner displayed his great overall talents in 14.1, Nine-Ball, One Pocket and Bank Pool by claiming the 1969 and 1970 National ACU-I collegiate titles, the World 14.1 Championship in 1980 and 1986 and the BCA National Eight-Ball Championships in 1980. Accumulating over 20 major titles in his career, he became only the second man to earn over $100,000 in prize winnings in the memorable 1989 season in which he won eight of the sixteen major Nine-Ball events. Winner of the Player of the Year in 1980 and 1989, and the first honoree of the MPBA Sports Person of the year in 1991, Varner has always been an exemplary role model and has enriched the sport of pocket billiards through his many years of dedication to excellence and sportsmanship.

Hall of Fame

Michael Phelan
1817-1871
Inducted 1993

MICHAEL PHELAN is considered by many to be the Father of American Billiards, as a player, inventor, manufacturer and tireless popularizer of billiards. He played in and won the first billiard stakes match in 1859. He held many patents for table designs and cushions. He is credited as being the first to put diamonds on tables. Phelan is the author of *Billiards Without A Master* (1850), the first American book on billiards. He set a trend for lavish billiard rooms through his New York room on Broadway.

Eddie Taylor
1918-Present
Inducted 1993

EDDIE TAYLOR is a two-time world all-around tournament champion. Defeated Hall-of-Famer Luther Lassiter in all-around finals in Johnston City, IL., in 1964. Defeated Danny Jones and Mike Eufemia at '67 Stardust Open finals in Las Vegas. Lost to Lassiter in '63 Johnston City all-around finals. Finished 7th in '67 World 14.1 Championship in New York. A Tennessee native, the "Knoxville Bear" was inducted into the Knoxville Sports Hall of Fame in 1987. He is an active promoter of billiards in Boys Clubs of America. Regarded as one of the greatest one-pocket and bank pool players of all time.

Ray Martin
1936-Present
Inducted 1994

RAY MARTIN'S world titles in straight pool in 1971, 1974 and 1978 make Martin one of only seven players in this century to win three or more world 14.1 titles. He has many Nine-Ball tournament wins to his credit as well, including the 1980 Caesar's Tahoe Invitational, the 1981 ESPN King of the Hill, and the 1983 Music City Open. Martin is one of only two players to win a world title on his first attempt. (Cisero Murphy is the other). While concentrating today more on teaching than playing, Martin is still a threat in straight pool tournaments, finishing fourth and fifth in the 1992 and 1993 BCA U.S. Opens. In collaboration with Rosser Reeves, Martin wrote *The 99 Critical Shots in Pool* (1977).

Jimmy Moore
1911-1999
Inducted 1994

JIMMY MOORE: Although Moore never won a world title, he claimed the National Pocket Billiards Championship in a 3,000 point match win over Luther Lassiter in 1958. At the National Invitational Pocket Billiards Championship in New York City in 1965 he easily outdistanced a straight-pool field which included the strongest players of the period such as Joe Balsis, Ed Kelly, Lou Butera, Luther Lassiter and Eddie Taylor. He is a five-time runner-up in world 14.1 championship play. He posted high finishes in many other major events in the '50s and '60s.

Cisero Murphy
1937-1996
Inducted 1995

CISERO MURPHY: James Cisero Murphy was the first and only African-American ever to win a World or U.S. National billiard title. He started by taking the New York City Championship at age 16. While in his '20s he won the Eastern States 14.1 Championship six straight times against top competition, but because of his race was not invited to compete in world title events until 1965, when he won the Burbank World Invitational 14.1 tournament, beating Joe Balsis, Jimmy Moore and Luther Lassiter. Murphy is one of only two players to win a World Title on his first attempt. (Ray Martin is the other). He continued to place near the top in straight pool events during the 1960's and, two decades later, had a winning record in the 1983 BCA U.S. Open 14.1 Championship. He posted several competitive high runs of over 250 balls.

Dallas West
1941-Present
Inducted 1996

DALLAS WEST, the only player to appear in every BCA U.S. Open straight pool championship, was born in 1941 in Rockford, Illinois. By age 13, he had run 97 balls at straight pool. The holder of several state pool titles, West was the U.S. Open champion in 1975 and 1983. An expert Nine-Ball player, he earned second place in the 1995 WPA World Championship. He also plays top-level three cushions. West has shared his extensive knowledge of straight pool on video-tapes, explaining in detail how long runs are made. He has been winning tournaments for over 20 years and has earned the respect of the best players in the game for his positive attitude, gentlemanly behavior, and competitive spirit.

Hall of Fame

157

Arthur Cranfield
1915-2004
Inducted 1997

ARTHUR "Babe" CRANFIELD is the only person ever to win the National Junior, National Amateur and World Professional pocket billiard titles. He was giving exhibitions by the age of 10, when it was predicted he would eventually beat Ralph Greenleaf. He won the New York City and National Junior titles at age 15, breaking previous high-run records, and was the National Amateur champion in 1938 and 1940. After serving in the Army Air Corps, he appeared frequently in World Tournament ranks. He took the world straight pool title from Luther Lassiter in 1964, making him the first left-handed champion since Alfredo DeOro.

Ruth McGinnis
1910-1974
Inducted 1997

RUTH McGINNIS began playing pool at age 7. At 14, she had defeated both Flower sisters, then world champions at straight pool. She was acclaimed the World Women's Champion for 1932-1940 and during that time she lost only 29 out of 1,532 exhibition matches. She entered the New York State Pocket Championship in 1942 and was invited to compete for the world title in 1948. Her high runs were 85 on a 10' table and 128 on a 9' table. She had a tournament high run of 125 and was inducted into the WPBA Hall of Fame in 1976. She was considered the best female player in the country from 1924 through 1960.

Larry Johnson
1929-2000
Inducted 1999

LARRY "Boston Shorty" JOHNSON studied the best players of his time and was able to beat them by age 20. Because pool waned in popularity during the 1940s and 50s, the record books don't fully credit his skills and accomplishments. Johnson was not only a top 9-Ball player, but among the best at Rotation, One-Pocket, Straight Pool, 3-Cushion Billiards, 8-Ball, Cribbage and Cowboy. During the famed the Johnston City and Las Vegas events of the early 1960s, Johnson captured the World All-Around Champion in the last staging of both events, and later collected many other titles. Johnson mastered all games early in his career and played at that speed for four decades.

Cecil "Buddy" Hall
1945-Present
Inducted 2000

CECIL "Buddy" HALL is known as "The Rifleman" for his straight shooting. Mr. Hall was born in 1945 in Metropolis, IL and has been recognized as a championship player for three decades, garnering over 50 professional titles. Titles include the Caesar's Tahoe 9-Ball Championship, the World Open, the Miller Time Open, the International 9-Ball Classic, Challenge of Champions and the U.S. Open 9-Ball Championship. Hall has also won three of the ten richest top prizes in pool. Many consider him to be one of the most fundamentally solid 9-Ball players of all time. He has been selected as Player of the Year in 1982, 1991, and 1998 and Senior Tour Player of the Year in 1998. *Rags to Rifleman*, a biography of his life and career, was published in 1995.

Raymond Ceulemans
1937-Present
Inducted 2001

RAYMOND CEULEMANS of Rijmenan, Belgium, is the greatest all-around carom player the world has ever seen. He won his first European championship in three-cushion in 1962, won the title 21 times in a row. In 1963, he won his first of 18 world championships. He has also won world titles in straight-rail, 47.1 balkline, pentathlon (five disciplines) and one-cushion. His more than 100 major titles gave rise to the nickname "Mr. 100", which is also the title of his book on the game. In 2001, His Royal Majesty King Albert II of Belgium knighted Mr. Ceulemans for his contribution to Belgium and international sports. In October of 2001, he won the world three-cushion championship again, at the age of 64.

Hall of Fame

159

Robert Byrne
1930-Present
Inducted 2001

ROBERT BYRNE is the most prolific billiard writer in history. More than 350,000 copies of *Byrne's New Standard Book of Pool and Billiards* have been sold. Other titles include: *Byrne's Treasury of Trick Shots, Byrne's Advanced Technique,* and *Byrne's Wonderful World.* He published *McGoorty* in 1972, and compiled *Byrne's Book of Great Pool Stories* in 1995. His billiard works and his six instructional videotapes make him the best-known instructor in the world. An accomplished three-cushion player, he won the National Senior and the National Athletic Club titles in 1999.

Loree Jon Jones
1965 - Present
Inducted 2002

LOREE JON JONES began playing at age 4, when her father built wooden boxes so she could reach the table. At age 11, she joined the Women's Professional Billiard Association and became known as "Queen of the Hill". At age 15, she won the World 9-Ball tournament, becoming the youngest player to win a world title. From 1987 to 1993, she won 18 tournaments, including her third National Championship. When she won the World Pool-Billiard Association World Championship, she had held every title possible in women's professional pocket billiards. Over the course of her career, Ms. Jones was recognized five times as "Player of the Year".

Jim Rempe
1947 - Present
Inducted 2002

JIM REMPE began to play billiards at age 6. He turned professional at age 22 and was crowned "King James". From 1972 until the early 1980s, he won more championships than any other player. He has won nearly 100 major championships and 11 world titles, including the World One-Pocket Championships, the World 9-Ball Championships, the World Straight Pool Championship, the All-Around Champion of the World, the World Bar Table 8-Ball Championships and the World English Pool Championships. Also known as the "Ambassador of Pool", he has traveled the world to promote modern pool.

Edwin Kelly
1938 - Present
Inducted 2003

EDWIN KELLY earned the nickname "Champagne Eddie" because of his smooth playing style and elegant attire. He entered his first tournament in 1963, placing second to Mr. Luther Lassiter. In 1965, he won the World 9-Ball Championship. In 1966, he won both the World One-Pocket and World Straight- Pool titles. The following year, he placed second in the Invitational World Open 14.1 Championship and, several months later, won the International One-Pocket title. In 1969, he won the L.A. Open World Pocket Billiard (14.1) title and, in 1971, took both the World One-Pocket and All-Around Championships. In 1985, he won the Nevada Open 3-Cushion Championship. In 1991, he won the Super One-Pocket Championship, giving him titles in four different games, in four decades.

Efren Reyes
1954 - Present
Inducted 2003

EFREN REYES is known as "The Magician" and was a star in the Philippines well before 1985, when he won his first tournament in the U.S. He has been awarded the Philippines Legion of Honor, the Outstanding Filipino Award from the Jaycees and is a Gold Medal winner in the Asian Games (9-Ball) and Southeast Asian Games (Snooker). In 2001, he won the richest first prize in pool history: $163,172 in the Tokyo 9-Ball Championship. He is also a champion at Rotation and Balkline. His many wins include the 1995 Pro Tour Championship, 1995 PBT World 8-Ball, 1999 Derby City One-Pocket, 1999 ESPN Ultimate Challenge, 2000 Camel Pro 8-Ball, the 2001 Masters 9-Ball and numerous other titles from 1985 to the present.

Hall of Fame

Ewa Laurance
1964 - Present
Inducted 2004

EWA MATAYA LAURANCE, "The Striking Viking", began her career by capturing the Swedish National 9-Ball Championship in 1980 and 1981. She won the World Open 9-Ball Championship in 1983 and 1984. In 1988, she won the International 9-Ball, the World 8-Ball and the U.S. Open Women's 9-Ball Championships. She set the Women's High Run record for Straight Pool in 1988. She has made many TV appearances, written four books, received the Billiard & Bowling Institute of America Industry Service award, visited U.S. troops in Bosnia and was featured on the cover of *The New York Times Magazine*.

George Balabushka
1912 - 1975
Inducted 2004

GEORGE BALABUSHKA arrived from Russia to the U.S. in 1924 to build children's wooden toys and educational materials. After 30 years as a woodworker and Straight Pool player, he began making pool cues. He was an innovator in cue construction, finishes and designs. He was quickly recognized as the premier cue maker, inspiring others and elevating the demand for custom cues. He was the first inductee into the American Cuemakers Association Hall of Fame in 1993. Because of their playability, design and rarity, Balabushka cues are highly collectible. A Balabushka cue was featured in the book and movie *The Color of Money*.

TOURNAMENT RESULTS & RECORDS

For past champions, please refer to the BCA website:
www.bca-pool.com

2004 Amateur Results

BCA NATIONAL 8-BALL CHAMPIONSHIPS

Men's Master Singles ....Tom McCluskey
Men's Open Singles ....Ben Diggs
Women's Master Singles..Tammie Jones
Women's Open Singles..Debbie Snook
Men's Senior Singles ....Richard Magaro
Women's Senior Singles................................Maryann McConnell
Men's Super Senior Singles ....Clyde Bowles
Master Scotch Doubles ....Rhonda Pierce/John Gabriel
Open Scotch Doubles ....Phyllis Fernandez/Harold Prine
Men's/Mixed Master Teams................................The Greene Machine
Women's Master Teams ....Back for More
Men's/Mixed Open Teams ....Smooth Operation
Women's Open Teams ....City Light Gate Keepers
Women's Trophy Teams ....Texas Angels
Men's/Mixed Trophy Teams ....Thelma's Rebels

BCA ARTISTIC POOL CHAMPIONSHIPS

Men's ....Hani Kamany
Women's..Judy Malm

BCA SPEED POOL I CHALLENGE

Men's - Josh Silva ....Samuel Prieto
Women's - Kelly Fisher..Bev Ashton

BCA CANADIAN NATIONAL 8-BALL CHAMPIONSHIPS

Men's Singles "A"..Steve Cherewyk
Men's Singles "B" ....Rob Brandenburg
Men's Singles "C" ....Chris Duke
Women's Singles "A" ....Bonnie Plowman
Women's Singles "B" ....Bev Littler
Scotch Doubles ....Marcie Dunbar/Vince McIntyre
Men's/Mixed Teams "A" ....The Rock
Men's/Mixed Teams "B" ....Sharp Shooters
Men's/Mixed Teams "C" ....Five Blind Mice
Women's Teams "A"..Back for More
Women's Teams "B" ....Wild Eights

164

BCA WESTERN CANADIAN 8-BALL CHAMPIONSHIPS

Men's Singles "A" ....Larry Wilson
Men's Singles "B" .... T.R. Olson
Men's Singles "C" ....Shawn Carroll
Women's Singles "A" ....Jana Montour
Women's Singles "B" ....Chantelle Farell
Scotch Doubles ....Josh Silva/Bev Ashton
Men's/Mixed Teams "A" ....Greene Machine
Men's/Mixed Teams "B" ....Broadway Bullies
Men's/Mixed Teams "C" ....No Fat Guys
Women's Teams "A" ....Cue Club Still Waiting
Women's Teams "B" ....Busting Loose

BCA JUNIOR NATIONAL 9-BALL CHAMPIONSHIPS

18 & Under Open..John Morra
14 & Under Open ....Christopher Futrell
18 & Under Girls ....Mary Rakin

BCA NATIONAL JUNIOR ARTISTIC POOL CHAMPIONSHIPS

18 & Under Open ....Daniel Rakin
14 & Under Open ....Nicolas Tafoya
18 & Under Girls ....Regina Rakin

ASSOCIATION OF COLLEGE UNIONS INTERNATIONAL (ACUI) POCKET BILLIARD CHAMPIONSHIPS

Men's ....Lars Vardaman - Southern Illinois University
Women's...Maria Juana - University of Wisconsin

BCA STATE ASSOCIATION CHAMPIONSHIPS

Arizona (AzBCA)
Men's Singles ....Ray Shobe III
Women's Singles ....Diana Clayton
Open Teams ....Knobby's Muchacho's
Women's Teams ....Northern Lounge

Colorado/Wyoming (CO/WY BCA Pool Association)
Men's "AA/AAA" Singles ....Steve Knight
Men's Open "A" Singles ....Dave Wells
Men's Open "B" Singles ....Sigifredo Chaparro
Women's "A" Singles ....Katrina Games
Women's "B" Singles ....Carol Radebaugh
Scotch Doubles...Gary Lameyer/Kim Seenae

Florida (Sunshine State BCA Pocket Billiards Association, Inc.)
Men's Singles...Corey Penrod
Women's Singles...Ellen VanBuren
Scotch Doubles ....Jamie Duncan/Autumn Duncan
Men's/Mixed Teams ....Power House
Women's Teams ....Hollywood Housewives

Iowa (Iowa State BCA Pool Players Association)
Men's Master Singles 8-Ball ....Josh Johnson
Mixed Open Singles 8-Ball ....Jason Chance
Women's Master Singles 8-Ball ....Karla Chorny
Women's Singles 8-Ball ....Kristien Carrillo
Men's Master Teams 8-Ball ....Can't Win
Mixed Open Teams 8-Ball...Snipers
Women's Master Teams 8-Ball...........................Corner Pocket Ladies
Women's Open Teams 8-Ball ....Fort Crook Ladies
Men's Master Singles 9-Ball ....Jesse Bowman
Mixed Open Singles 9-Ball ....Robert Huskey
Open Teams 2nd Chance ....Ballscratchers

Michigan (Michigan State BCA Association)
Men's Master Singles 8-Ball ....Kelly Espinosa
Men's Open Singles 8-Ball ....Joe Henry
Women's Singles 8-Ball ....Michell Press
Open Singles 9-Ball ....Juan Alcorta
Master Scotch Doubles ....Ian Joyce/C. J. Jerome
Open Scotch Doubles ....Mike Neighbors/Carol Disalvo
Men's Open Teams ....Hit & Run Billiards
Women's Teams ....Kiss My BCA

Minnesota (Minnesota State BCA Association)
Men's Masters Singles 8-Ball ....Lee Heuwagen
Men's "AA" Singles 8-Ball ....Jon Brown
Men's "A" Singles 8-Ball ....Matt Benton
Men's "B" Singles 8-Ball ....Joe Loscheider
Women's Masters Singles 8-Ball ....Pam Bell
Women's "A" Singles 8-Ball ....Jenni Benson
Women's "B" Singles 8-Ball ....Toni Johnson
Open Scotch Doubles 8-Ball.............................Tom Anderson/Robin Wellman
Men's "AA" Teams 8-Ball..Circus Monkeys
Men's Masters Teams 8-Ball ....Saba's Masters
Men's "A" Teams 8-Ball ....Underwood Legion Over Rated
Men's "B" Teams 8-Ball ....Glen Loch #1
Women's Masters Teams 8-Ball ....MNBilliards.com
Women's Open Teams 8-Ball ....Whiskey Shooters
Men's Masters Singles 9-Ball ....Derek McMaster
Men's "A/B" Singles 9-Ball ....Jared Bailey
Women's Masters Singles 9-Ball ....Pam Bell
Women's Open Singles 9-Ball...Dana Tonjum

Oklahoma (Black Gold BCA)
Men's Open Singles ....Barry Poole
Women's Open Singles ....Michele McDermoth
Men's Open Teams ....Team Muskogee
Women's Open Teams ....Time 4 Action

Texas (BCA Texas)

Men's Singles ....Jason Dutchover
Women's Singles ....Susan Bishop
Men's Teams ....Azteca Diablos
Women's Teams ....B & N Bad Company

Washington/Oregon (Western BCA Poolplayers Association)

Men's Master Singles 8-Ball ....Stan Tourangeau
Men's Open "A" Singles 8-Ball ....Dana Aldridge
Men's Open "B" Singles 8-Ball..................................Dillon Standley
Men's Novice Singles 8-Ball ....Bob Yunker
Men's Senior Singles 8-Ball ....Michael Stephens
Women's Master Singles 8-Ball ....Jackie Fitchner
Women's Open Singles 8-Ball ....Catherine Tran
Women's Novice Singles 8-Ball ....Natasha Hook
Women's Senior Singles 8-Ball..............................Jean Bartholomew
Master Scotch Doubles 8-Ball ....Stan Tourangeau/Wendy Sedlacek
Open Scotch Doubles 8-Ball........................Michael Stephens/Roxanne Oliver
Men's Master Teams 8-Ball ....Hi-Revving
Men's Open Teams 8-Ball ....Pure Insanity
Women's Master Teams 8-Ball ....Noti Heartbreakers
Women's Open Teams 8-Ball ....The Baltenders
Men's Master Singles 9-Ball ....Stan Tourangeau
Men's Open Singles 9-Ball ....Jim Dray
Women's Master Singles 9-Ball..................................Kris Robbins
Women's Open Singles 9-Ball ....Wanda Plummer
Master Scotch Doubles 9-Ball ....Stan Tourangeau/Michelle Barkdoll
Open Scotch Doubles 9-Ball................................Ken Welch/Bonnie Mahaffey
Men's Open Teams 9-Ball ....The Nuts
Women's Open Teams 9-Ball ....Noti Heartbreakers

Wisconsin (Wisconsin BCA Association)

Men's Master Singles ....Rob Mattson
Men's "AA" Singles ....Jeff Pots
Men's "A" Singles ....Billy Lasee
Men's "B" Singles ....Tom Soppa
Women's Master Singles ....Debbie Martin
Women's Open Singles..Wendy Ady
Women's Master Singles 9-Ball..Pam Bell
Women's Open Singles 9-Ball ....Toni Johnson
Men's Master Singles 9-Ball................................Duncan Kauffman
Men's Open Singles 9-Ball..Justin Volk
Men's Master Teams ....Sportsmens Bar

Men's "AA" Teams ....Lakerz Sports Bar
Men's "A" Teams ....Pourhouse
Men's "B" Teams ....Hurricane Alley II
Women's Master Teams ....Midwest Masters
Women's Open Teams ....Hurricane Alley #1
Master Scotch Doubles ....Scott Herbeck/Marti Lamar
Open Scotch Doubles............................Travis Seubert/Diance Jonas

JUNIOR WORLD 9-BALL CHAMPIONSHIPS

In 2004, a Girls Division was established.

Year	Champion	Runner-Up
Boys		
1992	Hui-Kai Hsia (Taiwan)	Michael Coltrain (USA)
1993	Hui-Kai Hsia (Taiwan)	Hsieh-Chun Wang (Taiwan)
1994	Jorn Kjolass (Norway)	Andreas Rindler (Austria)
1995	Kung-Chang Huang (ROC)	Alexander Dremsizis (Germany)
1996	Kung-Chang Huang (ROC)	Andreas Rindler (Austria)
1997	Christian Goteman (Germany)	Chi Hsiang Chuang (Taiwan)
1998	Hui-Chan Lu (Chinese Taipei)	Atthasit Mahitthi (Thailand)
1999	Hui-Chan Lu (Chinese Taipei)	John Vassalos (Greece)
2000	Dimitri Jungo (Switzerland)	Brian Naithani (Germany)
2001	Brian Naithani (Germany)	Jung-Lin Chang (Chinese Taipei)
2002	Ying-Chieh Chen (Chinese Taipei)	Shane Hennen (USA)
2003	Vilmos Foldes (Hungary)	Jung-Lin Chang (Chinese Taipei)
2004	Yu-Lun Wu (Taipei)	Chia-Ching Wu (Taipei)
Girls		
2004	Meng-Meng Zhou (China)	Chia-Ching Wu (Taipei)

PROFESSIONAL RESULTS & RECORDS

BCA OPEN 9-BALL CHAMPIONSHIPS

Year	Champion	Runner-Up
Women's		
1999	Allison Fisher	Gerda Hofstatter
2000	Gerda Hofstatter	Allison Fisher
2001	Jeanette Lee	Karen Corr
2002	Karen Corr	Vivian Villarreal
2003	Karen Corr	Allison Fisher
2004	Karen Corr	Allison Fisher
Men's		
1999	George San Souci	Jeremy Jones
2000	Johnny Archer	George San Souci
2001	Cory Deuel	Jose Parica
2002	Charlie Williams	Tony Robles
2003	Ralf Souquet	Francisco Bustamante
2004	Tony Robles	Santos Sambajon

YEAR-END RANKINGS
WOMEN'S PROFESSIONAL BILLIARD ASSOCIATION (WPBA)

Rank	Player	Points
1.	Allison Fisher	1,550
2.	Karen Corr	1,500
3.	Jeanette Lee	1,070
4.	Julie Kelly	805
5.	Monica Webb	665
6.	Helena Thornfeldt	645
7.	Gerda Hofstatter	625
8.	Ga Young Kim	565
9.	Vivian Villarreal	565
10.	Melissa Herndon	495

UNITED STATES PROFESSIONAL POOL PLAYERS ASSOCIATION (UPA)

Rank	Player	Points
1.	Johnny Archer	701
2.	Santos Sambajon	420
3.	Jose Parica	382
4.	Charlie Williams	378
5.	Mika Immonen	352
6.	Rodney Morris	314
7.	Tony Robles	306
8.	Ralf Souquet	275
9.	Ronnie Wisemen	272
10.	Jeremy Jones	271

WPBA NATIONAL CHAMPIONSHIPS

Year	Champion	Runner-Up
14.1		
1978	Jean Balukas	Billie Billing
1979	Jean Balukas	Mary Kenniston
9-Ball		
1980	Gloria Walker	Sabra MacArthur
1983	Jean Balukas	Belinda Bearden
1984	Jean Balukas	Mary Kenniston
1985	Belinda Bearden	Linda Haywood
1986	Jean Balukas	Mary Kenniston
1987	Mary Kenniston	Loree Jon Jones
1988	Loree Jon Jones	Robin Bell
1989	Robin Bell	Loree Jon Jones
1990	Loree Jon Jones	Ewa Mataya
1991	Ewa Mataya	Belinda Bearden
1992	Vivian Villarreal	Ewa Mataya
1993	Loree Jon Jones	Dawn Meurin
1994	Jeanette Lee	Loree Jon Jones
1995	Allison Fisher	Loree Jon Jones
1996	Allison Fisher	Loree Jon Jones
1997	Gerda Hofstatter	Allison Fisher
1998	Allison Fisher	Vivian Villarreal
1999	Allison Fisher	Vivian Villarreal
2000	Allison Fisher	Jeanette Lee
2001	Karen Corr	Jeanette Lee
2002	Karen Corr	Allison Fisher
2003	Allison Fisher	Jeanette Lee
2004	Karen Corr	Gerda Hofstatter

Results and Records

171

WPBA CLASSIC TOUR

Event	Champion
Brunswick Billiards Delta Classic	Allison Fisher
Brunswick Billiards San Diego Classic	Allison Fisher
WPBA Midwest Classic	Allison Fisher
Brunswick Billiards Midwest Classic	Allison Fisher
2004 Women's Trick Shot Challenge	Jeanette Lee
Cuetec Cues Canadian Classic	Julie Kelly
Brunswick Billiards U.S. Open 9-Ball	Ga Young Kim
Cuetec Cues WPBA National Championship	Karen Corr
Cuetec Cues Florida Classic	Jeanette Lee

UPA EVENTS

Event	Champion
UPA Pro Tour Championship	Mika Immonen
Brunswick Open 9-Ball Professional Players Championship	Johnny Archer
Master Billiard 9-Ball Challenge	Johnny Archer
World Summit of Pool	Santos Sambajon
3rd Annual UPA Atlanta Open	Mika Immonen
North American Open	Johnny Archer

NORTH AMERICAN PROFESSIONAL ARTISTIC POOL CHAMPIONSHIPS

Year	Champion	Runner-Up
2000	Mike Massey (Las Vegas, NV)	Tom Rossman
2001	Tom Rossman (Cloverdale, IN)	Charles Darling
2002	Mike Massey (Las Vegas, NV)	Tom Rossman
2003	Charles Darling (Washington, MO)	Tom Rossman
2004	Charles Darling (Washington, MO)	Mike Massey

WPA WORLD ARTISTIC POOL CHAMPIONSHIPS

Year	Champion	Runner-Up
2000	Mike Massey (USA)	Tom Rossman (USA)
2001	Charles Darling (USA)	Mike Massey (USA)
2002	Mike Massey (USA)	Tom Rossman (USA)
2003	Mike Massey (USA)	Stefano Pelinga (Italy)
2004	Lukasz Szywala (Poland)	Mike Massey (USA)

INDEPENDENT EVENTS

All Japan Championships
Men ....Ralf Souquet
Women ....Akimi Kajitani
Atlanta Women's Open..Jeanette Lee
Derby City Classic
9-Ball Banks ....Jason Miller
One-Pocket ....Efren Reyes
9-Ball ....Ralf Souquet
All Around Championship ....Efren Reyes
Diamond Nine Euro-Tour
Italy..Thomas Engert
Germany ....Oliver Ortmann
Austria ....Marcus Chamat
Netherlands ....Sandor Tot
Denmark..Samir Kaddur
Spain ....Sandor Tot
Glass City Open..Charlie Bryant
The Gulf Coast Classic
9-Ball..John Schmidt
Banks ....Buddy Hall
One Pocket..Marco Marquez
Bar Box 9-Ball ....Will Pay
International Challenge of Champions ....Thomas Engert
Master Billiard 9-Ball Challenge..............................Jonny Archer
Mosconi Cup
Team USA: Johnny Archer (captain), Rodney Morris, Gabe Owen,
Tony Robles, Earl Strickland, Charlie Williams
Music City 9-Ball Open
Midnight Madness ....Bobby Pickle
Scotch Doubles....................................Monica Webb/Barry Emerson
Men's 9-Ball ....Johnathan Hennessee
Women's 9-Ball..Helena Thornfeldt
NYC Open 9-Ball Championships ....Bruce Berrong
Predator Central Florida Pro Open ....Johnny Archer
Sands Regency Reno Open (June) ....Rodney Morris
Sands Regency Reno Open (November) ....Danny Basavich
Senior Masters V 9-Ball ....Howard Vickery
South Padre Island 2nd Annual International 9-Ball Championships
Men's ....Al Mason
Women's..Amanda Lampert
Seniors' ....Ron Griffus

WHEELCHAIR WORLD 9-BALL CHAMPIONSHIPS

Year	Champion	Runner-Up
1999	Robert Calderon (USA)	Mark Jones (USA)
2000	Fred Dinsmore (Ireland)	Tankred Volkmar (Germany)
2002	Jouni Tahti (Finland)	Henrik Larsson (Sweden)
2003	Henrik Larsson (Sweden)	Takahiro Terada (Japan)
2004	Shou-Wei Chu (Taiwan)	De-Ming Chou (Taiwan)

WHEELCHAIR WORLD 8-BALL CHAMPIONSHIPS

Year	Champion	Runner-Up
2004	Kurt DeKlerck (Belgium)	Shih-Long Chang (Taiwan)

NATIONAL WHEELCHAIR POOLPLAYERS ASSOCIATION (NWPA) U.S. NATIONAL 8-BALL CHAMPIONSHIPS

2004	Aaron Aragon	Charlie Hans

NWPA U.S. NATIONAL 9-BALL CHAMPIONSHIPS

2004	Aaron Aragon	Charlie Hans

NWPA HALL OF FAME

2002	Bob Calderon
2003	Mark Jones
2004	Aaron Aragon

MEN'S WORLD POCKET BILLIARD CHAMPIONSHIPS

Over the years, a variety of tournament formats have been used to determine the World Pocket Billiard Champion. For a detailed history of the evolution of the World Championships, please visit the BCA website (www.bca-pool.com).

61-Pool

Month/Year	Champion	Runner-Up
Apr. 1878	Cyrille Dion	Samuel F. Knight
Aug. 1878	Gotthard Walhstrom	Cyrille Dion
Apr. 1879	Samuel F. Knight	Gotthard Walhstrom
Aug. 1879	Alonzo Morris	Samuel F. Knight
Oct. 1879	Gotthard Walhstrom	Alonzo Morris
Feb. 1880	Samuel F. Knight	Gotthard Walhstrom
May 1880	Gotthard Walhstrom	Samuel F. Knight
Jan. 1881	Gotthard Walhstrom	Albert M. Frey
Jun. 1881	Gotthard Walhstrom	Albert M. Frey
Jan. 1884	James L. Malone	Albert M. Frey/Joseph T. King (tie)
Mar. 1886	Albert M. Frey	James L. Malone
May 1886	Albert M. Frey	James L. Malone
Feb. 1887	Albert M. Frey	James L. Malone
Apr. 1887	Albert M. Frey	James L. Malone
May 1887	James L. Malone	Albert M. Frey
May 1887	Alfredo DeOro	James L. Malone
Feb. 1888	Alfredo DeOro	James L. Malone

Continuous Pool

Month/Year	Champion	Runner-Up
Mar. 1889	Albert M. Frey	Alfredo DeOro
Apr. 1889	Title vacant	
Jun. 1889	Alfredo DeOro	Charles H. Manning
Apr. 1890	Alfredo DeOro	Charles H. Manning
May 1890	Albert G. Powers	Alfredo DeOro
Jun. 1890	Charles H. Manning	Albert G. Powers
Aug. 1890	Charles H. Manning	George N. Kuntzsch
Oct. 1890	Charles H. Manning	Albert G. Powers
Jan. 1891	Albert G. Powers	Charles H. Manning
Mar. 1891	Albert G. Powers	P. H. Walsh
May 1891	Alfredo DeOro	Albert G. Powers
Mar. 1892	Alfredo DeOro	Albert G. Powers
Mar. 1893	Alfredo DeOro	Frank Sherman
Jun. 1893	Alfredo DeOro	P. H. Walsh
Dec. 1895	William Clearwater	Alfredo DeOro
Mar. 1896	William Clearwater	Jerome Keogh
Apr. 1896	William Clearwater	Alfredo DeOro
May 1896	Alfredo DeOro	William Clearwater
Jun. 1896	Alfredo DeOro	Grant Eby

Fall	1896	Herman E. Stewart	Alfredo DeOro
May	1897	Grant Eby	Herman E. Stewart
Jun.	1897	Jerome Keogh	Grant Eby
Aug.	1897	Jerome Keogh	William Clearwater
Mar.	1898	William Clearwater	Jerome Keogh
Apr.	1898	Jerome Keogh	William Clearwater
Dec.	1898	Alfredo DeOro	Grant Eby/Frank Horgan(tie)
Jan.	1899	Alfredo DeOro	
Apr.	1899	Alfredo DeOro	Jerome Keogh
Dec.	1899	Alfredo DeOro	Fred Payton
Apr.	1900	Alfredo DeOro	Jerome Keogh
Mar.	1901	Frank Sherman	Alfredo DeOro
Apr.	1901	Alfredo DeOro	Frank Sherman
Mar.	1902	William Clearwater	Charles Weston
May	1902	Grant Eby	William Clearwater
Dec.	1902	Grant Eby	P. H. Walsh
May	1903	Title vacant	
Nov.	1904	Alfredo DeOro	Jerome Keogh
Nov.	1904	Alfredo DeOro	Jerome Keogh
Jan.	1905	Alfredo DeOro	Grant Eby
Mar.	1905	Jerome Keogh	Alfredo DeOro
May	1905	Alfredo DeOro	Jerome Keogh
Oct.	1905	Alfredo DeOro	William Clearwater
Dec.	1905	Thomas Hueston	Alfredo DeOro
Feb.	1906	Thomas Hueston	Charles Weston
Apr.	1906	Thomas Hueston	Joe W. Carney
May	1906	John Horgan	Thomas Hueston
Oct.	1906	John Horgan	Horace B. ("Jess") Lean
Oct.	1906	Jerome Keogh	John Horgan
Nov.	1906	Jerome Keogh	Fred Tallman
Dec.	1906	Thomas Hueston	Jerome Keogh
Feb.	1907	Thomas Hueston	Edward Dawson
Apr.	1907	Thomas Hueston	Jerome Keogh
Apr.	1907	Thomas Hueston	William Clearwater
Jan.	1908	Thomas Hueston	Jerome Keogh
Jan.	1908	Title vacant	
Apr.	1908	Frank Sherman	Charles Weston
May	1908	Alfredo DeOro	Frank Sherman
Oct.	1908	Alfredo DeOro	Bennie Allen
Nov.	1908	Thomas Hueston	Alfredo DeOro
Apr.	1909	Charles Weston	Thomas Hueston
May	1909	Charles Weston	Horace B. ("Jess") Lean
Oct.	1909	John G. Kling	Charles Weston
Nov.	1909	Thomas Hueston	John G. Kling

Dec.	1909	Thomas Hueston	Bennie Allen
Feb.	1910	Jerome Keogh	Thomas Hueston
Mar.	1910	Jerome Keogh	Charles Weston
Apr.	1910	Jerome Keogh	Thomas Safford
Sep.	1910	Jerome Keogh	Thomas Hueston
Oct.	1910	Jerome Keogh	Bennie Allen
Nov.	1910	Alfredo DeOro	Jerome Keogh
Jan.	1911	Alfredo DeOro	William Clearwater
Mar.	1911	Alfredo DeOro	Thomas Hueston
Apr.	1911	Alfredo DeOro	Jerome Keogh
May	1911	Alfredo DeOro	Charles Weston
Nov.	1911	Title vacant	

14.1 Continuous

Apr.	1912	Edward Ralph	James Maturo
Jun.	1912	Alfredo DeOro	Edward Ralph
Nov.	1912	Alfredo DeOro	Frank Sherman
Jan.	1913	Alfredo DeOro	James Maturo
Feb.	1913	Alfredo DeOro	Thomas Hueston
Oct.	1913	Bennie Allen	Alfredo DeOro
Dec.	1913	Bennie Allen	Charles Weston
Jan.	1914	Bennie Allen	James Maturo
Apr.	1914	Bennie Allen	Edward Ralph
Jun.	1914	Bennie Allen	Ray R. Pratt
Dec.	1914	Bennie Allen	James Maturo
Dec.	1915	Title vacant	
Mar.	1916	W. Emmett Blankenship	Johnny Layton
May	1916	Johnny Layton	W. Emmett Blankenship
Sep.	1916	Frank Taberski	Johnny Layton
Oct.	1916	Frank Taberski	Ralph Greenleaf
Nov.	1916	Frank Taberski	Edward Ralph
Jan.	1917	Frank Taberski	James Maturo
Feb.	1917	Frank Taberski	Louis Kreuter
Apr.	1917	Frank Taberski	Bennie Allen
May	1917	Frank Taberski	Larry Stoutenberg
Oct.	1917	Frank Taberski	Joe Concannon
Nov.	1917	Frank Taberski	Louis Kreuter
Jan.	1918	Frank Taberski	Ralph Greenleaf
Jan.	1918	Title vacant	
Dec.	1919	Ralph Greenleaf	Bennie Allen
Nov.	1920	Ralph Greenleaf	Arthur Woods
Oct.	1921	Ralph Greenleaf	Arthur Woods
Dec.	1921	Ralph Greenleaf	Arthur Woods
Feb.	1922	Ralph Greenleaf	Thomas Hueston
May	1922	Ralph Greenleaf	Walter Franklin

Oct.	1922	Ralph Greenleaf	Bennie Allen
Dec.	1922	Ralph Greenleaf	Arthur Church
Jan.	1923	Ralph Greenleaf	Thomas Huestonm
Apr.	1924	Ralph Greenleaf	Bennie Allen
Apr.	1925	Frank Taberski	Ralph Greenleaf
Apr.	1926	Title vacant	
Nov.	1926	Ralph Greenleaf	Erwin Rudolph
Jan.	1927	Erwin Rudolph	Ralph Greenleaf
Mar.	1927	Erwin Rudolph	Harry Oswald
May	1927	Thomas Hueston	Erwin Rudolph
Sep.	1927	Frank Taberski	Thomas Hueston
Nov.	1927	Frank Taberski	Pasquale Natalie
Jan.	1928	Frank Taberski	Arthur Woods
Mar.	1928	Ralph Greenleaf	Frank Taberski
May	1928	Ralph Greenleaf	Andrew St. Jean
Dec.	1928	Frank Taberski	Ralph Greenleaf
Dec.	1929	Ralph Greenleaf	Erwin Rudolph
Dec.	1930	Erwin Rudolph	Ralph Greenleaf
Dec.	1931	Ralph Greenleaf	George Kelly
Dec.	1932	Ralph Greenleaf	Jimmy Caras
May	1933	Ralph Greenleaf	Andrew Ponzi
Dec.	1933	Erwin Rudolph	Andrew Ponzi
Feb.	1934	Andrew Ponzi	Erwin Rudolph
Dec.	1935	Jimmy Caras	Erwin Rudolph
Apr.	1936	Jimmy Caras	Erwin Rudolph
Apr.	1937	Ralph Greenleaf	Andrew Ponzi
Nov.	1937	Ralph Greenleaf	Irving Crane
Dec.	1937	Ralph Greenleaf	Irving Crane
Mar.	1938	Jimmy Caras	Andrew Ponzi
Apr.	1938	Jimmy Caras	Andrew Ponzi
Apr.	1940	Andrew Ponzi	Jimmy Caras
May	1941	Willie Mosconi	Andrew Ponzi
Nov.	1941	Erwin Rudolph	Irving Crane
May	1942	Irving Crane	Erwin Rudolph
Dec.	1942	Willie Mosconi	Andrew Ponzi
Apr.	1943	Andrew Ponzi	Willie Mosconi
Dec.	1943	Andrew Ponzi	Irving Crane
Mar.	1944	Willie Mosconi	Andrew Ponzi
Feb.	1945	Willie Mosconi	Ralph Greenleaf
Mar.	1946	Willie Mosconi	Jimmy Caras
Nov.	1946	Willie Mosconi	Irving Crane
Dec.	1946	Irving Crane	Willie Mosconi
May	1947	Willie Mosconi	Irving Crane
Nov.	1947	Willie Mosconi	Jimmy Caras

Mar.	1948	Willie Mosconi	Andrew Ponzi
Feb.	1949	Jimmy Caras	Willie Mosconi
Feb.	1950	Willie Mosconi	Irving Crane
Jan.	1951	Willie Mosconi	Irving Crane
Feb.	1951	Willie Mosconi	Irving Crane
Apr.	1952	Willie Mosconi	Irving Crane
Mar.	1953	Willie Mosconi	Joe Procita
Mar.	1955	Willie Mosconi	Joe Procita
Apr.	1955	Irving Crane	Willie Mosconi
Dec.	1955	Willie Mosconi	Irving Crane
Feb.	1956	Willie Mosconi	Jimmy Caras
Mar.	1956	Willie Mosconi	Jimmy Moore
Apr.	1956	Willie Mosconi	Irving Crane
Apr.	1963	Luther Lassiter	Jimmy Moore
Aug.	1963	Luther Lassiter	Jimmy Moore
Mar.	1964	Luther Lassiter	Arthur Cranfield
Sep.	1964	Arthur Cranfield	Luther Lassiter
Mar.	1965	Joe Balsis	Jimmy Moore
Mar.	1965	Joe Balsis	Jimmy Moore
Mar.	1966	Luther Lassiter	Cisero Murphy
Dec.	1966	Luther Lassiter	Cisero Murphy
Apr.	1967	Luther Lassiter	Jack Breit
Dec.	1967	Luther Lassiter	Jack Breit
Apr.	1968	Irving Crane	Luther Lassiter
Feb.	1969	Ed Kelly	Cisero Murphy
Feb.	1970	Irving Crane	Steve Mizerak
Feb.	1971	Ray Martin	Joe Balsis
Feb.	1972	Irving Crane	Lou Butera
Feb.	1973	Lou Butera	Irving Crane
Feb.	1974	Ray Martin	Allen Hopkins
Aug.	1976	Larry Lisciotti	Steve Mizerak
Aug.	1977	Allen Hopkins	Pete Margo
Aug.	1978	Ray Martin	Allen Hopkins
Aug.	1979	Mike Sigel	Joe Balsis
Aug.	1980	Nick Varner	Mike Sigel
Aug.	1981	Mike Sigel	Nick Varner
Aug.	1982	Steve Mizerak	Danny DiLiberto
Aug.	1983	Steve Mizerak	Jimmy Fusco
Aug.	1985	Mike Sigel	Jim Rempe
Aug.	1986	Nick Varner	Allen Hopkins
Jan.	1990	Bobby Hunter	Ray Martin

Results and Records

9-Ball

Year	Champion	Runner-Up
1990	Earl Strickland (USA)	Jeff Carter (USA)
1991	Earl Strickland (USA)	Nick Varner (USA)
1992	Johnny Archer (USA)	Bobby Hunter (USA)
1993	Fong-Pang Chao (Taiwan)	Thomas Hasch (Germany)
1994	Takeshi Okumuru (Japan)	Yasunari Itsuzaki (Japan)
1995	Oliver Ortmann (Germany)	Dallas West (USA)
1996	Ralf Souquet (Germany)	Tom Storm (Sweden)
1997	Johnny Archer (USA)	Kun Fang Lee (Taiwan)
1998	Kunihiko Takahashi (Japan)	Johnny Archer (USA)
1999*	Nick Varner (USA)	Jeremy Jones (USA)
1999*	Efren Reyes (Philippines)	Hao-Ping Chang (Chinese Taipei)
2000	Fong-Pag Chao (Chinese Taipei)	Ismael Paea (Mexico)
2001	Mika Immonen (Finland)	Ralf Souquet (Germany)
2002	Earl Strickland (USA)	Francisco Bustamante (Philippines)
2003	Thorsten Hohmann (Germany)	Alex Pagulayan (Philippines)
2004	Alex Pagulayan (Philippines)	Pei-Wei Chang (Taipei)

* The WPA sanctioned two Men's World Championships in 1999

WOMEN'S WORLD POCKET BILLIARD CHAMPIONSHIPS

Year	Champion	Runner-Up

14.1 Continuous

Year	Champion	Runner-Up
1974	Meiko Harada	Jean Balukas
1977	Jean Balukas	Gloria Walker
1978	Jean Balukas	Billie Billing
1979	Jean Balukas	Mary Kenniston (WPBA Nationals)
1980	Jean Balukas	Billie Billing
1981	Loree Jon Ogonowski	Vicki Frechen
1982	Jean Balukas	Loree Jon Ogonowski
1983	Jean Balukas	Loree Jon Ogonowski
1985	Belinda Bearden	Mary Kenniston
1986	Loree Jon Jones	Mary Kenniston

9-Ball

Year	Champion	Runner-Up
1990	Robin Bell (USA)	Loree Jon Jones (USA)
1991	Robin Bell (USA)	Joann Mason (USA)
1992	Franziska Stark (Germany)	Vivian Villarreal (USA)
1993	Loree Jon Jones (USA)	Jeanette Lee (USA)
1994	Ewa Mataya-Laurance (USA)	Jeanette Lee (USA)
1995	Gerda Hofstatter (Austria)	Vivian Villarreal (USA)
1996	Allison Fisher (England)	Helena Thornfeldt (Sweden)
1997	Allison Fisher (England)	Chun Chen Chen (Taiwan)
1998	Allison Fisher (England)	Franziska Stark (Germany)
1999	Shin-Mei Liu (Chinese Taipei)	Allison Fisher (England)

2000 Julie Kelly (Ireland)..Karen Corr (Ireland)
2001 Allison Fisher (England) ....Karen Corr (Ireland)
2002 Shin-Mei Liu (Chinese Taipei) ....Karen Corr (Ireland)
2003 Not held
2004 Ga-Young Kim (Korea)..Hsin-Mei Liu (Taipei)

PYRAMID WORLD CHAMPIONSHIPS

Year	Champion
1999	....Evgeny Stalev (Russia)
2000	....Evgeny Stalev (Russia)
2001	....Kanibek Saghyndkov (Kazakhstan)
2002	....Ilya Kirichkov (Russia)
2003	....Yaroslav Vinokur (Ukraine)

BCA US OPEN 14.1 POCKET BILLIARDS CHAMPIONSHIPS

Year	Champion	Runner-Up

Men's

Year	Champion	Runner-Up
1966	Irving Crane (Chicago, IL)	Joe Balsis
1967	Jimmy Caras (St. Louis, MO)	Luther Lassiter
1968	Joe Balsis (Lansing, MI)	Danny DiLiberto
1969	Luther Lassiter (Las Vegas, NV)	Jack Breit
1970	Steve Mizerak (Chicago, IL)	Luther Lassiter
1971	Steve Mizerak (Chicago, IL)	Joe Balsis
1972	Steve Mizerak (Chicago, IL)	Dan DiLiberto
1973	Steve Mizerak (Chicago, IL)	Luther Lassiter
1974	Joe Balsis (Chicago, IL)	Jim Rempe
1975	Dallas West (Chicago, IL)	Pete Margo
1976	Tom Jennings (Chicago, IL)	Joe Balsis
1977	Tom Jennings (Dayton, OH)	Richard Lane
1983	Dallas West (Detroit, MI)	Nick Varner
1989	Oliver Ortmann(Chicago, IL)	Steve Mizerak
1992	Mike Sigel (New York, NY)	Dallas West
1993	Oliver Ortmann (New York, NY)	Chien Sheng Lee
2000	Ralf Souquet (Germany)	Min-Wai Chin (Chinese Taipei)

Women's

Year	Champion	Runner-Up
1967	Dorothy Wise (St. Louis, MO)	San Lynn Merrick
1968	Dorothy Wise (Lansing, MI)	San Lynn Merrick
1969	Dorothy Wise (Las Vegas, NV)	San Lynn Merrick
1970	Dorothy Wise (Chicago, IL)	Sheila Bohm
1971	Dorothy Wise (Chicago, IL)	Geraldine Titcomb
1972	Jean Balukas (Chicago, IL)	Madelyn Whitlow
1973	Jean Balukas (Chicago, IL)	Donna Ries
1974	Jean Balukas (Chicago, IL)	Mieko Harada
1983	Jean Balukas (Detroit, MI)	Loree Jon Ogonowski
1989	Loree Jon Jones (Chicago, IL)	Robin Bell
1992	Loree Jon Jones (New York, NY)	Ewa Mataya
1993	Hsin-Mei Liu (New York, NY)	Loree Jon Jones
2000	Allison Fisher (England)	Loree Jon Jones

BILLIARD FEDERATION USA (BFUSA) NATIONAL CHAMPIONSHIPS

1968 ....Allen Gilbert	1979 ....Eddie Robbin
1969 ....Bill Hynes	1980 ....Harry Sims
1970 ....Allen Gilbert	1981 ....George Ashby
1971 ....Allen Gilbert	1982 ....Carlos Hallon
1972 ....Eddie Robin	1983 ....Harry Sims
1973 ....John Bonner	1984 ....George Ashby
1974 ....Frank Torres	1985 ....Frank Torres
1975 ....John Bonner	1986 ....Carlos Hallon
1976 ....George Ashby	1987 ....Allen Gilbert
1977 ....Allen Gilbert	1988 ....Allen Gilbert
1978 ....Frank Torres	

AMERICAN BILLIARDS ASSOCIATION (ABA) NATIONAL CHAMPIONSHIPS*

1969 ....Bud Harris	1975 ....George Ashby
1970 ....Bud Harris	1976 ....Allen Gilbert
1971 ....Jim Cattrano	1977 ....Allen Gilbert
1972 ....Jim Cattrano	1978 ....George Ashby
1973 ....Allen Gilbert	1979 ....George Ashby
1974 ....Not held	1980 ....George Ashby

Regional tournaments only were held in 1981-1988

1981 Carlos Hallon, Eastern	1985 Bill Maloney, Eastern*
George Ashby, Central	Dick Reid, Eastern*
Allen Gilbert, Western	Ira Goldberg, Eastern*
	George Ashby, Central
	Rick Bryck, Western
	3-way tie for first place

1982 Chris Bartzos, Eastern	1986 Dick Reid, Eastern
Bill Hawkins, Central	Bill Smith, Central
Allen Gilbert, Western	Nahib Yousri, Western

1983 Dick Reid, Eastern	1987 Dick Reid, Eastern
George Ashby, Central	George Ashby, Central
Allen Gilbert, Western	Harry Sims, Western

1984 Carlos Hallon, Eastern	1988 Carols Hallon, Eastern
George Ashby, Central	Mike Donnelly, Central
Not held, Western	Allen Gilbert, Western

In September 1988, BFUSA and ABA merged to form the United States Billiard Association (USBA).

Results and Records

U.S. BILLIARD ASSOCIATION (USBA)
NATIONAL CHAMPIONSHIPS

Year	Champion	Grand Average
1989	Carlos Hallon	1.103
1990	Sang Chun Lee	1.471
1991	Sang Chun Lee	1.416
1992	Sang Chun Lee	1.476
1993	Sang Chun Lee	1.596
1994	Sang Chun Lee	1.422
1995	Sang Chun Lee	1.665
1996	Sang Chun Lee	1.552
1997	Sang Chun Lee	1.492
1998	Sang Chun Lee	1.477
1999	Sang Chun Lee	1.503
2000	Sang Chun Lee	1.216
2001	Sang Chun Lee	1.756
2002	Pedro Piedrabuena	1.190
2003	Hugo Patino	1.223
2004	Pedro Piedrabuena	1.439

U.S. BILLIARD ASSOCIATION (USBA)
JUNIOR 3-CUSHION NATIONAL CHAMPIONSHIP

Year	Champion	
2003	Justin Gennaro	Charles McMillan
2004	Justin Gennaro	Ryan Taramona

WORLD THREE-CUSHION CHAMPIONSHIPS (WOMEN)

2004	Orie Hida (Japan)

WORLD TEAM THREE-CUSHION CHAMPIONSHIPS

2004	Turkey

WORLD THREE-CUSHION CHAMPIONSHIPS
(Professional - Billiard Worldcup Association)

1878	Leon Magnus	1931	Arthur Thurnblad
1899	W. H. Catton	1932	Augie Kieckhefer
1900	Eugene Carter	1933	Welker Cochran
1900	Lloyd Jevne	1934	John Layton
1907	Harry P. Cline	1935	Welker Cochran
1908	John W. Daly	1936	William Hoppe
1908	Thomas Hueston	1936-37	Welker Cochran
1908-09	Alfredo DeOro	1938	Roger Conti*
1910	Fred Eames	1939	Joseph Chamaco
1910	Thomas Hueston	1940-43	William Hoppe
1910	Alfredo DeOro	1944-46	Welker Cochran
1910	John W. Daly	1947-52	William F. Hoppe
1911	Alfredo DeOro	1953	Raymond Kilgore
1912	Joseph W. Carney	1954	Harold Worst
1912	John Horgan	1964	Arthur Rubin
1913-14	Alfredo DeOro	1969, 72	Juan Navarra
1915	George Moore	1984	Ludo Dielis
1915	William H. Huey	1986-87	Raymond Ceulemans**
1915	Alfredo DeOro	1988-89	Ludo Dielis
1916	Charles Ellis	1990	Raymond Ceulemans
1916	Charles McCourt	1991-92	Torbjorn Blomdahl
1916	Hugh Heal	1993	Sang Chun Lee
1916	George Moore	1994-96	Torbjorn Blomdahl
1917	Robert L. Cannefax	1997	Dick Jaspers
1917	Alfredo DeOro	1998	Torbjorn Blomdahl
1918	Augie Kieckhefer	1999	Dick Jaspers
1919	Alfredo DeOro	2000-01	Torbjorn Blomdahl
1919	Robert L. Cannefax	2004	Dick Jaspers
1920	John Layton		
1921	Augie Kieckhefer		
1921-22	John Layton		
1923	Tiff Denton		
1924-25	Robert L. Cannefax		
1926	Otto Reiselt		
1927	Augie Kieckhefer		
1927	Otto Reiselt		
1928-30	John Layton		

*Tournament held in Paris, France, with Welker Cochran and Jake Schaefer in the field.

**The Billiard Worldcup Champion, determined through a series of Billiard Worldcup Assn. events held annually, was regarded as the world professional champion since its inception in 1986 until 2001.

WORLD THREE-CUSHION CHAMPIONSHIPS
(Union Mondiale de Billard)

1927-29	Edmond Soussa, Egypt	1983	Raymond Ceulemans, Belgium
1930	H. J. Robijns, Holland	1984	Nabuaki Kobayashi, Japan
1931	Enrique Miro, Spain	1985	Raymond Ceulemans, Belgium
1932-33	H. J. Robijns, Holland	1986	Avelino Rico, Spain
1934	Claudio Puigvert, Spain	1987	Torbjorn Blomdahl, Sweden
1935	Alfred Lagache, France	1988	Ludo Dielis, Belgium
1936	Edward L. Lee, U.S.A.	1989	Torbjorn Blomdahl, Sweden
1937	Alfred Lagache, France	1990	Raymond Ceulemans, Belgium
1938	Augusto Vergez, Argentina	1991-92	Torbjorn Blomdahl, Sweden
1948	Rene Vingerhoedt, Belgium	1994	Rini Van Bracht, Netherlands
1952	Pedro L. Carrera, Argentina	1995	J. Philipoom, Belgium
1953, 58	Enrique Navarra, Argentina	1996	Christian Rudolph, Germany
1960	Rene Vingerhoedt, Belgium	1997	Torbjorn Blomdahl, Sweden
1961	Adolfo Suarez, Peru	1998	Daniel Sanchez, Spain
1963-73	Raymond Ceulemans, Belgium	1999	Fredric Cauldron, Belgium
1974	Nobuaki Kobayashi, Japan	2000	Dick Jaspers, Netherlands
1975-80	Raymond Ceulemans, Belgium	2001	Raymond Ceulemans, Belgium
1981	Ludo Dielis, Belgium	2002	Marco Zanetti, Italy
1982	Rini Van Bracht, Holland	2003	Semih Sayginer, Turkey

THREE-CUSHION RECORDS
CLASSIC ERA (BEFORE 1960) - IVORY BALLS
Best Tournament Grand Average
1950   Willie Hoppe 1.333
Best League Game
1926   Otto Reiselt ....50 pts. in 16 innings
Best Tournament Game
1949   Jay Bozeman ....50 pts. in 23 innings
1952   Jay Bozeman ....50 pts. in 23 innings
High Run, Exhibition
1918   Willie Hoppe 25
1926   John Layton 18
1939   Joe Chamaco 18
High Run, Tournament
1915   Charles Morin 18
1930   Gus Copulus 17
1940   Tiff Denton 17
High Run, Match
1945   Willie Hoppe 20
High Run, Practice Games
Gus Copulos and Welker Cochran 22

MODERN ERA (AFTER 1960) - CAST PHENOLIC BALLS
Top Ten Tournament Grand Average (minimum 4 games played)

1995	Torbjorn Blomdahl (Sweden), Zundert, Netherlands	2.506 (4)
1995	Torbjorn Blomdahl (Sweden), Monte Carlo, Monaco	2.324 (7)
1998	Dick Jaspers (Netherlands), Hooglede, Belgium	2.314 (5)
1995	Torbjorn Blomdahl (Sweden), Istanbul, Turkey	2.308 (4)
1997	Marco Zanetti (Italy), Izmir, Turkey	2.290 (4)
1993	Torbjorn Blomdahl (Sweden), Rotterdam, Netherlands	2.252 (5)
1994	Torbjorn Blomdahl (Sweden), Oosterhout, Netherlands	2.250 (4)
1995	Raymond Ceulemans (Belgium), Ghent, Belgium	2.222 (6)
1996	Semih Sayginer (Turkey), Mersin, Turkey	2.217 (4)
1992	Torbjorn Blomdahl (Sweden), Tokyo, Japan	2.250 (4)

Best Tournament Games — Points in Innings

1996	Torbjorn Blomdahl (vs. Tay Quoc Co)	5.000 (50 in 10)
1996	Frederic Caudron (vs. Semih Sayginer)	5.000 (45 in 9)
1995	Torbjorn Blomdahl	4.167 (50 in 12)
1994	Semih Sayginer	4.091 (45 in 11)
1985	Raymond Ceulemans	4.000 (40 in 10)
1996	Raymond Ceulemans (vs. Ralf Kostner)	4.000 (40 in 10)
1990	Christ van der Smissen	4.000 (40 in 10)
1996	Eddy Merckx	4.000 (40 in 10)
1996	Torbjorn Blomdahl (vs. Raymond Ceulemans)	4.000 (60 in 15)
1994	Torbjorn Blomdahl (vs. Dick Jaspers)	3.846 (50 in 13)
1995	Raymond Ceulemans (vs. Mark Donvil)	3.636 (40 in 11)
1995	Torbjorn Blomdahl (vs. Richard Bitalis)	3.571 (50 in 14)
1994	Semih Sayginer (vs. Sang Lee)	3.571 (50 in 14)
1994	Torbjorn Blomdahl (vs. Sang Lee)	3.333 (60 in 18)
1995	Sang Chun Lee (vs. Michael Garcia)	3.333 (50 in 15)
1994	Torbjorn Blomdahl (vs. Tonny Carlsen)	3.214 (45 in 14)
1994	Dick Jaspers (vs. Tonny Carlsen)	3.214 (45 in 14)
1992	Sang Lee (vs. Torbjorn Blomdahl)	3.125 (50 in 16)
1992	Raymond Ceulemans (vs. Frederic Caudron)	3.125 (50 in 16)
1995	Sang Lee (vs. Tommy Thomsen)	3.076 (40 in 13)
1994	Sang Lee (vs. Frederic Caudron)	2.812 (45 in 16)
1992	Torbjorn Blomdahl	2.812 (45 in 16)
1991	Torbjorn Blomdahl	2.812 (45 in 16)
1988	Nobuaki Kobayashi	2.812 (45 in 16)
1998	Dick Jasper (vs. Roland Rorthomme)	4.545 (50 in 11)
1998	Torbjorn Blomdahl (vs. Mikael Nilsson)	4.166 (50 in 12)
1998	Raymond Ceulemans (vs. Michel Van Camp)	3.461 (45 in 13)
1998	Torbjorn Blomdahl (vs. Wim Van Cromvoirt)	3.750 (45 in 12)

1998	Peter de Becker (vs. Marc de Sutter)	2.857 (40 in 14)
1998	Bert Van Manen (vs. Danny Jansen)	4.000 (40 in 10)
1998	Dick Jaspers (vs. Ludo Dielis)	4.166 (50 in 12)
1998	Henk Habraken (vs. Jan Arnouts)	2.941 (50 in 17)
1997	Raymond Ceulemans	5.000 (40 in 8)
1998	Daniel Sanchez (vs. Sang Chun Lee)	2.812 (45 in 16)
1998	Dick Jaspers (vs. Maged Elias)	3.333 (30 in 9)

High Run, Tournament
1968   Raymond Ceulemans in Simonis Cup 26
High Run, League
1993   Junichi Komori, Dutch League..28
1998   Raymond Ceulemans, Dutch League 28
High Run, Inter-Club Match
1969   Raymond Ceulemans 23
High Run, USA Regional Tournament
1977   Bill Hawkins...19
1998   Semih Sayginer..20
High Run, Exhibition
1992   Torbjorn Blomdahl (vs. Sang Lee) 22
High Runs, Not Scored in Major Tournaments or Exhibitions
Raymond Ceulemans (Belgium) 32
Yoshio Yoshihara (Japan)...31
Torbjorn Blomdahl (Sweeden) 24
Allen Gilbert (USA) 22

WORLD PROFESSIONAL BILLIARD AND SNOOKER ASSOCIATION WORLD CHAMPIONSHIPS

1927-40	Joe Davis
1941-45	Not held
1946	Joe Davis
1947	Walter Donaldson
1948-49	Fred Davis
1950	Walter Donaldson
1951-56	Fred Davis
1957	John Pulman
1958-63	Not held
1964-66	John Pulman
1967	Not held
1968	John Pulman
1969	John Spencer
1970	Ray Reardon
1971	John Spencer
1972	Alex Higgins
1973-76	Ray Reardon
1977	John Spencer
1978	Ray Reardon
1979	Terry Griffiths
1980	Cliff Thorburn
1981	Steve Davis
1982	Alex Higgins
1983-84	Steve Davis
1985	Dennis Taylor
1986	Joe Johnson
1987-89	Steve Davis
1990	Stephen Hendry
1991	John Parrot
1992-96	Stephen Hendry
1997	Ken Doherty
1998	John Higgins
1999	Stephen Hendry
2000	Mark Williams
2001	Ronnie O'Sullivan
2002	Peter Ebdon
2003	Mark Williams
2004	Ronnie O'Sullivan

Results and Records

U.S. SNOOKER ASSOCIATION NATIONAL CHAMPIONSHIPS

1991-92	Tom Kollins
1993-94	David Yao
1995	Tang Hoa
1996	Peter Ong
1997	George Lai
1998-99	Tom Kollins
2000	Ajeya Prabhaker
2001	Tom Kollins
2002	Not held
2003	Not held
2004	Kenny Kwok

INTERNATIONAL BILLIARD & SNOOKER FEDERATION WORLD AMATEUR CHAMPIONSHIPS

1963, 66	Gary Owen (England)
1968	David Taylor (England)
1970	Jonathan Barron (England)
1972, 74	Ray Edmonds (England)
1976	Doug Mountjoy (Wales)
1978	Cliff Wilson (Wales)
1980	Jimmy White (England)
1982	Terry Parsons (Wales)
1984	O.B. Agrawal (India)
1985-86	Paul Mifsud (Malta)
1987	Darren Morgan (Wales)
1988	James Wattana (Thailand)
1989	Ken Doherty (Ireland)
1990	Stephen O'Connor (Ireland)
1991	Noppadon Noppachorn (Thailand)
1992	Neil Mosley (England)
1993	Chucat Triratanapradit (Thailand)
1994	Mohammed Yusuf (Pakistan)
1995	Sakchai Sim-Ngam (Thailand)
1996	Stuart Bingham (England)
1997	Marco Fu (Hong Kong)
1998	Luke Simmonds (England)
1999	Ian Preece (Wales)
2000	Stephen Maguire (Scotland)
2001	Not held
2002	Steve Mifsud (Australia)
2003	Pankaj Advani (India)
2004	Mark Allen (Ireland)

WORLD LADIES BILLIARD AND SNOOKER ASSOCIATION WORLD CHAMPIONSHIPS

1976	Vera Selby
1977-1979	Not held
1980	Lesley McIlrath
1981	Vera Selby
1982	Stacey Hillyard
1983	Sue Foster
1984	Not held
1985-1986	Allison Fisher
1987	Ann-Marie Farren
1988-1989	Allison Fisher
1990	Karen Corr
1991	Allison Fisher
1992	Not held
1993-1994	Allison Fisher
1995	Karen Corr
1996	Not held
1997	Karen Corr
1998-2000	Kelly Fisher
2001	Lisa Quick
2002	Kelly Fisher
2003	Kelly Fisher
2004	Reanne Evans (England)

WORLD SENIORS BILLIARD AND SNOOKER ASSOCIATION WORLD CHAMPIONSHIPS

2004	Dene O'Kane (New Zealand)

Foot Rail

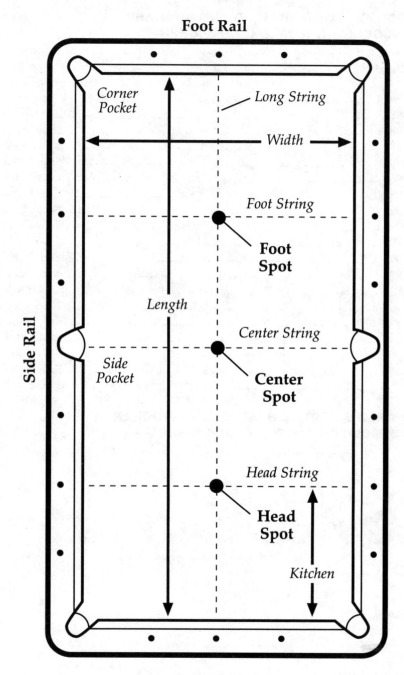

Head Rail

GLOSSARY OF BILLIARD TERMS

This glossary contains billiard terms and definitions essential to playing by the rules provided in this book. In addition to the definitions of these terms, there are references to equipment, accessories and phrases commonly used by billiard players. Each definition begins with the term in bold face type, followed by italicized notation of the game or classification in which the term is used. Where a diagram or other supplemental information is available elsewhere in this book, it is referenced following the definition. Many terms reference specific rules for further clarification.

ANGLED

(*Snooker, Pocket Games*) When the corner of a pocket prevents a player shooting the cue ball directly at an object ball. (See "CORNER-HOOKED")

ANGLE SHOT

(*Pocket Games*) A shot that requires the cue ball to drive the object ball other than straight ahead. (*See "CUT SHOT"*)

APEX OF TRIANGLE

(*Pocket Games*) The position in the grouping of object balls that is on the foot spot; the front ball position of the pyramid or rack.

AROUND THE TABLE

(*Carom Games*) Describes shots in which the cue ball contacts three or more cushions, usually including the two short cushions, in an effort to score.

BALANCE POINT

(*General*) The point on a cue at which it would remain level if held by a single support, usually about 18" from the butt end of the cue.

BAD HIT

(*General*) A foul in which the cue ball strikes the wrong object ball.
▲ 5.8

BALL IN HAND

(*General*) When the cue ball may be put into play anywhere on the playing surface after the other play commits a specific foul (rules vary by game being played). (*See "CUE BALL IN HAND"*)
▲ 3.10 ▲ 3.40 ▲ 4.9 ▲ 4.14 ▲ 5.7 ▲ 7.5 ▲ 7.7

BALLS JUMPED OFF TABLE

(*General*) A ball that comes to rest on a surface other than the bed of the table after a stroke or a ball that comes to rest on the bed of the table after striking an object that is not a part of the table, such as a light fixture, cue, player or piece of chalk.
▲ 3.6-d ▲ 3.28 ▲ 4.7

Glossary

193

BALLS MOVING SPONTANEOUSLY

(*General*) If a ball shifts, settles, turns or otherwise moves "by itself", the balls shall remain in the position they assumed and play continues. A hanging ball that falls into a pocket "by itself" after being motionless for 5 seconds or longer shall be replaced as closely as possible to its position prior to falling, and play shall continue.

BALL ON

(*Snooker*) A colored (non-red) ball a player intends to legally pocket; same as on ball.

BANK SHOT

(*Pocket Games*) A shot in which the object ball is driven to one or more cushions before it is pocketed; incidental contact as a ball moves along and adjacent to a cushion does not qualify as a cushion or bank. It is not an obvious shot and must be called in games requiring called shots. (*See "KICK SHOT"*)

▲ 4.2 ▲ 4.11

BAULK

(*Snooker*) The intervening space between the bottom cushion and the baulk-line.

BAULK-LINE

(*Snooker*) A straight line drawn 29" from the face of the bottom cushion and parallel to it.

BED OF TABLE

(*General*) The flat, cloth-covered surface of the table within the cushions; the playing area exclusive of the cushions.

BEHIND THE HEAD STRING

(*General*) The area of the table between the cushion on the head end of the table and the head string; also known as "the kitchen".

▲ 3.8 ▲ 3.39 ▲ 6.7 #'s 5-7 ▲ 6.10 ▲ 7.8#-5 ▲ 7.11 ▲ 7.14

BILLIARD

(*Carom Games*) A count or score; a successful shot.

BLIND DRAW

(*General*) A method used to determine pairings or bracketing of players in tournaments that assures random placement or pairing of contestants.

BOTTLE

(*Pocket Games*) A specially shaped leather or plastic container used in various games. (*See "SHAKE BOTTLE"*)

BOTTOM CUSHION

(*Snooker*) The cushion located at the head of a snooker table - closest to the half circle.

BREAK

(*Pocket Games*) The opening shot of pocket billiard games. (*See "OPEN BREAK" and "OPENING BREAK SHOT"*)

▲ 3.6 ▲ 3.7 ▲ 3.8 ▲ 3.9 ▲ 3.36 ▲ 4.2 ▲ 4.4 ▲ 4.5 ▲ 4.6 ▲ 4.7 ▲ 4.8 ▲ 4.10 ▲ 4.11 ▲ 4.14 ▲ 4.20 #-1 ▲ 4.21 ▲ 5.4 #-3

BREAK

(*Snooker*) Total scored in one inning.

BREAK AND RUN

(*General*) When a player breaks the balls and continues to shoot until pocketing the 8-ball (when playing Eight-Ball) or 9-ball (when playing Nine-Ball).

BREAKING VIOLATION

(*Pocket Games*) A violation of special rules which apply only to the opening break shot of certain games. Unless specified in individual game rules, a breaking violation is not a foul.
▲ 6.6

BRIDGE

(*General*) The hand configuration that holds and guides the shaft-end of the cue during play. (*See "MECHANICAL BRIDGE"*)
▲ 3.21 ▲ 3.25 ▲ Wheel Chair General Rules #'s 1-2 ▲ 4.18 ▲ 5.12

BURST

(*Forty-One Pocket Billiards*) Scoring a total of more than 41 points.

BUTT OF CUE

(*General*) The larger end of a cue, opposite the tip. On a two-piece cue, the butt extends up to the joint.

CALL SHOT

(*Pocket Games*) Requirement that a player designate, in advance of each shot, the ball to be made and the pocket into which it will be made. In calling the shot, it is NEVER necessary to indicate details such as the number of cushions, banks, kisses, caroms, etc. The rules of "Bank Pool" are an exception.
▲ 3.4 ▲ 4.1 ▲ 4.2 ▲ 6.7

CALLED BALL

(*Pocket Games*) The ball the player has designated to be pocketed on a shot.

CALLED POCKET

(*Pocket Games*) The pocket in which a player has designated a ball to be shot.
▲ 6.7 #-1

CAROM

(*General*) To bounce off or glance off an object ball or cushion; a shot in which the cue ball bounces off one ball into another is termed a carom.
▲ 3.4 ▲ 6.7 #'s 1-2

CAROM, SCORING

(*General*) Contact by the cue ball with object balls, the bottle or cushions in such a way that a legal score is made, according to specific game rules.

CENTER SPOT

(*General*) The exact center point of a table's playing surface.

CHALK

(*General*) A dry, slightly abrasive substance that is applied to the cue tip to help assure a nonslip contact between the cue tip and the cue ball.

▲ 3.43

CHOICE OF GROUP

(*Pocket Games*) The choice of stripes or solids is not determined on the break even if balls are made from only one or both groups. *THE TABLE IS ALWAYS OPEN IMMEDIATELY AFTER THE BREAK SHOT.* The choice of group is determined only when a player legally pockets a called object ball after the break shot.

CHUCK NURSE

(*Straight Rail Billiards*) A scoring technique used when one object ball rests against the cushion and the second object ball is to one side of the first ball and away from the cushion. Cue ball strikes the object ball at the cushion so that the cue ball just comes back to touch (carom) the second object ball without moving it out of position for a similar subsequent shot.

CLEAN BANK

(*Bank Pocket Billiards*) A shot in which the object ball being played does not touch any other object balls (*i.e., no kisses, no combinations*).

CLEAR BALL

(*Carom Games*) The all-white ball, devoid of any markings, used in carom games. (*See* "*SPOT BALL*")

COMBINATION

(*Pocket Games*) Shot in which the cue ball first strikes a ball other than the one to be pocketed, with the ball initially contacted in turn striking one or more other balls in an effort to score.

▲ 3.4 ▲ 4.2 ▲ 6.7 #1

COMBINATION ON

(*Pocket Games*) Two or more balls positioned in such a way that a ball can be driven into a called pocket with a combination shot, often called a "dead combo" or an "on combo".

COMBINATION ON

(*Snooker*) A position of two or more red balls that allows a ball to be driven into a pocket with a combination shot. (*See* "*PLANT*")

CONTACT POINT

(*General*) The precise point of contact between the cue ball and the object ball when the cue ball strikes the object ball. (*See "Instructional Playing Tips"*)

CORNER-HOOKED

(*Pocket Games, Snooker*) When the corner of a pocket prevents shooting the cue ball in a straight path directly to an object ball, the cue ball is corner-hooked; same as angled.

COUNT

(*General*) A score; a successful shot.
▲ 3.4 ▲ 3.15 ▲ 3.7-b ▲ 3.34 ▲ 3.36-c ▲ 4.4-c ▲ 5.3-c ▲ 6.5 ▲ 7.6 ▲ 7.8

COUNT, THE

(*General*) The running score at any point during a player's inning in games where numerous points are scored successively.

CROSS CORNER

(*Pocket Games*) Term used to describe a bank shot that will rebound from a cushion and into a corner pocket.

CROSS SIDE

(*Pocket Games*) Term used to describe a bank shot that will rebound from a side cushion and into a side pocket.

CROSS TABLE SHOT

(*Carom Games*) Shot in which scoring is accomplished by driving the cue ball across the table between the long cushions.

CROTCH

(*Carom Games*) The corner area of a carom table in straight-rail billiards in which a player may score no more than three successive counts with the balls before driving at least one object ball out of the area. The four crotches are defined as those spaces within crotch lines drawn between the first diamond on the end rail to the second diamond on the side rail.

CRUTCH

(*General*) Slang term for the mechanical bridge.

CUE

(*General*) Tapered device, usually wooden, used to strike the cue ball to execute carom or pocket billiard shots. (*Also called "cue stick"*)

CUE BALL

(*General*) The white, unnumbered ball that is always struck by the cue during play.
▲ 7.6 ▲ 7.7 ▲ 7.8 ▲ 7.8 #1-4 ▲ 7.10

CUE BALL FOUL

(*General*) A foul specific to the cue ball: 1) player drops the cue ball from their hand and it makes contact with an object ball; 2) player double hits the cue ball with the tip of the stick while executing a shot; or 3) player mistakenly picks up the cue ball thinking the opposing player has committed a foul.

▲ 3.28 ▲ 4.18 ▲ 5.12

CUE BALL IN HAND

(*Pocket Games*) When the cue ball may be put into play anywhere on the playing surface after the other play commits a specific foul (*rules vary by game being played*).

▲ 3.9 ▲ 3.10 ▲ 3.22 ▲ 3.39 ▲ 3.40 ▲ 4.9 ▲ 4.14 ▲ 4.19 ▲ 5.4 #'s 5-7 ▲ 5.10

CUE BALL IN HAND BEHIND THE HEAD STRING

(*Pocket Games*) Cue ball may be put into play anywhere between the head string and the cushion on the head end of the table not in contact with an object ball. (*See Diagram 40, page 192*)

▲ 3.8 ▲ 3.9 ▲ 3.10 ▲ 3.16 ▲ 3.39 ▲ 5.2 ▲ 6.6 ▲ 6.7 #'s 5-7 ▲ 6.10

CUE BALL IN HAND WITHIN THE "D"
(also known as the "Half-Circle")

(*Snooker*) The cue ball is in hand within the half-circle when it has entered a pocket or has been forced off the table. The base of the cue ball may be placed anywhere within or on the half-circle. It remains in hand until the player strikes the cue ball with the tip of the cue or a foul is committed while the ball is on the table.

CUE TIP

(*General*) A piece of specially processed leather or other fibrous or pliable material attached to the shaft end of the cue that contacts the cue ball when the shot is executed.

▲ 3.3 ▲ 3.8 ▲ 3.13 ▲ 3.21 ▲ 3.24

CUSHION

(*General*) The cloth-covered rubber which borders the inside of the rails on carom and pocket billiard tables; together the cushions form the outer perimeter of the basic playing surface.

▲ 3.6 ▲ 3.6-b-c-e ▲ 3.19-b ▲ 3.28 ▲ 3.32 ▲ 3.38 ▲ 3.38-b-c-d ▲ 3.39 ▲ Wheel Chair General Rules #1 ▲ 4.2 ▲ 6.6 s 6.7 #' ▲ 1-2 ▲ 7.7 ▲ 7.8 #1

CUT SHOT

(*Pocket Games*) A shot in which the cue ball contacts the object ball to one side of full center, thus driving it in a direction other than that of the initial cue ball path. (*See "Instructional Playing Tips"*)

D

(*Snooker*) an area, semicircular in shape, with the straight side formed by the line drawn between the spot for the yellow and the spot for the green measured 29 inches out from the face of the bottom cushion (sometimes referred to as the baulk-line) and the semicircle is determined by the size of the table being used. (*See Diagram 30 in "Snooker Games"*)

DEAD BALL

(*Pocket Games*) A cue ball stroked in such a manner that virtually all of the speed and/or spin of the cue ball is transferred to the object ball, the cue ball retaining very little or none after contact.

DEAD BALL SHOT

(*Pocket Games*) A shot in which a dead ball stroke is employed; often called a kill shot, because of the relative lack of cue ball motion after contact with the object ball.

DEAD COMBINATION

(*Pocket Games*) Two or more balls positioned in such a way that a ball can be driven into a called pocket with a combination shot, often called a "dead combo" or an "on combo". (*See "COMBINATION ON"*) When the cue ball may be put into play anywhere on the playing surface after the other play commits a specific foul (*rules vary by game being played*).

DIAMONDS

(*General*) Inlays or markings on the table rails that are used as references or target points. The diamonds are essential for the utilization of numerous mathematical systems employed by carom and pocket games players. (*See "The Diamond System"*)

DECIDING GAME

(*General*) The game (determined ahead of time by the players or the tournament director) that results in a player winning the match or set. (*See "MATCH", "RACE" and "SET"*)

DEVICES

(*General*) Players are not allowed to use a ball, the triangle or any other width-measuring device to see if the cue ball or an object ball would travel through a gap, etc. Only the cue stick may be used as an aid to judge gaps, etc. So long as the cue is held by the hand. To do so otherwise is a foul and unsportsmanlike conduct.

DRAW SHOT

(*General*) A shot in which the cue ball is struck below center and the resulting backspin causes the cue ball to return towards the player after full contact with an object ball.

DROP POCKETS

(*Pocket Games*) Type of pockets with no automatic return of the balls to the foot end of the table; balls must be removed manually.

DOUBLE ELIMINATION

(*General*) A tournament format in which a player is not eliminated until sustaining two match losses.

DOUBLE HIT

(*General*) A shot on which the cue ball is struck twice by the cue tip on the same stroke. (*See "General Rules of Pocket Billiards" and "Carom Billiards"*)

▲ 3.23

DOUBLE ROUND ROBIN

(*General*) A tournament format in which each contestant in a field plays each of the other players twice.

ENGLISH

(*General*) Sidespin applied to the cue ball by striking it off center; used to alter the natural roll of the cue ball and/or the object ball. (*See "SIDE"*)

FEATHER SHOT

(*General*) A shot in which the cue ball barely touches or grazes the object ball; an extremely thin cut.

FERRULE

(*General*) A piece of protective material (usually plastic, horn, or metal) at the end of the cue shaft, onto which the cue tip is attached.

▲ 3.26 ▲ 3.29

FOLLOW SHOT

(*General*) A shot in which the cue ball is struck above center and the resulting forward spin causes the cue ball to roll forward after contact with an object ball.

FOLLOW-THROUGH

(*General*) The movement of the cue after contact with the cue ball through the area previously occupied by the cue ball. (*See "Instructional Playing Tips"*)

▲ 5.12

FOOT OF TABLE

(*General*) The end of a carom or pocket billiard table at which the balls are racked or positioned at the start of a game.

FOOT SPOT

(*General*) The point on the foot end of the table where imaginary lines drawn between the center diamonds of the short rails and the second diamonds of the long rails intersect. (*See Diagram 40, page 192*)

▲ 3.2 ▲ 3.32 ▲ 4.3 ▲ 5.2 ▲ 6.4 ▲ 6.7 #3

FOOT STRING

(*General*) A line on the foot end of the table between the second diamonds of the long rails, passing through the foot spot. (*See Diagram 40, page 192*) The foot string is never drawn on the table and has no use in play.

FORCE

(*General*) The power applied on the stroke to the cue ball, which may result in distortion and altering of natural angles and action of the ball.
▲ 3.38-d

FORCE FOLLOW

(*General*) A follow shot with extreme overspin applied to the cue ball, with the term generally used in reference to shots in which the cue ball is shot directly at and then "through" an object ball, with a pronounced hesitation or stop before the overspin propels the cue ball forward in the general direction of the stroke.

FOUL

(*General*) An infraction of the rules of play, as defined in either the general or the specific game rules. Fouls result in a penalty, and are also dependent on specific game rules. Not all rule infractions are "fouls".
▲ 3.3 ▲ 3.9 ▲ 3.13 ▲ 3.14 ▲ 3.17 ▲ 3.18 ▲ 3.19-b ▲ 3.20 ▲ 3.21 ▲ 3.22 ▲ 3.23 ▲ 3.24 ▲ 3.25 ▲ 3.26 ▲ 3.27 ▲ 3.28 ▲ 3.29 ▲ 3.30 ▲ 3.37 ▲ 3.38-d ▲ 3.39 ▲ 3.40 ▲ 3.41 ▲ 3.42 ▲ 3.43 ▲ *wheelchair competition general rules* #'s1-2 ▲ 4.2 ▲ 4.5 ▲ 4.6 ▲ 4.7 ▲ 4.9 ▲ 4.11 ▲ 4.14 ▲ 4.15 ▲ 4.16 ▲ 4.17 ▲ 4.18 ▲ 4.19 ▲ 4.20 #1 ▲ 5.1 ▲ 5.4 #'s 2-3 ▲ 5.5 ▲ 5.6 ▲ 5.7 ▲ 5.8 ▲ 5.9 ▲ 5.11 ▲ 5.12 ▲ 5.13 ▲ 5.14 ▲ 6.1 ▲ 6.6 ▲ 6.7 #'s 2-5 ▲ 6.9 ▲ 6.10 ▲ 6.11 ▲ 6.12 ▲ 6.13 ▲ 7.6 ▲ 7.7 ▲ 7.8 #'s 1-4 ▲ 7.10 ▲ 7.13

FOUL STROKE

(*General*) A stroke on which a foul takes place.
▲ 3.26

FRAME

(*Snooker*) The equivalent of one game in snooker.

FREE BALL

(*Snooker*) After a foul, if the cue ball is snookered, the referee shall state "Free Ball". If the non-offending player takes the next stroke, he may nominate any ball as on, and for this stroke, such ball shall be regarded as, and acquire the value of, the ball on. (*See "International Snooker Rules"*)

FREE BREAK

(*Pocket Games*) An opening break shot in which a wide spread of the object balls may be achieved without penalty or risk. Free breaks are detailed in individual game rules.

FROZEN

(*General*) A ball touching another ball or cushion.
▲ 3.32 ▲ 3.38 ▲ 3.38-c-d ▲ 6.7 #-2

FULL BALL

(*General*) Contact of the cue ball with an object ball at a contact point on a line joining the centers of the cue ball and object ball. (*See "Instructional Playing Tips"*)

Glossary

GAME

The course of play that starts when the referee has finished racking the balls, and ends at the conclusion of a legal shot which pockets the last required ball. In 14.1 Continuous, a game lasts several racks.

GAME BALL

(*General*) The ball which, if pocketed legally, would produce victory in a game.

GATHER SHOT

(*Carom Games*) A shot on which appropriate technique and speed are employed to drive one or more balls away from the other(s) in such a manner that when the stroke is complete, the balls have come back together closely enough to present a comparatively easy scoring opportunity for the next shot.

GRIP

(*General*) The manner in which the butt of the cue is held in the hand. (*See "Instructional Playing Tips"*)

GULLY TABLE

(*Pocket Games*) a table with pockets and a return system that delivers the balls as they are pocketed to a collection bin on the foot end of the table.

HANDICAPPING

(*General*) Modifications in the scoring and/or rules of games to enable players of differing abilities to compete on more even terms.

HEAD OF TABLE

(*General*) The end of a carom or pocket billiard table from which the opening break is performed; the end normally marked with the manufacturer's nameplate.

HEAD SPOT

(*General*) The point on the head of the table where imaginary lines drawn between the center diamonds of the short rails and the second diamonds of the long rails intersect. (*See Diagram 40, page 192*)
▲ 3.6

HEAD STRING

(*General*) A line on the head end of the table between the second diamonds of the long rails, passing through the head spot. (*See Diagram 40, page 192*)
▲ 3.10 ▲ 3.16 ▲ 3.39 ▲ 5.14 ▲ 7.8 #5

HICKEY

(*Snooker Golf*) Any foul.

HIGH RUN

(*14.1 Continuous*) During a specified segment of play, the greatest number of balls scored in one turn (*inning*) at the table.

HILL

(*General*) A player is "on the hill" when he or she is one game away from winning the set or match.

HILL - HILL

(*General*) Term used when both players are tied in games and each is one game away from winning the set or match.

HOLD

(*General*) English which stops the cue ball from continuing the course of natural roll it would take after having been driven in a certain direction.

HOT SEAT

(*General*) In a Double elimination tournament, the team that has come through the winner's bracket and therefore has to win only one match to win the tournament is "in the hot seat".

ILLEGAL MARKING

(*General*) If a player intentionally marks the table in any way to assist in executing the shot, whether by wetting the cloth, by placing a cube of chalk on the rail, or by any other means, he has fouled. If the player removes the mark prior to the shot, no penalty is imposed.

ILLEGALLY POCKETED

(*General*) Object ball(s) pocketed on a shot when 1) a foul is committed, 2) the called ball does not go into the designated pocket or 3) a safety is called prior to the shot. See specific game rules to determine if and how to spot the illegally pocketed ball(s).
▲ 4.9 ▲ 4.16 ▲ 6.8 ▲ 7.8 #3 ▲ 7.9

INFRACTION

(*General*) A violation of the rules. (*See* "*FOUL*")
▲ 4.20 ▲ 5.5 ▲ 6.7 #2

INNING

(*General*) A turn at the table by a player, and which may last for several racks in some pocket games.
▲ 3.5 ▲ 3.7-a ▲ 3.30 ▲ 3.37 ▲ 3.41 ▲ 5.5 ▲ 5.13 ▲ 6.7 #4 6.12 ▲ 6.13 ▲ 7.6 ▲ 7.8 #4 ▲ 7.9 ▲ 7.12 ▲ 7.13

IN HAND

(*Pocket Games*) When the cue ball may be put into play anywhere on the playing surface after the other play commits a specific foul (rules vary by game being played). (*See* "*CUE BALL IN HAND*")

IN HAND BEHIND THE HEAD STRING

(*Pocket Games*) Cue ball may be put into play anywhere between the head string and the cushion on the head end of the table not in contact with an object ball. (*See Diagram 40, page 192 and* "*CUE BALL IN HAND BEHIND THE HEAD STRING*")

Glossary

203

IN-OFF

(*Snooker*) A losing hazard; that is, when the cue ball enters a pocket. The snooker equivalent of a scratch.

IN THE RACK

(*14.1 Continuous*) A ball that would interfere with the re-racking of the object balls in 14.1 Continuous that extends past one rack.

INTERFERENCE

(*General*) If the nonshooting player distracts his opponent or interferes with his play, he has fouled. If player shoots out of turn, or moves any balls except during his inning, it is considered to be interference.

JAW

(*Pocket Games*) The slanted part of the cushion that is cut at an angle to form the opening from the bed of the table into the pocket.

JAWED BALL

(*Pocket Games*) Generally refers to a ball that fails to drop because it bounces back and forth against the jaws of a pocket.
▲ 3.33

JOINT

(*General*) On two-piece cues, the screw-and-thread device, approximately midway in the cue, that permits it to be separated into two sections.

JUMP SHOT

(*General*) A shot in which the cue ball or object ball is caused to rise off the bed of the table.
▲ 3.26 ▲ 3.27 ▲ 4.20 #1 ▲ 4.18 ▲ 5.11 ▲ 5.1

JUMPED BALL

(*General*) A ball that has left and remained off the playing surface as the result of a stroke or a ball that is stroked in a manner that causes it to jump over another ball.
▲ 3.28

KEY BALL

(*14.1 Continuous*) The 14th ball of each rack; called the key ball because it is critical in obtaining position for the all important first (or break) shot of each re-racking of the balls.

KICK SHOT

(*General*) A shot in which the cue ball banks off a cushion(s) prior to making contact with an object ball or scoring.

KILL SHOT

(*Pocket Games*) A shot in which a dead ball stroke is employed; often called a kill shot, because of the relative lack of cue ball motion after contact with the object ball.
(*See "DEAD BALL SHOT"*)

204

KISS

(*General*) A shot in which more than one contact with object balls is made by the cue ball; for example, the cue ball might kiss from one object ball into another to score the latter ball. Shots in which object balls carom off one or more other object balls to be pocketed. (*Also called "CAROM" shots*) Contact between balls. (*See "KISS SHOT"*)

▲ 3.4 ▲ 6.7 #1

KISS SHOT

(*Pocket Games*) A shot in which more than one contact with object balls is made by the cue ball; for example, the cue ball might kiss from one object ball into another to score the latter ball. Shots in which object balls carom off one or more other object balls to be pocketed. (*Also called "CAROM" shots*)

KISS-OUT

(*General*) Accidental contact between balls that causes a shot to fail.

KITCHEN

(*Pocket Games*) A slang term used to describe the area of the table between the head string and the cushion on the head end of the table. (*Also called the area above the "HEAD STRING"*)

▲ 3.10 ▲ 3.39

LAG

(*Carom Games*) A shot in which the cue ball is shot three or more cushions before contacting the object balls.

▲ 3.6 ▲ 3.6-g ▲ 3.7 ▲ 3.35 ▲ 4.4 ▲ 5.3

LAG FOR BREAK

(*General*) Procedure used to determine starting player of game. Each player shoots a ball from behind the head string to the foot cushion, attempting to return the ball as closely as possible to the head cushion. (*See "General Rules of Pocket Billiards" and "Carom Billiards"*)

LEAVE

(*Pocket Games*) The position of the balls after a player's shot.

LEGAL BREAK SHOT

(*General*) (Defined) To execute a legal break shot, the breaker (with cue ball behind the headstring must either (1) pocket a ball, or (2) drive at least 4 ball to a rail. If the player fails to make a legal breaks, it is a foul, and the incoming player has the option of (1) accepting the table in position and shooting, or (2) having the balls reracked and having the option of shooting the opening break himself or allowing the offending player to rebreak.

▲ 4.5 ▲ 4.6 ▲ 5.4 ▲ 6.6

LEGAL SHOT

(*General*) A shot that is in accordance with the rules of the game being played and does not result in a foul.

▲ 3.3 ▲ 3.11 ▲ 3.19 ▲ 3.21 ▲ 3.40 ▲ 4.14 ▲ 5.1 ▲ 5.5 ▲ 5.13 ▲ 5.14 ▲ 7.8

LEGALLY POCKETED

(*General*) When an object ball is pocketed in accordance with the rules of the game being played.

▲ 3.37 ▲ 4.1 ▲ 4.2 ▲ 4.10 ▲ 4.13 ▲ 4.19 ▲ 6.5 ▲ 6.7 ▲ 6.12 ▲ 7.6 ▲ 7.7 ▲ 7.8 #'s 2-4

LONG

(*General*) Usually refers to a ball that, due to English and speed, travels a path with wider angles than those that are standard for such a ball if struck with natural English and moderate speed.

LONG STRING

(*Pocket Games*) A line drawn from the center of the foot cushion to the foot spot (and beyond if necessary) on which balls are spotted.

LOSS OF GAME

(*General*) When a player loses the game by committing a number of different infractions.

▲ 4.17 ▲ 4.19 ▲ 4.20 ▲ 4.21 ▲ 7.8 #6

LOSS OF TURN

(*General*) When a player commits a foul and must end his or her turn at the table.

▲ 4.17

LOSING HAZARD

(*Snooker*) Occurs when the cue ball is pocketed after contact with an object ball.

LOT

(*General*) Procedures used, not involving billiard skills, to determine starting player or order of play. Common methods used are flipping coins, drawing straws, drawing cards, or drawing peas or pills.

▲ 3.7

MASSÉ SHOT

(*General*) A shot in which extreme spin is applied to the cue ball by elevating the cue butt at an angle with the bed of the table of anywhere between 30 and 90 degrees. The cue ball usually takes a curved path, with more curve resulting from increasing cue stick elevation.

▲ 4.18 ▲ 5.12

MATCH

(*General*) The course of play that starts when the players are ready to lag and ends when the deciding game ends.

▲ 3.9 ▲ 3.21 ▲ 3.25 ▲ 3.29 ▲ 3.35 ▲ 3.36 ▲ 3.39 ▲ 4.18 ▲ 5.1 ▲ 5.12 ▲ 7.14

MECHANICAL BRIDGE

(*General*) A grooved device mounted on a handle providing support for the shaft of the cue during shots difficult to reach with a normal bridge hand. Also called a crutch or rake.

▲ 3.21 ▲ 3.25

MISCUE

(*General*) A stroke that results in the cue tip contact with cue ball being faulty. Usually the cue tip slides off the cue ball without full transmission of the desired stroke. The stroke usually results in a sharp sound and discoloration of the tip and/or the cue ball at the point of contact.
▲ 3.27

MISS

(*General*) Failure to execute a completed shot.
▲ 5.1 ▲ 5.5 ▲ 5.13

MISS

(*Snooker*) The call the referee makes in snooker if it is judged the player has not endeavored to the best of his ability to hit the ball on. (*See "Rules for International Snooker"*)

NATURAL

(*Carom Games*) A shot with only natural angle and stroke required for successful execution; a simple or easily visualized, and accomplished, scoring opportunity.

NATURAL ENGLISH

(*General*) Moderate sidespin applied to the cue ball that favors the direction of the cue ball path, giving the cue ball a natural roll and a bit more speed than a center hit.

NATURAL ROLL

(*General*) Movement of the cue ball with no English applied.

NIP DRAW

(*General*) A short, sharp stroke employed when a normal draw stroke would result in a foul due to drawing the cue ball back into the cue tip.

NURSES

(*Carom Games*) Techniques whereby the balls are kept close to the cushions and each other, creating a succession of relatively easy scoring opportunities.

NOMINATION

(*14.1 Continuous*) To designate a specified ball in a specific pocket.
▲ 6.1

OBJECT BALLS

(*General*) The balls other than the cue ball on a shot.

OBJECT BALL, THE

(*Pocket Games*) The particular object ball being played on a shot.
▲ 3.6 ▲ 3.8 ▲ 3.20 ▲ 3.21 ▲ 3.28 ▲ 3.31 ▲ 4.1 ▲ 4.2 ▲ 4.6 ▲ 4.7 ▲ 4.10 ▲ 4.11 ▲ 4.12 ▲ 4.15 ▲ 4.16 ▲ 4.17 ▲ 4.19 ▲ 4.20 #5 ▲ 4.21 ▲ 5.1 ▲ 5.2 ▲ 5.11 ▲ 6.3 ▲ 6.6 ▲ 6.7 #7 ▲ 6.9 ▲ 7.2 ▲ 7.4 ▲ 7.8 #5 ▲ 7.10

ON BALL

(*Snooker*) A colored (non-red) ball a player intends to legally pocket; same as on ball. (*See "BALL ON"*)

ON THE HILL

(*General*) Term used when a player is one game away from winning a set or match. (*See "HILL" and "HILL - HILL"*)

OPEN BREAK

(*Pocket Games*) The requirement in certain games that a player must drive a minimum of four object balls out of the rack to the cushions in order for the shot to be legal.

OPENING BREAK SHOT

(*General*) The first shot of a game.
▲ 3.7 ▲ 3.8 ▲ 6.6 ▲ 7.5

PEAS

(*Pocket Games*) Small plastic or wooden balls numbered 1 through 15 or 16; use defined in specific game rules. (*See "PILLS"*)

PILLS

(*Pocket Games*) Equipment used in pocket games. (*See "PEAS"*)

PLANT

(*Snooker*) A position of two or more red balls that allows a ball to be driven into a pocket with a combination shot.

POSITION

(*General*) The placement of the cue ball on each shot relative to the next planned shot. Also called "SHAPE".
▲ 3.10 ▲ 3.12 ▲ 3.21 ▲ 3.31 ▲ 3.33 ▲ 3.35 ▲ 3.37 ▲ 3.39 ▲ 3.40 ▲ 4.5 ▲ 4.7 ▲ 4.14 ▲ 7.10 ▲ 7.12

POT

(*Snooker*) The pocketing of an object ball.

POWDER

(*General*) Talc or other fine, powdery substance used to facilitate free, easy movement of the cue shaft through the bridge.

POWER DRAW SHOT

(*General*) Extreme draw applied to the cue ball. (See "FORCE DRAW").

PUSH OUT

(Nine-Ball) A strategic safety shot that a player may take in Nine-Ball on the shot immediately following their legal break. The player must call the "push out" but does not have to contact an object ball or a rail on the shot.
▲ 5.5 ▲ 5.6

PUSH SHOT

(*General*) A shot in which the cue tip maintains contact with the cue ball beyond the split second allowed for a normal and legally stroked shot.

▲ 3.24

PYRAMID

(*Pocket Games*) Positioning of the object balls in a triangular grouping (with the front apex ball on the foot spot), used to begin many pocket billiard games.

PYRAMID SPOT

(*Snooker*) The same as the pink spot. The spot is marked midway between the center spot and the face of the top cushion.

RACE

(*General*) Predetermined number of games necessary to win a match or set of games. For example, a match that is the best 11 out of 21 games is called a race to 11, and ends when one player has won 11 games.

▲ 3.24

RACK

The device used for gathering the balls into the formation required by the game being played.

▲ 3.2 ▲ 3.35 ▲ 3.36 ▲ 4.3 ▲ 7.3 ▲ 7.14

RAILS

(*General*) The top surface of the table not covered by cloth, from which the cushions protrude toward the playing surface. The head and foot rails are the short rails on those ends of the table; the right and left rails are the long rails, dictated by standing at the head end of the table and facing the foot end.

▲ 3.10 ▲ 3.28 ▲ 4.11 ▲ 5.4 ▲ 5.6 ▲ 5. 9 ▲ 6.7 #2 ▲ 7.7

RED BALL

(*Carom Games*) The red-colored object ball. Also the name of a particular 3-cushion billiard game.

REST

(*Snooker*) The mechanical bridge.

RESPOTTED

(*General*) To place an object ball back on the table, in accordance with the rules of the game being played. (See "SPOTTED")

▲ 3.17-c ▲ 4.17 ▲ 5.4 #3 ▲ 5.7 ▲ 5.11

RERACK

(*General*) To rack the balls again after an illegal break in accordance with the rules of the game being played.

▲ 4.5 ▲ 4.8 ▲ 4.21 ▲ 6.6 ▲ 6.7 #2 ▲ 6.12

Glossary

REVERSE ENGLISH

(*General*) Sidespin applied to the cue ball that favors the opposite direction of the natural cue ball path, i.e., inside English.

ROUND ROBIN

(*General*) A tournament format in which each contestant plays each of the other players one time.

RUNNING ENGLISH

(*General*) Sidespin applied to the cue ball which causes it to rebound from a cushion at a narrower angle and at a faster speed than it would if struck at the same speed and direction without English.

RUN

(*General*) The total of consecutive scores, points or counts made by a player in one inning. The term is also used to indicate the total number of full short-rack games won without a missed shot in a match or tournament.

SAFETY

(*General*) Defensive positioning of the balls that minimizes the opponent's chance to score. (*The nature and rules concerning safety play are decidedly different in specific games; see individual game rules regarding safety play.*) A player's inning usually ends after a safety play.
▲ 4.12 ▲ 4.16 ▲ 6.7 #'s 2-4 ▲ 6.12

SCRATCH

(*Carom Games*) To score a point largely by accident, due to an unanticipated kiss, unplanned time-shot, etc.

SCRATCH

(*Pocket Games*) The cue ball goes into a pocket on a stroke.
▲ 3.10 ▲ 3.20 ▲ 4.6 ▲ 4.19 ▲ 5.6 ▲ 6.6 ▲ 6.7 #7 ▲ 6.10 ▲ 6.11 ▲ 6.12 ▲ 7.6 ▲ 7.8 #'s 4-5 ▲ 7.11 ▲ 7.12

SEEDING

(*General*) Predetermined initial pairings or advanced positioning of players in a field of tournament competition.

SET

(*General*) A subdivision of a match consisting of a pre-determined number of games. For example, a match might be best 3 of 5 sets with each set a race to 7 games.
▲ 7.14

SHAFT

(*General*) The thinner part of a cue on which the cue tip is attached. On a two-piece cue, the shaft extends from the cue tip to the joint.
▲ 3.21 ▲ 3.26 ▲ 3.29

SHAKE BOTTLE
(*Pocket Games*) A specially shaped leather or plastic container used in various games. (*See "BOTTLE"*)

SHOT
An action that begins the instant the cue tip contacts the cue ball and ends when all balls in play stop rolling and spinning.

SHOT CLOCK
(*General*) Any timing device used to gauge the time limit in which a player is allowed to play a shot. The timing device must have at least the functions of a stopwatch: reset to zero, start and stop. A simple wristwatch without timing functions is not sufficient.

SHORT
(*General*) Usually refers to a ball that, due to English and stroke, travels a path closer to perpendicular to the rail than those for a ball struck without English.
▲ 3.32 ▲ 3.38 ▲ 4.2 ▲ 7.5 ▲ 7.6 ▲ 7.8 ▲ 7.8 #2 ▲ 7.13 ▲ 7.1

SHORT-RACK
(*Pocket Games*) The set of balls for games that utilize fewer than 15 countable object balls (*i.e. Nine-Ball*).
▲ 3.36

SPIN
(*General*) Side applied to the cue ball by striking it off center; used to alter the natural roll of the cue ball and/or the object ball.

SIDE
(*General*) Sidespin applied to the cue ball by striking it off center; used to alter the natural roll of the cue ball and/or the object ball. (*See "ENGLISH"*)

SIDESPIN
(*General*) Force applied to the cue ball by striking it off center; used to alter the natural roll of the cue ball and/or the object ball. (*See "ENGLISH"*)

SINGLE ELIMINATION
(*General*) A tournament format in which a single loss eliminates a player from the competition.

SNAKE
(*Carom Games*) A shot in which the use of English causes the cue ball to make three or more cushion contacts, though utilizing only two different cushions. Also called a double-the-rail shot.

SNOOKERED
(*Snooker*) The condition of an incoming player's cue ball position when he cannot shoot in a straight line and contact all portions of an on ball directly facing the cue ball (*because of balls not "on" that block the path*).

211

SPLIT DOUBLE ELIMINATION

(*General*) A modification of the double elimination tournament format, in which the field is divided into sections, with one player emerging from each of the sections to compete for the championship, in a single showdown match for the championship.

SPLIT HIT

A shot in which it cannot be determined which object ball(s) the cue ball contacted first, due to the close proximity of the object balls.

SPOT

(*General*) The thin, circular piece of cloth or paper glued onto the cloth to indicate the spot locality (*i.e., head spot, center spot, foot spot*); also an expression to describe a handicap.
▲ 3.31 ▲ 3.32 ▲ 7.12

SPOT BALL

(*Carom Games*) The white ball differentiated from the clear by one or more markings; usually spots, dots or circles.

SPOT SHOT

(*Pocket Games*) Player shoots a ball on the foot spot with the cue ball in hand behind the head string.

SPOTTING BALLS

(*General*) Replacing balls to the table in positions as dictated by specific game rules.

STALEMATED GAME

If, after 3 consecutive turns at the table by each player (6 turns total), the referee judges that attempting to pocket or move an object ball will result in loss of game, the balls will be reracked with the original breaker of the stalemated game breaking again. The stalemate rule may be applied regardless of the number of balls on the table. **Please Note**: Three consecutive fouls by one player in 8-Ball is not a loss of game.

STANCE

(*General*) The position of the body during shooting. (*See "Instructional Playing Tips"*)

STOP SHOT

(*Pocket Games*) A shot in which the cue ball stops immediately upon striking the object ball.

STRIKER

(*Snooker*) The player who is about to shoot and has yet to complete an inning.

STROKE

(*General*) The movement of the cue as a shot is executed. (See Instructional Playing Tips Chapter)

▲ 3.4 ▲ 3.15 ▲ 3.17-b ▲ 3.18 ▲ 3.20 ▲ 3.24 ▲ 3.27 ▲ 3.28 ▲ 3.31 ▲ 3.32 ▲ 3.34 ▲ 3.40 ▲ 6.1 #'s 1-3 ▲ 6.7 #3 ▲ 6.9 ▲ 6.12 ▲ 7.8 #'s 2-4 ▲ 7.10

SUCCESSIVE FOULS

(*Pocket Games*) Fouls made on consecutive strokes by the same player, also called consecutive fouls.

▲ 5.13 ▲ 6.6 ▲ 6.7 #2 ▲ 6.11 ▲ 6.12 ▲ 7.8 #6

TABLE IN POSITION

(*General*) Term used to indicate that the object balls remain unmoved following a shot.

TABLE RUN

(*General*) After the breaking player fails to pocket a ball on the break, the incoming player shoots his group of ball with out missing and completes the game.

THROW SHOT

(*Pocket Games*)

1. A shot in which English alters the path of the object ball.
2. A combination shot of frozen or near frozen balls in which the rubbing of the first ball across the second ball pulls the shot away from the line joining the centers of the two balls.

TIME SHOT

(*General*) A shot in which the cue ball (most often) moves another ball into a different position and then continues on to meet one of the moved balls for a score.

TOP CUSHION

(*Snooker*) The cushion located at the foot of a snooker table - closest to the black spot.

TRIANGLE

(*Pocket Games*) The triangular device used to place the balls in position for the start of most games (See "RACK")

▲ 3.32 ▲ 6.4 ▲ 6.7 #'s 3-6 ▲ 7.3

YELLOW BALL

(*Carom Games*) In international competition, the spot ball has been replaced by a yellow ball without any markings.

UNSPORTSMANLIKE CONDUCT

(*General*) An action by a player that is not in accordance with the rules of the game being played and may result in a foul, loss of game.

▲ 3.39 ▲ 3.42

Glossary

BECOME A BCA MEMBER TODAY!

Business Membership

Manufacturers, retailers, room operators, publications and service companies all benefit greatly from a BCA Business Membership. The BCA provides marketing support, industry information and special events designed to promote and grow cue sports worldwide. Benefits include:

- Free badges to the International Billiard & Home Recreation Expo
- Discounted tickets to the *Business of Billiard* Seminars
- Sponsorship opportunities
- *52 Ways to Make Pool Everybody's Game* promotional booklets
- Billiard Creative Agency marketing support materials
- Product & service discounts
- Voting rights and board representation opportunities
- Complimentary product for promotional use or resale
- Website links
- Online directory listings

Junior Membership

A special Junior Membership is available to billiard enthusiasts under the age of 18. Benefits include:

- *Billiards: The Official Rules and Records Book*
- *How to Play Pool Right* booklet
- BCA window decal, letter opener and pen
- Member patch and pin
- Membership card
- Discounts from BCA Business Members
- *Chalk it Up*, the online quarterly Junior newsletter
- Eligibility to enter a BCA Junior National Qualifier
- Sample issue of *Billiards Digest*, *Pool & Billiard Magazine* or *National Billiard News* (first-time members only)

For membership details and applications, please visit www.bca-pool.com.

League Play

Looking to meet new people and enjoy fun, competitive matches? Contact any of the BCA Members below and get in the game!

BCA Pool Leagues ....www.playbca.com

American Poolplayers Association (APA).......................www.poolplayers.com

American CueSports Alliance (ACS)....................www.americancuesports.org

BCA PRESIDENT'S AWARD RECIPIENTS

Year	Recipient	President
2004	Butch Olhausen	Skip Nemecek
2003	Michael Di Motta	Skip Nemecek
2002	Harold Simonsen	Larry Johns
2001	Nancy Hart	Larry Johns
2000	Jerry Briesath	Michael Di Motta
1999	David Maidment	Michael Di Motta
1998	Don Shimel*	Michael Di Motta
1997	Daniel Gauci	Don Shimel
1996	Michael Geiger	Raoul Rubalcava
1995	James Bakula	Raoul Rubalcava
1994	Mort Luby	Daniel Gauci
1993	Euroslate S.R.L.	Daniel Gauci
	Italardesia S.R.L.	
	L.E.A.N.I. Slate	
1992	Paul Huebler	David Maidment
	Charles Robertson*	
1991	Jorgen Sandman	James Bakula
	Horst Vondenhoff	
1990	Charles Milhelm	James Bakula
1989	Bob Froeschle*	Charles Robertson
1988	Pierre Wilhelm	Charles Robertson
1987	William Gunklach	Charles Robertson
	Red Jones*	

The President's Award is presented yearly to an individual who has made significant contributions to the billiard industry. The award ceremony takes place just prior to the Hall of Fame induction ceremony at the International Billiard & Home Recreation Expo.

The President's Award is inscribed with the phrase: "Sursum et Porsum ad Excellentium", which means: "Onward and Upward Toward Excellence".

BCA PAST PRESIDENTS

John Stransky	2004-Present
Skip Nemecek	2002-03
Larry Johns	2000-01
Michael Di Motta	1998-99
Don Shimel*	1996-97
Raoul Rubalcava	1994-95
Daniel Gauci	1992-93
David Maidment	1991
James Bakula	1989-90
Charles Robertson*	1986-88
David Maidment	1985
Paul Huebler	1982-84
James F. Wilhem*	1980-81
Darrell Lawless	1979
Paul Lucchesi*	1978
Kim Gandy	1976-77
Michael Geiger	1974-75
Charles L. Bailey	1972-73
James F. Wilhem*	1969-71
William Gunklach	1968
Bud Hobbs	1967
William Gunklach	1966

Deceased